I0061356

Power and Probity in a DC Cooperative

By the same author:

VYGOTSKY'S CHILDREN: Georgetown and Oxbridge Students Meet Urban Youth

MEDIEVAL LYRIC: Middle English Lyrics, Ballads and Carols

CHAUCER AND THE CANTERBURY TALES: A Short Introduction

THE BOUNDARIES OF FAITH: The Development and Transmission of Medieval Spirituality

SURSUM CORDA: Teaching Urban Youth to Read

THE REVELATIONS OF MARGERY KEMPE: Paramystical Practices in Late Medieval England

HOPE EMILY ALLEN: Medieval Scholarship and Feminism

BARLAM AND IOSAPHAT: A Middle English Life of Buddha

WESTERN MANUSCRIPTS OF THE TWELFTH THROUGH THE SIXTEENTH CENTURY IN LEHIGH UNIVERSITY LIBRARIES: A Guide to the Exhibition

Power and Probity in a DC Cooperative

The Life and Death of Sursum Corda

JOHN C. HIRSH

with Photographs by Harry Mattison

NNP NEW ACADEMIA PUBLISHING VELLUM

Washington DC

Copyright © 2017 by John C. Hirsh
Photographs Copyright © Harry Mattison
New Academia Publishing, 2018

All rights reserved. No part of this book may be reproduced or transmitted in any form or by any means, electronic or mechanical, including photocopying, recording, or by any information storage and retrieval system.

Printed in the United States of America

Library of Congress Control Number: 2017953889
ISBN 978-0-9986433-8-0 paperback (alk. paper)

VELLUM   An imprint of New Academia Publishing

NAP
NEW ACADEMIA
PUBLISHING   New Academia Publishing, 4401-A Connecticut Ave. NW, #236,
                  Washington, DC 20008
                  info@newacademia.com - www.newacademia.com

For
Shiv Newaldass, Darrin Bates, Christine Nicholson,

To the Memory of
Allene Harper

And To
All the Georgetown and Sursum Corda Students
Who Worked Together in Our Program

Contents

Preface

This is an account of the ways in which an inner-city community called Sursum Corda (the name, taken from the Preface of the Latin mass, means "Lift up your hearts") had the bad luck to find itself situated on suddenly valuable land, sought to contend with its changed circumstances, and both failed and succeeded in its designs. The community consisted of 199 units, grouped around and off a central U-shaped street (First Place, NW, otherwise "the horseshoe"), all completed by 1970, and consisting of between one and six bedroom apartments located in connected low-rise town houses, a real departure at the time when the usual practice in public housing was to construct two bedroom apartments for all families, whatever their size. But Sursum Corda, as envisioned and as realized, was a private development, albeit one supported and sponsored by HUD. As the name implies, it was envisioned and constructed by a small group of Catholic laymen, ably supported by an equally small group of priests and nuns, to offer affordable housing to disadvantaged Washingtonians, particularly single mothers with children, and those recently dislocated by what was then called "urban renewal." What follows is a record of events that took place some thirty-five years later, when the suddenly-valuable land on which the community stood became attractive to property developers, who fixed their eye on it. This then is a record, written at the time but subsequently considered and polished, less of what transpired than of what seemed to some of those who were involved to have been happening at the time. Henry James said "The whole of anything is never told. You can only take what groups together." And a drama teacher I knew would instruct his students to act on stage so as to suggest that the events they were presenting "could always have been otherwise." During the years I kept this journal, I would remember both the observation and the injunction, even when the crush of events seemed all too predictable. The book concludes with the community's end.

Because I am as much concerned with the process as the result, a journal emerged as the best way to record what appeared, from my limited perspective, to be happening, and to consider what at least seemed to be the reasons why. I say from "my perspective" because throughout this period I, like almost everyone involved in the process, lived in a world of limited knowledge, in which doubt and uncertainty played a part in everything we undertook – or tried to. Like very many of the Sursum Corda residents, like almost all of the on-lookers (including those from the press), like most of those who were otherwise involved, I never really knew what was going to happen next, nor was it entirely clear who, if anyone, was in charge. Such uncertainty is probably endemic to such undertakings, and here it has led to an account in which epistemology figures almost as importantly as ethics. I urge this perspective lest what follows be mistaken for social or political science, particularly since I have been at pains to include in my narrative many events that, at first blush, seem not connected to the continuing, indeed still continuing, narrative.

My text is not without quotation, whether implicit and explicit, and these inform the meaning, though the most important may be Henry James' warning that the whole of anything is never told. Like him, however, I have sought to represent what grouped together, not excepting the pedagogical enterprise that brought me there, the Georgetown University – Sursum Corda Tutoring Program, and to do so in a way intended to reveal formal and thematic, as well as actual, difficulties. Thus my concern for "housing policy" fights shy of dwelling upon intentions and past practices, and is invested rather in the ways in which it fell upon these homes, at that time. Its effects indeed registered, but led to no general conclusion, nor have I invented one, the odd *cri de coeur* apart, in order to make an ending that will satisfy. I suppose it is inevitable that what follows will be called "participant observation," though could I dodge that particular cliché I would happily do so. Specifically, I here renounce any claims to greater knowledge, academic authority, and, as far as I am able, the simple vanity, born of method, that seizes on the advantaged when they address the circumstances of the poor. It may be that no one can commit class suicide, but we are men and women, boys and girls together, and together we complicate law and practice, religion and education, power and probity. My larger objection is that such is the way the advantaged ever serve the disadvantaged. That is why our little program, invested in learning and ethics, informed by ordinary practice, is part of this particular equation. The individual's tale is of meaning and circumstance, customary and socio-legal practice, and without it nothing happens. Those are my methods, and that is my data.

Partly because Sursum Corda became a cooperative, one in which the residents themselves, and not some distant owner, owned their homes, it enjoyed a certain legal standing denied to many apparently similar projects. But that standing was never entirely understood by many, and the actions of the Board set up to represent them were often opaque, and seemed to many never subject to question. The result was that alternative versions of what was going on, and sometimes outright fictions, drove events forward. The first challenge that our adversaries (for so they became) had to confront concerned ownership, and that was what the City and HUD had to overcome. But there seemed to some residents no real certainty in anything, at least none that could be taken to the bank. In any case, our ground was ever uncertain, and whatever the issue may have been, there were always those who thought otherwise. I hope I have represented that doubt and uncertainty in what I have written here: it was what we lived with, though there were other kinds of knowing present too.

Here and there throughout this narrative I have employed the words "power" and "probity" as a way of describing the constructions and operations that gradually became apparent in the course of things, sometimes all too apparent. I appropriated these words, as I have acknowledged below, from the nineteenth-century American writer and intellectual Ralph Waldo Emerson, and yet in doing so have developed, for better or worse, my own inflection. Writing in 1848, Emerson understood the representation, but also the actuality, of present power in largely technological terms

– railways, steamships, telegraphs – and believed that humankind had already more power than it could contend with. Steeped in a concern for the individual as he was – including a concern that the concept itself may have had its day – Emerson also concluded that without a growth of human understanding rooted in probity, a kind of mental revolution, such power was all but certain to turn on its creator. For him, 'probity' effectively implied something like 'honesty,' a personal virtue that commanded respect, but one that, sympathetically united with power, might lead to better persons. I have employed the words in a very different context, one more attentive to social, and even administrative authority, than to that of the individual, and the words, while admitting of private virtue (and vice), here reflect an extended and communal sensitivity most of all. Mindful of the competing circumstances we all encountered, I have of course sought neither to disparage nor, candidly, to fully describe, the character, still less the integrity, of those with whom I have been concerned – the point here is not that bad people did bad things, or that good ones did so – but I hope I have not been inattentive to the social dynamic and several oppositions present in our mutual interactions – at least as I have understood them.

I wrote these pages not only as a non-voting (because non-resident) member of the Board of Trustees, but also and very much as a friend of the community, a bias for which I make no apology. For the past twenty-seven years I oversaw a tutoring program (it began in 1970 and we believed it to be one of the oldest such in the country between an American university and a specific urban community), in which Georgetown University undergraduates worked, one-on-one, with some of the primary school aged children who live in Sursum Corda. An account of our work runs, I hope like a leitmotif, through these pages, supplying some insight not only into our program, but also, through its youngest members, into the life of the community itself.

The perspective here will appear resolutely secular, involving as it does the deprivations visited on a particular community at a particular time, and touching as well the legal, ethical, social and individual challenges its members confronted. The Sursum Corda / Georgetown University tutoring program, on the other hand, faced none of these difficulties, though my own concern for what was happening deepened some of the associations on which it rested, and some of these were less secular than others. Georgetown is the oldest Catholic university in the United States, and about half of its students come from Catholic families, though many are of an age when they are considering what they themselves both believe and consider intrinsically meaningful, and in some cases at least, their work in our program contributed to their reflection. But in spite of topics that I sometimes introduced into our weekly seminars (we tutored in the community for an hour on Tuesday and Thursday evening, and the students and I met on campus on Wednesday), religious consideration as such entered only very, very occasionally into our discussions. As a group we maintained a loosely Kantian belief that every child we seek to teach has an inherent human dignity that makes each one an end in himself or herself, and not, as is sometimes implied on campus, a means of securing a kind of secular moral salvation for the individual tutor. Such explanations may suffice in the classroom, where such theory so often flourishes, but they can neither explain nor inform the sometimes complex motivation, the necessary commitment, or the intellectual cut and thrust involved in a year's serious tutoring.

I do not of course believe that the actions and the attitudes of our program were without significance. For one thing, and partly because of the ages of the persons involved, there was a mutual assumption of a certain non-academic equality between tutor and learner, one grounded in felt and mutual experiences, and that included largely unspoken ethical and even moral implications. It is not right to say that the exchange between tutor and learner itself confers integrity on either one or upon the interaction itself, which are rather determined by individual motivation and academic understanding. But done right, our work involved a degree of intellectual application and creativity that informed both tutor and learner, producing an affectionate exchange that advantaged both, and that lasted beyond the moment. Still, the discourse and engagement we began were not necessarily permanent, important as they often were to those who took part in them. In most cases, they did not endure unless they were made to do so, even though they can, and often did, inform the most intimate of considerations. But for these to last beyond graduation requires an act of will and mind, as well, as I have come to understand, of heart.

As will appear, in the larger discourse to which we in the program, and I in particular, were sometimes party, other community voices spoke out loudly, and often with confidence, though intermittently, and rarely in unison. As a result of my attachment through the program I had come to a certain insight into, and an historical understanding of, the Sursum Corda community, though not into the many governmental agencies present in these pages, whether HUD, the City, or into the several development firms which, taken together, will determine what is to come.

No doubt these powerful entities, which seem so monolithic and intractable from without, have their own internal dynamic and dissensions, closed to outsiders. Were there those in the City administration who thought a fourth inspection (or even a third) should not have been allowed, and that the foreclosure should go ahead as planned? Were there, among the developers or their putative partners, or among the members of the Sursum Corda Board, some who came to consider that their actions may have had a dubious moral edge? If so, they are known to God, not me. Effectively at least, those bodies never blinked, and seemed to turn thumbs down whenever it was in their interest so to do. The individual actors involved, while often disclaiming personal responsibility, simply advanced the apparently advancing cause, while in some cases at least, advancing their own cause too. One man may indeed make a difference, but it doesn't always happen that he does so. Those bleak impersonal forces that you despise are real enough, and they will have their way: only read on.

But there were larger forces working too. The role of two important, by which I mean very powerful, federal entities played dramatically upon the fortunes of the community at Sursum Corda, precipitating and focusing the crisis here described, and all but determining its outcome. Still, the putative relationship between these two bodies, HUD and the Supreme Court, is nothing if not complex. Unlike the other subterranean if possibly putative relationships that complicate these pages – between HUD and the City; between a developer and this Board member or that one; between the Mayor's Office and one or more Sursum Corda officers – the connection between HUD and the Supreme Court exists without a phone call or a nod, and is legitimately denied, or could be, by either or both. But in the context of the contest present here, it is real indeed.

When the Supreme Court handed eminent domain to cities, more or less for the asking, that action finally struck against the poor. Claim the land of the wealthy and they will hire lawyers, negotiate, and if they really must surrender what they own, obtain the fairest of fair price for every inch. But who in America will defend the putative prerogatives of the lawyerless? The law does no such thing, and the Court's hard ruling proved hardest of all on them. Could they, should they, resist the rows of lawyers massed against them? They must give way to HUD, which now has turned against them, and quickly, since the great Court says so too.

At Sursum Corda, however, HUD's menace was a good deal more precise: pass our inspection or we'll end your ability to be one with Section 8, and voucher all your residents away. Faced with such an ending, the drowning ones clutched at a developer to help them out. The City's plan was apparent from the first: the community would fail HUD's inspection, and soon thereafter, its residents scattered, lose all its land as well. A few favored ones would be fobbed off with this or that – a new apartment elsewhere, and a better one at that. But as things stood, the Board could no more meet HUD's specifications than the residents could pay market rate for their homes. And so a Faustian bargain was agreed, mistaken if not more in certain ways, but without it all the walls would soon be down, and the community scattered to HUD's strong and sudden winds.

As a sign of deference and accuracy I have been most sparing with quotation marks, using them only when I am quite certain of the words they enclose, otherwise allowing an approximation, or my best memory, or a report I trust, to show what (in effect) was probably said. I have been as concerned here to register the impersonal forces that drove these issues forward, as the role for good or ill of any single actor. Part of any "lesson" here is that, as a cooperative, it has taken other kinds of cooperation to bring Sursum Corda down, urban and federal processes, denigration in the press, the presence of sometimes well-meaning partners, of management companies, or directors of various sorts, no less than dissension and distraction from within.

What happened at Sursum Corda happened in a country that, collectively at least, honestly does seek justice for its poor, equity in its housing, and a way of preventing the rich from exploiting others. Even with political crisis and our many wars abroad, the poor do not disappear – they only recede from view. My concern here has been to report what it actually means to move the disadvantaged on, the difficulties it poses for all concerned, particularly when the disadvantaged are, as they are here, in a fairly strong legal position. This has often meant rewriting widely. Sometimes I began rewriting an entry before I finished it, and especially when I was standing with my friends, my shout went up with theirs. More often I have revisited my lines to clarify or to refine their meaning, though taking care to keep what happened then. The result is that there are two voices here, one greener than the other; both are mine.

I have thus let events unfold from day to day. "A foolish consistency is the hobgoblin of little minds," said Emerson, and what I say one day, I may reconsider or contradict the next. I did not know what Sursum Corda's fate would be as I was writing these words. Even so, the book that follows has a certain structure, and it would be best if I said what it is. The first three chapters reveal, albeit with false starts, a largely uninstructed grassroots attempt to save a community that, through no fault of its own, but rather through the rapaciousness and mismanagement of others, found itself in debt to HUD, and needed to discover a way out. What finally registers in these pages is less the methods we explored – mortgages, bank loans and the like – than the reasons for attempting what we did, and the limits that we found ever about us.

Finance is theory; we were concerned with those with lives to lead. Mortgages (we discovered) would hardly work for everyone, and the idea of trying to impose them on everyone would have been transparently mistaken.   In any case, we never found a bank that would do so. No doubt this circumstance is unsurprising, since to do so the bank would have had to lock horns with our adversaries, and, as a favor to our residents, help to frustrate the City's interests. Not an attractive proposition. But we started with the wrong that was before us, the one that was being done, brushed aside the stereotypes so often used against the poor (including the comforting illusion that they don't exist, or if they do it's only temporary), and tried to estimate if and how we might contain the perfect storm that rose against our co-op. HUD and the City meant every word they said – they were quite prepared to do whatever was needed in order to have their way. At first perhaps, our swords were tinfoil to their tempered steel, and it may be that we failed to spot an opening or two, or misconstrued a financial remedy, but if we slipped, it was not for want of trying.

But it was trying that gave rise to chapters four and five, and if the first three arise from the ground up, these two are top down, and with a vengeance. If there were residents who thought the City would deal generously with them, after the events recorded in chapter four, they largely held their peace, and waited for an end that has now come to pass. But as I say somewhere below, Sursum Corda is more a tar baby than a damsel in distress. Only touch it, and you will never quite be free.

I will discuss aspects of the Georgetown program I have already mentioned in the course of things. But it might be well to sound one question here – one to which I will return – since, as I insist, the learning in our program is mutual, then what did I expect the Georgetown students to take away with them? I really try not to expect too much, but my short answer is based upon different assumptions. Many, indeed most of those who came to us,` are already well-disposed young men and women, perceptive and really quite bright, thoughtful to a degree, inclined both toward success and thinking well of others. But like all of us, they were no strangers to the media, and to the lessons that it teaches about violence and broken families, drugs and early death, events associated not with their families, where these things also happen, but with the disadvantaged, and especially with the poor.

During the first meeting of our classroom seminar I would invite some of last year's tutors, those still in the program, to come and speak to the new tutors, and make it a practice to leave the room when they do so. This allows the neophytes to ask whatever they like, though as the program has become better known their questions have begun to turn on grading, and less on what was asked before, "Is it really safe there?" Implicit in both is an understanding that our program raises questions that are intended for those who will, one day, be busy in the world, and not for monks.

But if they will but allow it, and only then, the assumptions that replace the ones they have can last, and so allow a different way of seeing. And that is why we made tutor competence, by no means a Georgetown preoccupation in those days, the hallmark of our work. Knowing that they have a useful skill – the ability to read and understand – gives tutors the confidence to learn what those they teach have to teach them, so both undo the lessons of the past.

Introduction

In the early evening of the 23rd of January, 2004, a fourteen-year-old African American girl named Jahkema Princess Hansen was shot to death, at very close range, inside a town house in a Washington, D.C. apartment complex known as Sursum Corda. The murder attracted media attention – far more so than another murder, committed soon after, of a seventeen-year-old boy in a city high school – and for several days thereafter the *Washington Post* pursued Princess' murder, reporting both on its circumstances and soon thereafter on the community of Sursum Corda itself. The facts of the murder were at once simple and gruesome. Fourteen years old and only recently arrived in the community, Princess had acquired a boyfriend several years older than herself, or so the story ran, one who, since he was involved in the drug trade, could entertain her as he liked. That entertainment ended on the day she saw him shoot and kill a competitor. Being fourteen, she was without fear, and told her friends what she had seen, though in the closed world of Sursum Corda it was not long before the police (and others) found out as well. Directed by them, according to this report, her mother brought her daughter to a police station some distance from Sursum Corda (the point is important because another report suggests that the police had visited her at home, thus indicating her vulnerability). Once at the station they asked Princess to bear witness as to what she had seen. Anticipating the refusal to speak that she at once produced, the police offered to protect her anyway, only to be told, it is said, "I'm fourteen and can look after myself." "But really you can't," they insisted. "Your boyfriend is going to believe that he has a choice between spending 60 years in prison or shooting you. He's going to shoot you." Meeting a refusal still, they turned to her mother: "She's a minor," they pointed out. "If you permit it, we can protect her anyway." "Leave my daughter alone," came the reported reply.

Back at Sursum Corda things did not improve. Princess, or someone close to her, reported a version of the conversation at the police station to her boyfriend or to one of his crew, with the result that Princess came to believe that she was going to be remunerated for her faithfulness. Her mother subsequently denied any knowledge of what her daughter had been told. How could I know it?, she asked. But if there was a threat involved as well, neither Princess nor her mother understood it. In the end a friend of her boyfriend came to her, but not with the reward she was expecting.

Or at least such was the account we allowed ourselves to believe soon after the crime. But there is another perspective to pursue, one that began to emerge during the 2006 trial, and was reported both in the *Washington Post* and in Jonathan York's article in the October 13, 2006 issue of Washington's free *City Paper*, my source for the details that now follow. Suddenly it is January, 2004 again, and Princess Hansen, aged 14, and a friend with whom she was living, Timika Holiday, aged 18, returned from a go-go bar to a nearby apartment complex called Temple Courts in order to see what was going on, what could be had, and for how much. There Mario Evans had set up shop by the door to the stairs on the sixth floor, selling dippers – cigarettes, sold singly, but dipped in a bottle of PCP when the customer produced twenty dollars. The girls stood by and watched.

Marquette Ward came in, stocky, dressed in black and with some members of his crew, but he wanted a half-price deal, a dipper for ten dollars, not twenty. He had a bundle of greenbacks with him, and knowing that he could pay full price, Evans said No, disrespecting him in front of his friends, probably a mistake, though with so many people present it might have ended there. The cause for subsequent events was never entirely clear to the participants, nor was it inevitable. But salient points came out at the trial, more than a year and a half later, and these suggest some of the reasons for what followed. Evans' refusal of a discount put Ward in a bind: he could not back down and play poor without losing face in front of his friends, including the two girls. He had slept with both of them, and it is possible that their presence as witnesses may have encouraged him not to haggle, just as it encouraged Evans to hold out for the full twenty dollars. On the other hand, when Ward paid up then Evans had won, and worse still, he had treated Ward like a cheap mug, not like a friendly equal. Choosing the simpler course, Ward paid the twenty dollars and left down the stairway with his friends, though no doubt their conversation continued, probably to Evans' detriment.

Back on the sixth floor, things got no better. Bernard Smith, already present together with the girls, came forward. He also wanted a half-price dipper, and Evans again refused. But now all accommodation had been thrust aside, and nothing was as it should be. Smith drew his gun to gain respect and power. Knowing his man, Evans didn't believe that he would use it, and stood his ground. Words followed. Then the stairway door suddenly opened again and Ward reappeared, gun in hand. The girls retreated, leaving the men to do their worst. Ward and Smith fired almost at once. Mario Evans died where he fell.

But this was a murder that could be solved. There were too many people involved in it, and the police caught up with the confused and frightened girls in the Temple Courts lobby soon after. They had seen everything. And everybody knew they had.

Initially, Ward may have thought that he could ignore the threat the girls posed, perhaps because he knew them so very well. Holiday he had paid (a point for the defense at the trial): but even so, he called her with a warning and a threat. But by the next week things hadn't settled down at all, and the police, who were actively pursuing an investigation, soon knew what had happened. Not long thereafter Princess ran into Bernard Smith again, who let her see his gun and warned her to keep her mouth shut. Taken to the police station with her mother, she remembered his admonition. It was there that, explaining her naive lack of fear, she told the police that she was safe because, "I have the best pussy in Sursum Corda." It sounded as though she was quoting Ward. After her interview she returned to Sursum Corda and called Ward to report her loyalty. He promised her that his friend Frank Thompson would bring her and Holiday some money, and she was naively delighted. Holiday knew better.

But then Frank Thompson ran into both of the girls on the street. Looking directly at Princess, he warned her that she had better not tell anything to anybody, but as he spoke he thought that she was too young really to understand what he was saying, and what she had to do. Now Holiday was well and truly frightened. When Princess was late coming home that night she sent her sisters out to look for her, and cooked half-smokes for dinner. Then at last Princess came home and all seemed well. But suddenly Thompson pushed through the front door. He had a ski-mask pulled down over his face, a gun in his hand, and he began shooting as soon as he was inside, in his fear and agitation shooting wildly, so that his bullets sprayed everywhere, striking a bucket, the floor, a chair, the wall, and Holiday's twelve-year-old sister, who was hit in the leg. The older girls, Princess Hansen and Timika Holiday, rushed behind a sofa in the living room to hide, but they were too slow. Frank Thompson stood directly over them and, at point blank range, shot Princess repeatedly until she was dead. He then pointed the gun at Holiday, but it clicked empty. Now without bullets and suddenly terrified, he rushed back through the house and out into the night. This is where my story begins.

Sursum Corda covers 5.8 acres and is separated from the rest of Washington both by roadways and by black metal fences intended to make life difficult for fleeing drug dealers. It is a short distance from Union Station, the main railway station in Washington, and is made up of 199 light brown stone townhouses built in the late 1960's, completed in 1970, a little small by today's standards, though most contain between one and six bedrooms and a living space of between 1200 and 1500 square feet, usually on two floors. These circumstances make the units easy to heat in the winter and, since the units are centrally air conditioned, easy to cool in the summer. Room sizes differ, but many measure about 10 by 8 feet, and are entered through a narrow hallway which runs, often bending at an angle, from the front door. The room in which Princess was trapped with her friend was one of these, and the closeness of the space in which she confronted her murderer only added to the extraordinary viciousness of the crime.

It was hardly the first murder to take place at Sursum Corda, though in fact the killing of a child is rare. Some years ago a former tutor and I were discussing with two of our young learners what they liked about their community. Aware of the homelessness present about them, both boys indicated that the best thing about Sursum Corda was its houses, and prompted only a little by my colleague, were willing to add the Georgetown tutorial program to the list. Another thing I like about it, one boy said, is that when they shoot people here, they usually don't shoot children.

A fair point, though not entirely true. A few years ago in a complex not far from Sursum Corda, a six-year-old was shot (but not killed) with an automatic handgun in the hands of another boy, aged fifteen. I was alarmed when I heard the story, since it is quite true that there is a taboo against harming children seriously (though a few years earlier a big-for-his-age and aggressive fourteen-year-old had been, with calculation, shot in the leg to teach him not to interfere with drug transactions), and I was concerned that the inhibition might be breaking down. It wasn't, at least not then. The shooter had been aiming at one of his colleagues in the drug trade, but like many such he was a simply terrible shot, the result of little if any target practice. But bad marksmanship is only one of the dangers here. Shortly before I began working at Sursum Corda one killer had inadvertently murdered his intended victim's brother. Two weeks later he returned and finished what he had begun. During the period of violence at Sursum Corda, roughly from the late 1980's to the mid 1990's, most of the executions I heard about had taken place in the small hours, and usually at point blank range.

I have begun my narrative with this recitation of violence because that is what you expect of me. Accounts of violence in inner-city communities, many a good deal less true than the ones I have just told, are legion, and shortly after Princess' murder several newspaper articles sought thus to stigmatize the community, to represent it as a place of drugs, murder, disorder and crime generally, and though interesting enough in its way, nothing that should be encouraged or preserved. The attractiveness of inner-city violence is particularly apparent in print, where it can be regarded from a distance, and isolated from the very many other aspects of urban life which the disadvantaged confront daily: a concern for their children and the rent, an apprehension of standing authority and of the simple arbitrariness of life which affects all of us, a desire to understand the world, particularly as it registers upon whatever it is that life gives. Violence has a small place too, but one that is diminished by the daily grind. Elsewhere, it is what such places as Sursum Corda, once stigmatized, are known for, and all residents are deemed somehow culpable, if not by active participation than by indirect acquiescence. Usually we look away from the poor, except when they threaten, frighten or entertain us.

But the issue of drugs was a large one in Sursum Corda, and probably I should write about it now. In one of his short stories, James Joyce creates a character who "deals with moral problems the way a cleaver deals with meat," and it has sometimes seemed to me that he might have been describing many a Sursum Corda critic. But not all of them. The hardest criticism to answer comes from a person of like background who has prospered through intelligence, perseverance, and opportunity, and now looks back at the world left behind, and judges it. Such a one is usually willing to encourage others to follow in his or her footsteps, but that encouragement comes at a price, one involving a certain attitude toward the community left behind. In the worst case, for example Princess' murder, it would not be impossible to argue that the community was complicit in her death, and this in fact was sometimes done in the days following. Her murder, like many before it, turned on the muted struggle among drug dealers and users, and it is true that the community has not often sought help from the police, a circumstance that has occasioned ill will. Drug dealers, sons of the community or not, are almost never handed over to the authorities, but even so they are generally unwelcome, and made to feel so. At the same time, except perhaps for those who stand to benefit, such persons are not really approved of, and it is uncommon for a mother to watch her young take up with them with equanimity, though it does happen.

No cause for celebration, to be sure. For forty-seven years our little program encouraged children to look beyond the schemata which had been prepared for them, and our chief adversaries were the drug guys. Some years ago Allene, a woman working with our program, saw a boy talking with one such when it was time for tutoring; no question what they were discussing. She walked over to them and told our young learner that it was time to come inside for tutoring. You make me sick, the other one replied. No I don't, Allene answered, careful not to deny what he had said. It's that white stuff you take that makes you sick. And walked away with her young learner. Another boy was friends with them as well: his grandmother, the only anchor in his life, was much concerned, and he would not reject her love for him, so always came to tutoring on time. But his friends advised him: Pound on the piano. (There was a piano in the room in which we worked.) That way they'll kick you out and it won't be your fault. No question which side we are on.

But in the past it was impossible not to observe the way the community countenanced – from fear, from indifference, from a sense that they are ours – the presence of these dreadful and unwelcome people. Sursum Corda is a short walk from Capitol Hill, and in the nineteenth century a large slave market stood between the two – Frederick Douglass used to cite it when he spoke, forcefully objecting to the sale of persons at the very threshold of the Capitol. Two centuries of slavery, another of neglect, cannot vanish with the stroke of a pen. We hold these truths, as we have come to know them. Try to wrest them from us as you have before, but we will make you use brute force to do so.

I do not wish to romanticize the choices made. Intelligence and perseverance have led some residents away from Sursum Corda – but not all who have left it can lay claim those good qualities. And it is these other ones who give the place its roots and its direction. They live in a world that they themselves have only made in part, yet it bears the impress of their certainties. No plea for the community will move the great ones now, since it was that they set out to escape. Remember the friends you had when you were young, especially those who could not follow you. They are the ones who do not choose you now.

And finally this. A tutor long since graduated kept up with her young learner, and helped him find a place in a private school, known to be sympathetic to such as he, where he could live and find his way in life. When Princess' murder appeared in the press his headmaster made the connection, and invited the young man to speak in chapel about his life at Sursum Corda, and what, thanks to the school, he had replaced it with. But the headmaster didn't get the thanks he was expecting. Instead, the young man said that Sursum Corda was a part of him, that he would not desert it, even now. He didn't praise the murder, but knowing what he did (which was a lot) wouldn't accept that the community was complicit in the crime, and wouldn't desert it (as others had) now that it was vulnerable. To prudence he preferred this truth, this courage. Not long thereafter, and driven by that speech, he left the school, unwilling to forget the rock from which he was hewn.

Sursum Corda was founded on different principles. In the late 1960's an energetic ex-army-officer who was also a devout Catholic, Eugene Stewart, together with certain friends, took the then extraordinary step of making themselves personally responsible for establishing a place where the disadvantaged and the poor could live together with respect and dignity. There is no doubt at all that he was responding to Catholic social teaching when he did so, but the action seemed too almost utopian, a distant echo of those nineteenth-century communes that sprang up in response to a search for a new and better world, places to redeem the human race. It is usual, when referring to the early days of Sursum Corda, to point out the federal assistance that proved useful to the early residents, first of all in the person of Robert F. Kennedy, then Senator from New York, who supported ex-officer Stewart and recommended him to HUD, which approved one of the low-interest loans that the federal government had made available to groups and individuals interested in building low and moderate income housing in the city. On the other hand, there are those both inside Sursum Corda and outside it who do not regard the dedication of "Northwest 1," as the area is known, to support the urban disadvantaged as an act of civic generosity so much as a somewhat cynical way of containing the poor in one place, so that their presence would not lessen property values elsewhere in the city. Apparently HUD's more recent thinking has moved away from supporting such enclaves, even now sometimes represented as the haunt of criminals, so that present policy emphasizes mixed developments, with a portion of HUD supported developments now set aside for the disadvantaged, rather than seeking to contain them all in one place.

But the difficulties such developments posed seem to have been understood by those who sought to establish the community, and one of them was a well known Catholic priest, Horace McKenna, a Jesuit, and then a curate at near-by St. Aloysius Gonzaga church on North Capitol Street, whence he had come after his energetic work on behalf of his African-Americans parishioners in the Maryland countryside had made it imperative for him to leave. His connection with the founders was deep if sometimes continuous – McKenna Walk, on the Sursum Corda property, is named for him – but what drew the men together was what I have already alluded to, an understanding of Catholic social teaching, which had recently been both informed and encouraged by the twenty-first ecumenical council of the Catholic church, known as Vatican II, that took place in Rome between 1962 and 1965. Vatican II was concerned with Church renewal, a dialogue with the modern world, and a quest for unity among Christian churches, but what was as important as any of these as far as Sursum Corda is concerned was its emphasis on pastoral, not dogmatic, teaching. Catholic social teaching has its roots in the medieval university, but since the end of the nineteenth century it has focused on the poor and the disadvantaged, and on the responsibilities of the Christian towards them. Concerned less with individual salvation than with a considered social good, the teaching now seeks to realize a kind of covenant, not a contract, between and among persons, one that can work to their mutual advantage, and realize whatever common good can be agreed upon. It insists upon the dignity of the individual, and the importance of the family in the social order. But it is also concerned with the demands of justice and equity, and in recent years at least, has come to promote what has been called a "preferential option for the poor," which can mean many things to many people.

There is no doubt that both the founders of Sursum Corda and Fr. McKenna had an understanding of this teaching, and sought to instill it in their new community. The fact that relatively few of the residents were Catholic certainly did not dissuade them, which is not surprising since three of the other four developments constructed in Northwest 1 at about the same time, equally had religious roots, though Temple Courts was constructed by the Masons. Throughout much of the 1970's the community at Sursum Corda flourished, though its founder's style of management owed much

– some thought too much – to his army days, and as time went on he acquired the reputation of a man who did not suffer fools gladly. Of his own integrity, commitment, energy and persistence, however, there could be no doubt. He placed his own money into the project, and was given to confronting HUD officials on some of their regulations, which, much to the officials' credit, they often then proved willing to adjust. Resisting the two-bedrooms-per-unit model so much in use at the time, Stewart put the architectural contract out to tender, and his selection of town houses – with between one and six bedrooms in the 199 unit development – owed much to his Catholic commitment to the family, though perhaps it owed something to common sense as well. In any event, it is unique in the area. One other physical aspect of the place which has caused recent comment is the U-shaped street that runs through the complex – sometimes, rarely now, called the horseshoe – which, together with five or six separated areas (depending on how you count), some built around parking lots, make up Sursum Corda. These too would have been the architect's design, but they lent a sense of closeness, even intimacy, to the residences they enclosed which, in theory at least, would have accorded well with the idea of Christian community which the founders were pursuing.

I have already remarked that the style of management the early days witnessed could be abrasive. Minutes of early meetings of the Tenants' Association, preserved among Father McKenna's papers in Georgetown's Special Collections, record the difficulties the community encountered, sometimes at its meetings in an open air "meeting place," now a children's playground built into the project. It was here that the sense of covenant at which the founders had been aiming came up against the reality of residents who preferred not to take direction, as some understood it, from the white owners, and so would stay away. Evictions were to follow when a resident had amassed 25 points, and 12 and ½ points were assigned for missing a community meeting. Once opened, the split between founder and residents could only grow.

Finally the founder sold the property (which he owned) to a California company whose promises seemed fair. As the 1980's progressed, the company's interest in the property seemed at least to lessen, but when it became apparent that the plan was to evict the remaining residents and sell the land on which the property stood for offices, the Tenants Association sprang into action. A rent strike was organized, with the rent monies placed in escrow; HUD was alerted; and the California company backed down, and agreed that the development could remain, and with a new resident manager, too.

This successful strike was led by a group of people including a woman, often in the papers, who will figure later in these pages, Ms. Jane Walters (as I shall call her), a well known community advocate and then a resident, of keen mind and sure political instincts, who worked in close association with a Roman Catholic nun, Sister Diane Roche, then living with five other nuns on the property. Together, and not without an effort, they secured Sister Roche's appointment as the new resident manager, so that by the late 1980's the community seemed refreshed and renewed. True enough, what Sister Roche found when she took up her appointment was an extraordinary record of neglect, of requests for repairs ignored, of tools sold, so she learned, to support drug habits, of studied and intentional neglect. She, too, had to contend with the expectations of the residents. She had, some years earlier, lived in the community as its servant; how could she now, some foolishly and wrongly estimated, countenance as un-Christian an act as eviction? No need to pay the rent, then. However, Sister Roche lived in the community and helped to guide it during what can only be described as its best years. Yet quite paradoxically these were also the years during which violence in and around the community reached its peak. Shortly before, at the direction of her order, leaving the community to assume other and greater responsibilities, Sister Roche was one of those who assisted with the creation of a resident-owned cooperative at Sursum Corda, which came about with a pepper-corn payment to the California company, and created a legal hurdle that set the stage for everything that is to follow in these pages.

And yet I fear that these representations of confrontation and strife will misrepresent the experience of many a resident. In its early days Sursum Corda was known, and not only to its residents, as "poor people's paradise." In the late 1980's, when I began working with the tutoring program there, tales of "Fr. McKinny" (as Fr. McKenna was known in the neighborhood) were everywhere present: he had turned up the day before Thanksgiving with a turkey. He had paid the rent for the last two months. He bought our children clothes. The image of Fr. McKenna as a servant of the poor is so well established now, that it is difficult to convince those who know of him that his work was guided by a settled understanding of Catholic social teaching, and that it was social justice, not charity, that informed his days. A former Georgetown president, who knew and admired him, is one of the few I have met who referred to him first of all for his intellect, and remembered him as one who fully and accurately understood the philosophical implications of his work.

In fact, it is hard to think otherwise. The exact origins of the Georgetown tutoring program at Sursum Corda are unknown (I have tried hard to find them out), but I have always considered Fr. McKenna its founder, and that in office he had acted with several (unknown) brother Jesuits at Georgetown. Certainly in the very early 1970's it was in operation, a school bus bringing Georgetown students into the community to work with the children in their homes and on their homework. This book is only partly about that tutoring program, which I shall discuss in the course of things, but also about more recent matters, though it is from the vantage point of that program that I observed the community over the past twenty-seven years. When I joined it, the sudden development of the drug trade had necessitated moving the tutors from the homes into the Community Center, where, as it turned out, it became possible to undertake academic work of a far higher quality, while retaining the tradition of actually working with the children of Sursum Corda in their community, which many of the tutors come in time to prize, and somewhat to understand. Now begins my journal. The date given indicates the day I actually wrote my usually retrospective entry.

1

Sursum Corda. The End.

Reality, however one interprets it, lies behind a screen of clichés.
Every culture produces such a screen, partly to facilitate its own
practices (to establish habits) and partly to consolidate its own
power. Reality is inimical to those with power.
–John Berger

A long day's dying, to augment our pain.
–Milton

Saturday February 5, 2005

Thursday had dawned grey and cold, and stayed so throughout.
Snow showers possibly mixed with rain had been predicted on the
morning radio, and by 3pm the snow from the window of my third
floor office in New North looked heavy, so I called the weather
bureau and looked on the internet, only to find them both confidently predicting that it would end by 5pm, and that accumulation
would be minimal, "mainly on the grass." Still undecided, I called
Christine Nicholson, the Resident Manager and the chief connection and guide that our tutoring program has at Sursum Corda, to
see whether she thought we should still come to the Community
Center and tutor, as we regularly do on Tuesday and Thursday.
The two sessions before had both gone well, with almost everyone
on task and, though in the beginning of a new semester, settling in
nicely. Still, it was cold and damp, and I wouldn't have been sorry

to be told that the snow made tutoring impossible, as it sometimes did. Instead what I heard was that it was "your call," and that perhaps we should talk again just before 5pm. I had a 4:15 class which runs until 5:30, but said I'd call again after that, and reach Christine at home.

In fact, the snow stopped not long after 4:30pm – I could see it ending through the window in Walsh 390 where I was teaching -- so that the decision to go was easy, indeed I felt a little chagrined at my earlier hesitation. I stopped in the Tombs for a bowl of chili and a coke, and then went back to my office to call Christine and say that we would be coming. But this time she objected. No, really you can't, she said. We're having an emergency meeting of the community. We'll need the upstairs, and anyway, it might be best if you weren't here. I felt a tug at my heart, and knew what was coming. Had there been some news, I asked? There had. The community was going to be told that, in due course but soon, their homes were going to be foreclosed. Some time thereafter the buildings would be leveled and new ones built, probably better ones and for different people. In any case, and after 35 years, Sursum Corda would soon be no more.

The last sentence, to be sure, went unspoken. The purpose of the meeting was really to say that HUD had decided to withdraw its crucial Section 8 financial support on the basis of three failed inspections, but many of us believed HUD had acted in no small part with the support of the negative publicity spearheaded in the *Washington Post*. The *Post* had followed the murder of Princess Hansen on January 23rd, 2004 closely, and, weaving news and editorial together, effectively blamed the community for the deed. But there was no time to talk about that now. I met the student tutors at 6:30 by the Library steps and told them, if briefly, what had happened. That there would be no tutoring tonight. That we would have a meeting of all the tutors on the following Wednesday. I say somewhat more than this to Justin Campbell, Elizabeth Hall and David O'Brien, the students closest to, and most involved in our tutoring program, but don't say everything (I didn't know a lot myself at this point), and register their concern. They ask, What can we do? I have no answer.

Later that night I called Shiv Newaldass, Hindu and Trinidadian by birth and a markedly intelligent young man whom I had come to know well, and who is, thus far at least, the only George-town graduate to have come to us from Sursum Corda, where he and his family still live. How had the meeting had gone, I asked, not entirely innocently. He read to me from some of the documents that had been handed out – xeroxed copies of the letter from HUD saying that the community had failed the inspections (the commu-nity is now said to have been in default since January 26th), and how the decision to withdraw support could be appealed (within 7 days, though any meeting resulting from the appeal would have to take place in Atlanta, Georgia), another from the lawyer the Board had retained seeking information and delay among them. During the meeting, and as the effect of the letter from HUD was becoming clear, a woman stood up and looked at one of the Board members. "Who are you?," she asked. And to another, "I don't know you. What is all this? What's happening?"

But now it is Saturday morning, and I have just phoned Chris-tine at home to talk about where things actually stand. The decision has been made, she says, "Within two years Sursum Corda will be torn down." The Board is now, she says, "trying to get the best deal they can," and find a development company to do the work, but it will be very different in the future. The present plan is for each family to receive perhaps 40 or 50 thousand dollars and get a voucher for HUD-approved housing elsewhere in Washington, and to be offered the right of refusal of a unit in the newly rebuilt property when it is ready. All this comes, of course, with strings attached. As of now about 160 of the 199 units at Sursum Corda are occupied, and in recent weeks 16 families (which will be excluded from any settlement) have moved out. The present management company is also a development company, and they want to "do the work," but two members of the Board are opposing their appoint-ment. But if they are not appointed, the company insists, it will disengage from its management duties as soon as possible.

Of course, once the residents have left the community their re-turn is anything but certain. The new units will be sold, not rented or leased, and it is thought that the asking price would be about $300,000. A number of units (perhaps 20 percent) could of course be set aside, at least in the beginning, for present residents, but in order to be eligible to return they will have to pass a criminal check on themselves and their children, and find mortgage support for a percentage (51? 49?) of the asking price. The long and the short of it is that very few of the present residents will be able to return. Against these depredations the Board is holding out a final straw of hope: if support could somewhere be found, perhaps from a housing group which they have approached, then families could be moved temporarily and 30 units could be reconditioned at a time, then the families moved back in and the next 30 units taken on. This, evidently, is what the Board would prefer. But very sadly, the hope, at this point, and this late in the day, looks unrealistic. But maybe. Time will tell.

I ask about how the residents are reacting to the news, and am told that it is hard to say, but variously. Some are fatalistic (my sense is that Christine herself may be becoming one of these: I hope, so far, not me, and will try to resist the temptation). These realize that the pounding the community has been taking for over a year now – from *The Washington Post*, from former friends and former residents, from HUD itself – could not but have its effect. Others are really quite stunned and shaken. "It will be very hard for some of them," Christine observes. We agree that if all the residents had stood together after the murder a year ago, things might possibly be better now. But many people could not then understand, or not believe, that the homes that they thought they owned (Sursum Corda is a cooperative, owned by the residents) would be taken from them and torn down, and they themselves forced out, for nothing they had done. This is America. Things like that don't happen here. And in their fear, and hurt, and incomprehension some now turn against the Board. Hit those at hand. Or in a different form, pose again the question John Steinbeck's dispossessed farmers ask in *The Grapes of Wrath*, "Who should we shoot?" But there is no answer in the language spoken here.

I tell Christine that we will keep the tutorial program going to the end, and as long there are children there to teach. She says Good, and before we hang up, we agree, quite unnecessarily, to keep in touch. I then begin this account, and having some idea (I think) of what is to come, choose my mottos, in spite of the promise I have made myself, from John Berger, and from Milton.

Monday February 8, 2005

Over the weekend I email the tutors giving them a general sense of what has been going on, so that they will be able to deal with what they will hear from their young learners on Tuesday, and also think about themselves. I advise support and sympathy, but say too that the Board is working on things so that we should not assume the worst, and say we will have a meeting on Wednesday in which we discuss these things. Afterwards I have a return email from Sara, one of our best and most experienced tutors, saying among other things that she is upset at what has happened, and I realize that I am too, and have been making myself think about contingencies so as to avoid the larger issue. But I was impressed too that Sara had both the maturity and sensitivity to write back, and answer her as best I can.

Later that evening...

This seems a good point to offer a fuller account not only of Sursum Corda, but of the Georgetown tutoring program there too. As I have already said, the community was established by a group of Catholic laymen in the late 1960's, partly in response to the way the homes of the poor and disadvantaged were being appropriated in the interests of what was then called "Urban Renewal" (Gonzaga High School gained a football field thereby, and many of the new buildings around North Capitol Street stand on land once occupied by private homes), but partly too because of some low interest loans which HUD had then made available to groups and individuals who wished to invest in low and moderate income housing in an area not then thought to have much commercial value. In the course of things five properties were developed, one ("Temple Courts") by the Masons, the other four by various church groups. These included "Sibley Plaza," on North Capitol Street, which combined young families and retired persons, and "Tyler House," also on North Capitol, which was assisted at one point in its history by a group of Republican lawmakers who took an interest, and found funds to rebuild it.

As I have already indicated, the founder of Sursum Corda was a dedicated Catholic businessman and former army officer named Eugene Stewart, who had become President of the Georgetown Alumni Association, which he hoped to involve in the work of establishing the community. He found willing allies among his friends and others, one in the person of Richard McCooey, a fellow Catholic businessman who likewise had Georgetown associations, and another in the Rev. Horace McKenna, S.J. Once Sursum Corda was built, Fr. McKenna became a familiar visitor to many of the families who lived there, so much so that he is still remembered today as "Fr. McKinny," who brought food and help to those who needed it. But it was Gene Stewart who led the charge, so that without him the community would not exist.

Perhaps Gene Stewart's greatest innovation was to move away from the two bedroom units which convention had assigned to low and moderate income housing elsewhere, and put the architecture contract of the project out to tender. The result was that, instead of the high-rise buildings elsewhere apparent, Stewart built town houses, a construction rarely employed in low-income housing in the late 1960's. These had the effect of both privileging and encouraging family units, and building community. But in order to do so he needed to secure federal funds, and that was made possible only after he had gained the endorsement of the then-senator Robert F. Kennedy. To that endorsement he had hoped to add support from the Georgetown University Alumni Association, but here he was frustrated by those among its membership who objected that the organization had been founded for other purposes, and should not thus concern itself with the poor. Honorable man that he was, Stewart at once offered his resignation, and though persuaded to withdraw it, thereafter distanced himself from the group. Fortunately, though, Gonzaga College High School, whose campus lies close to St. Aloysius church and the projected project, came to his rescue, and stood in as a local sponsor.

The early years at Sursum Corda are still remembered as good ones. Before the properties were constructed, but when their first occupants had been identified, certain of the first residents pitched tents on the site so as to secure their homes, and the attention they attracted added to the visibility, and the viability, of the project. Some residents even called it a "poor people's paradise," since so it first seemed, when many of the residents were related to each other, and many came from the Carolinas. But that was before the rapacious 1980's when the drug trade came roaring into town, encouraged in Washington, so some believed, by the absence of those criminal organizations which at once advanced and regulated it in other places, so that crew contended with crew. In the conflicts which the quest for market share evoked, the murder of members of another crew (as the competing gangs were called) became an almost daily practice, and by the late 1980's the "D.C." following Washington's city name was reported variously as "Death City," "Dodge City," "Drug City," among many expansions of the acronym. There was one period in which Sursum Corda and the blocks around it experienced about a murder a month, and though almost all were drug assassinations and restricted to the small hours, one took place on a warm Saturday afternoon, another between 7 and 8pm, while tutors were working there. Tutoring continued between Monday and Thursday nights during this time, though each child was tutored only once a week, but when the tutors were enrolled in a class that required them to tutor the same child twice a week their work became a good deal more effective.

The tutoring program was likely begun by the Rev. Horace McKenna, S.J. in 1970. He had a school bus at his disposal, which he used to bring Georgetown students to teach the children of whichever parents would welcome them into their homes. The arrangement, unsatisfactory as it was, remained in force for years. The tutor would arrive; the parents, sometimes at least, would thereafter leave the house. The tutorial hour would pass, with or without effective tutoring, most of which was attached to homework, being accomplished. The tutor would then leave, too often abandoning a child or a group of other children, who were all thus left unattended. From the early years there developed a further Steinbeckian sense that the children of one were the children of all, so that, with all faults, the arrangement appeared at least to work. But by the mid-1980's, some think before, things had begun to change. The number of tutors and learners shrank dramatically. Drugs came in and consequently, relationships hardened. Walking back to the car (as with falling numbers the bus which brought them there had become), young women tutors would sometimes find themselves noticed and called after. Sometimes though, if directed by their parents, children would accompany their tutors to the car.

In 1989 a new office at Georgetown called the Office of Volunteer and Public Service took over the tutoring program and began to organize the transportation of the students, and the Sursum Corda Board not unreasonably took the opportunity to move the program out of the residents' houses, and install it in the Sursum Corda Community Center instead. In that Center, a large and open room made serious tutoring possible in a way it had not been in the period of home visits. It was shortly before then that, formerly appointed by the then Dean of Students John J. DeGioia (he is now the university's President), I became faculty advisor to the group, and in due course developed the program of instruction that I shall describe. But it is in the Sursum Corda Community Center that the program took root, attached to an English Department elective class that I offered for many years, and that became the program I shall describe here. In the late 1990's the Volunteer and Public Service Office withdrew from the Sursum Corda program in the Community Center, in favor of a largely student-run tutoring program at the nearby Perry School, an historic building that had been rebuilt as a center for neighborhood social services.

There have been certain constants in the operation of the program which have developed as the years progressed. In the first year we partly took direction from an accomplished, energetic and now retired primary school teacher, who strongly believed in phonics, and who, drawing on many years of experience, encouraged the program in ways that were certainly most helpful. Her focus on phonics offered clear direction when we were beginning to address the issues which training inexperienced undergraduates poses, and her own evident enthusiasm supplied its own support. During that first year it became apparent, from reactions among the tutors and the children both, that other methods of instruction were probably called for as well. For one thing, the program as envisioned largely repeated methods familiar to the children from their K-6 classrooms, but which seemed to interest them in neither setting; the tutors brought with them a lively willingness to engage their young learners which the phonics books hardly seemed to answer, and it was soon evident that there were probably different, possibly better, methods which might prove not less effective. But these reservations should not mask the vitality of those early days, when it seemed for all the world that we were inventing education, though in retrospect we were actually feeling our way, following, at least in the beginning, well worn paths, and it was not until we left them that the program began to blossom.

Thus it was that, thanks to financial assistance first supplied by Fr. Robert Lawton, S.J., Dean of the College, without which I doubt I would have embarked upon the course I took. I enrolled in courses in the School of Education at the University of California at Berkeley during three separate summers, living the while at the university's excellent International House, or I-House, as it is universally known. Even in the summer, I-House, a large graduate dorm built in the neo-Spanish style, retains some of the international and multicultural ambiance for which it is well known. I made good friends there, mostly German and Japanese, some of whom I have happily managed to keep. I much enjoyed the tone, the spirit, the apparent innocence of the place, and though as an institution it was perhaps more self-congratulatory than self-critical, I retain fond memories of it, only partly qualified by events years later, when I sought, with a friend, to introduce a program that would enable those I-House students who wished it, to work with disadvantaged children in near-by Oakland. Embraced warmly by the then-Director, the project was effectively scuttled, if rumor and report can be believed, by those of his subordinates who saw in it only an increase in their responsibilities. Academically, I chose Berkeley because it seemed to offer the best opportunity to study childhood literacy with a prejudice in favor of the socially and economically disadvantaged, and also, through instruction in a modified whole language approach to literacy, that could supply a different approach to the subject than what we had been doing. I say modified because the reading of whole language methodology I encountered in my classes was by no means uncritical, though it was sympathetic and astute, and when a fellow student put to the excellent professor in whose class I was enrolled that she was allowing a role for phonics as well, the woman candidly acknowledged that that was so. And yet in every way the methods taught were lively and engaging, and, with their focus on comprehension and understanding, would prove a great boon to our program. Though my own scholarly and critical writing certainly declined in quantity during those summer months, I found both the courses and I-House welcoming and stimulating, and never really regretted the choices I had made.

The difficulty with such an arrangement at Sursum Corda partly lies in the schools – and one in particular – which the majority of the children attend. This particular school has in the past represented, in a somewhat extreme form, many of the difficulties which beset inner-city education, beginning with a principal who purchased a doctoral degree in educational administration from a mail-order institution which federal authorities in the form of the FBI subsequently closed down. When this fact was understood, the woman represented that she was unaware that she had done anything wrong, and the school system accepted her assurances, only reducing her salary, which was in excess of $100,000 by about $3,000, since her doctorate was, by action of the authorities, now unrecognized. Even so, she continued for a while in office, and during her tenure effectively sequestered her school from the surrounding community, effectively forcing out of it a volunteer group of retired primary school teachers and others that had long been working there, by all accounts very commendably. It was widely conjectured that she had thus eliminated a possible source of criticism, but if that was her intention it proved ineffective, since the *Washington Post* published a column on her education and practices that ended her usefulness in office. Because Georgetown's tutoring program began within the community itself, it has enjoyed a measure of support which could not have accrued to it in any other circumstances, and that sustained it when times were hard, as they became after Princess' murder.

The program became more effective when we began going to Sursum twice a week (the same tutor with the same child), and added a weekly seminar in which the tutors both learned their craft and discussed their progress. Though attentive to pedagogical practice, and to those responsive to the thinking of the great Russian psychologist Lev Vygotsky (1896-1934) in particular, our program was not predicated on any social theory, whether one or many. Though separate from the schools which our young learners attend, we tried to remain attentive to the strategies employed there, some of which certainly are in accord with the focus on comprehension we work to maintain, and it is to everyone's advantage to have the children encouraged and instructed in comprehension whether favored in their home rooms or not.

In those days too, I was myself much interested in Vygotsky's work, and believed, with a degree of certainty and a somewhat lesser degree of truth, that, changes having been made, our program at Sursum Corda could reasonably be described as indebted to his thinking, to his insight, perhaps particularly through his description of the role of interaction. I thought of a mutual interaction amounting to an exchange, between student and learner, one that was particularly in evidence when social and economic issues were present. Although I studied several of Vygotsky's texts in order to understand his thinking, I may not invariably have observed the differences in practice, though I believed then and still believe that the model we worked toward was informed by Vygotsky's, albeit in a different tone. I have, if briefly, written about this experience elsewhere, focusing on the nature of the exchange that seemed to me implicit in our work, and the extent to which social interaction could inform cognition. But my concern here is rather with the nature of the Sursum Corda community, and the trials it underwent, and I will defer further comment for another time.

In general though, we encouraged the tutors to structure their tutorial in this pattern, which was largely without Russian nuance:

1. Introduction: In practice, we learned to allow time for greetings and even embraces, before we settled down to work. Our tutors dealt regularly with an "affective filter," attitudes born of confrontations and other circumstances that their learners had encountered before coming to tutoring. Time and familiarity helped, and it was most often the nature of the relationship between tutor and learner which let us proceed.

2. As a general rule we followed an old book – new book organization, in which a book read at the last tutorial meeting becomes the first one read this time, and once we began meeting twice a week this practice gained ground. All the tutors engage in previewing and predicting strategies, and in what we call the FIAT questions: factual, interpretive, applicative and transactive ques-

tions, but the last three in particular. We encouraged the tutors to read to their learners, and especially to the younger learners, for part of the tutorial hour, and to try to find high-interest material the better to engage them.

3. Writing figured with greater prominence as the learner, and perhaps also the tutor, gained in confidence, but even the youngest child could be encouraged to write a note to his or her mother, even if it only says "I love you." We encouraged as well dictated stories, which the tutors would type up and bring back for their learners to read the next time, and, with varying degrees of success, I have also encouraged tutors to compose their own stories, ones in which the learners figure prominently. We encouraged children to write out of their reading – what happened when the lion and the boy met the next day – and even children too young to write in sentences can draw a picture of what happened, thus processing what they have read themselves, or heard read to them. Further to encourage such efforts we published at the end of each semester a "Sursum Corda Literary Magazine," sponsored (that is, paid for) originally by the Georgetown English Department, more recently by two generous donations from parents, which effectively saved the program when money ran short. In any case, it has been our lit mag as much as anything that has turned our learners into writers, and also showed the larger community what we are all about.

4. There is a web of other things we urged as well: that tutors should praise their learners' work at every meeting, but only in specific terms, even very specific ones ("it was excellent the way you..."), not in general ones: ("good job"). We experimented with personal computers, but tilted rather, in the limited time we had (2 hours of instruction a week), toward one-on-one hands on instruction. And I regularly urged that when the tutors say good-bye that they try to remind their young learner of one good thing that they have accomplished this time, and praise that.

While it is not true that there are as many ways for such interaction as there are tutors and children, it is certainly true that circumstances alter cases.   One tutor engages a six-year-old boy whose mother has become deeply addicted, and who has, as a result, lost interest in her children.   Her chief attachment now is to her supplier who uses her roughly, particularly when she does not meet her quota of sales or his other expectations.   Ignored by his mother, her young son comes to identify with the cold bastard who beats her, but in time his tutor offered him another model.   Another tutor met his young learner's mother on the first day of tutoring, but when he saw her three weeks later, on a Saturday movie-trip, his young learner denies that the waving woman at whom his tutor is also waving towards is his mother, and it is not until they close the gap between them that the tutor finally understands the reason why.   But he greets her warmly, and reminds her that he is taking her son to the movies.   In the summer following my first year with the program three of our young learners had been arrested for shop-lifting in Maryland, and when I reported the fact to a child psychologist I know, I added ironically that their tutors had not, perhaps, been so very effective.   No, he said, that wasn't it at all. The motives for such behavior are many, but what their tutors had offered was another choice, one which, soon or not, one or more of the children might adapt.   When they decided to act otherwise, it was to that example that some at least could have reason to resort.

Wednesday February 9, 2005

Tutoring did not go particularly well last night, though the tutors who persevered were rewarded (as were their young learners), so that some good work got done in spite of the evident distraction, which sat like a 700 pound gorilla in the middle of the room.   A group that is engaged at the nearby Perry School, which confusingly clings to the name Sursum Corda, was not in evidence when we left the Georgetown campus, but after we arrived in the Sursum Corda community, I spotted a tutor I had not seen before, and had a word.   She was a member of the Perry School group, but not understanding the drill had simply asked "Is this the Sursum Corda van?," been told yes, and climbed aboard. She had found a boy from Temple Courts (or perhaps he had found her) who asked her to tutor him, and they were reading together, if without much sense of what they were doing. I went back to her at the end of the session, really just to be friendly and to tell her a little about the place (though she had been tutoring in Perry School all year, this was her first time into Sursum Corda itself) as the session broke up. Towards the end of our brief conversation one of the Sursum Corda Board members whom I had met before came in holding two bottles of soda which one of the children evidently had stolen (her word), and she was very angry about it. I excused myself and went over to her as she was putting them back, apologized for the child's depredation, and gave her ten of the eleven dollars I had with me to make it good. She took the money without hesitation, but was not going to be mollified, and later outside I heard her continuing her representations to a friend. Once home I called Christine and explained what had happened. She thanked me for calling, and said she would do what was needed.

Friday February 11, 2005

Wednesday night I had a meeting with the tutors to see if I could help them to gain some insight into what is now developing, and to encourage, what they have already begun to show, patience and sensitivity with their young learners. They all came, but except for Justin there were no questions afterwards, and I came away with the sense that they do not really understand what is happening, that circumstances of age and affluence have embarrassed some, and made the rest, for now at least, not eager to look too closely. This is not an uncommon reaction when young tutors first go to Sursum Corda, and first become aware of the evident differences between their own world and the one now before them. But it is a mistake to think that they stop at that reaction: sometimes it takes time, but in the end most tumble to the nature of the place, and the reasons for it, whatever use they finally make of it.

Tutoring last night went well, better (by which I mean more on task) than on Tuesday, when the children were really quite distracted, though perhaps because of the cold they were at first slow to come, including four grandchildren of Ms. H's, a longtime and active resident, who live with her. Somewhat unsure of my ground, I took the four tutors back to Ms. H's house (they had been put off with promises when they first called there for their learners), and as Christine happened to be passing as we were waiting outside for the children to come down, I engaged her in conversation about the difficulty, after which she put her head (and then her person) into the house itself, which greatly speeded the process. In the Community Center there are notices up for another meeting of the community on Tuesday at 6pm at St. Aloysius Gonzaga church on I Street. "What will the future hold for us?" the flyer asks. "Will we be forced to move? This is a very important meeting. Please come out, get all the facts about what is going on; this could mean displacement. All residents are welcome. Please forward this information to your neighbors." On the van ride home I discover that Justin's parents are coming down from New Hampshire for the weekend, and, partly since I may not be in Washington for graduation this year, contrive to invite them to visit on the Friday afternoon they will be here.

Monday February 14, 2005

Yesterday I went with a former student to lunch in Annapolis. I had known him as an undergraduate tutor in the program, and in the course of our conversation we discussed what seemed to be happening at Sursum Corda, and our apprehensions for the future. Almost at once, he suggested a plan to defend the community, one which (somewhat improbably, as it transpired) involved a bank issuing mortgages to individual tenants, basing the loans not on credit histories, but on the now much higher land and property valuations. Such a plan would only work, he thought, when property values increase dramatically, so that the mortgages could be based on that, but that seemed to be what was happening anyway, with the shift in property values brought about by the construction of the new Convention Center nearby. But what was useful about his intervention was his absolute conviction that the die was *not* cast, and that there were other possibilities than the ones that HUD, the City and soon after the developers, were holding out to us. This encouragement was very useful in those early hectic hours, where up was down and left was right, and who knew what was what.

I had arranged to have dinner a few days later with Shiv, whom

I have already mentioned, and whom I had come to know well during the years he was associated with our program, first as a learner and then years later as a particularly able and effective tutor. I resolve to discuss these ideas with him. After our cheering lunch my friend and I stop off at a pottery shop on State Circle where I bought a set of salt and pepper shakers shaped of two right whales ("right" because they were the "right" whales to hunt!), but these ones painted an unusual shade of light blue, which seems to presage an odd kind of unlikely hope, perhaps leading me away from nature and toward human constructions instead.

When Shiv and I finally get together, he opines that the best outcome would be for each resident to be allowed to continue to live where he or she is, and in peace, and he reveals how he thinks that might be accomplished. The mortgages would of course give the residents an equity they seem to lack now, and so leave them far wealthier than they would be with the modest $40K or $50K payment which is being prepared for them, since their individual homes are already worth far more than that, and they could thus retain ownership as the value continues to increase. We agree that Shiv will sound out the President of the Board, Wilma Holden, a powerful, direct and plain-spoken woman who has lived at Sursum for many years, raising two children there with hardly any income at all.

Later Shiv considers that there may be a danger that personal mortgages could prove the beginning of the end of that sense of community which, in spite of everything, still animates Sursum Corda. But I find myself wondering how such things will actually play out, if they do. In the course of our conversation I express concern at the continuing presence of drugs and violence, and am somewhat afraid that these may be used to support the current plan, which seems to want again to seize the houses of the poor, pay their owners a fraction of their value, and then pull them down so that a "development company" can build palaces for the affluent on the newly valuable land. My own sense is that we must consider carefully what surely lies in store for the community or we will be building on sand. Shiv wants to talk to certain members of the Board away from Sursum Corda, and I agree to invite whomever he wants to lunch at Georgetown on Friday, if they can come. He is sure they can.

Wednesday February 16, 2005

At tutoring last night Justin's young learner, Lewis (aged 7), brings in his second grade report card which sports not only good grades, but a particular commendation for Lewis' grasp of and response to previewing and predicting strategies, ones which, because of our program's focus on comprehension, Justin had been carefully cultivating. Justin was highly pleased and promised a celebratory visit to the Candy Lady after tutoring (a woman who sells candy to the children from her house, and to whom tutors sometimes, perhaps too often, resort when they have had a particularly good session – though not only then). In the event, alas, she was closed. But what struck me too was how the whole report, and with it Lewis' own assumptions about learning owe much to Justin's interventions. It is usually difficult to predict with confidence when, reading strategies apart, a tutor's work will inform his or her learner, but it is less difficult to observe it in practice, and when it does appear, the result can be very satisfying. Still, as I never tire of pointing out, both influences, academic and social, will prosper better if the tutor knows what he or she is about, and is able to deploy the teaching strategies appropriate to the learner and the hour.

At the very end of the session, as I am locking up and making my way out, Shiv comes back from the residents meeting which was being held at St. Aloysius Church on Eye Street, and quickly tells me what has gone on. No Board members were present this time, nor any from Management, but HUD was there (mostly to listen and observe, he thinks), along with reps from Northwest 1, and best of all, he thinks, from Boon, a tenants' rights association which has taken an interest in the case and had been assisting the Board informally. Shiv invited the woman from Boon, of whom he came to think highly, to our Friday lunch, and asked her to induce Wilma Holden, President of the Sursum Corda Board, to come as well. He also established (he thinks) that Sursum Corda owes HUD a nine million dollar debt, but that ownership is vested entirely in the Board, which alone has the power to act.

Friday February 18, 2005

The lunch with Wilma, Shiv and their colleague from the progressive urban housing group that is Boon went very well. Shiv had arrived early, partly to announce that he had just got himself officially appointed to the Sursum Corda Board, but also to note that Wilma might be bringing her grandchild with her, so I asked the waiter where we might best eat, and she suggested we sit in the open passageway outside the lunchroom proper, where the space would allow a child to cry or sleep, and kindly pushed two tables together to accommodate us. In fact Wilma came without the baby, but the table where we sat was well apart from any other (though at a nearby table the first judges from the new Man Booker International Prize for fiction, today visiting the campus, were themselves planning for a somewhat different outcome), a short walk from the buffet, and, unlike those in the darkened lunchroom, bathed in sunlight, all of which contributed to the conversation. We discussed the possibility of turning Sursum Corda into a condominium, a proposal which allows each party to own, absolutely, his or her own residence, but also to set rules so as to limit access by drug dealers and others who would harm the community. The hoped-for effect would be to make all the residents home owners, holding property they could sell for profit, or pass on to their children or grandchildren, and the last of these objectives in particular seemed to register with our guests.

Wilma Holden, the President of the Sursum Corda Board, is a tall, forceful black woman, whose often silent presence frequently registers, but always, when she does speak, is direct and to the point. She knows the community as well as anyone, and has neither forgotten the good (and bad) times of the past, nor closed her eyes to present realities, however painful. She listened, I thought attentively, to what we were discussing, asked few but pointed questions, and, only after considering, indicated that she liked what she had heard. A young and sympathetic colleague, not resident at Sursum Corda, accompanied her and seconded her approval as did Shiv, now the newest Board member, whose grasp of the particulars seemed to me also to have deepened apace. Towards the end of the conversation, Wilma remarked that Sursum Corda had "saved her life" some years ago, and I asked her what she meant. It was when she was a young mother, she said. Her daughter's tutor would take her up to Georgetown for a weekend, and entertain and look after her there. She was the only one I could trust to do that, she said, and it gave me time for myself, when I could be alone.

It became clear as we talked that although many groups, including the city, are approaching the Sursum Corda Board to seek either a partnership in, or ownership of, their newly valuable land, all are seeking, with varying degrees of candor, to feather their own nests. The first of these seems to be the present management team which is now "running" Sursum Corda, and which is a development company too, working in Sursum Corda without fee, and managing two adjacent properties, Turn Key, which runs between Sursum Corda and K Street, and Sibley Plaza, which lies between Sursum Corda and North Capitol Street. If by some fluke, we speculated, the company could acquire both of these properties as well as Sursum Corda, this effectively would place at their disposal a city block, bounded by North Capitol, K Street, First Street NW and New York Avenue, a block which lies almost midpoint between the new Convention Center and Capitol Hill, and one which is soon to be serviced with its own Metro stop. The potential profits would not be small, far more than the $80 million profit which, at a guess, might be realized from the sale of Sursum Corda alone. I hope that all of this is quite legal, and for those who would reap the profits such behavior falls under the heading of business, even business as usual. But now and again – if not more often – the law's an ass, and the ethical implications of separating the poor from their homes in the interests of the affluent may one day awake the conscience even of this rich, well-meaning and rapacious nation. Let it be now.

But we also talked about Fr. Horace McKenna, who is still warmly remembered (though often as "Fr. McKinney"), and the founding of Sursum Corda itself, about my eighteen years there, and with that the part Georgetown University had played over the years. Both women said that they had been praying over the decisions Wilma and the Board would have to make, as had their families, praying that God would show them a way, and put someone in their path who could help. My sense was that they were still looking, which, in retrospect, seems to me a very good thing indeed.

Monday February 21, 2005

HUD, otherwise the Department of Housing and Urban Development, was founded by President Franklin Delano Roosevelt in 1937 through the U.S. Housing Act of that year, as part of his program to confront and finally end the Depression. Though always a player, it grew in importance and influence only slowly, emerging as the mega-agency it has now become only in 1965, when under President Lyndon Johnson it attained the dignity of a cabinet-level agency, an integral part of the "Great Society" program. In 1968 it further acquired, under the Fair Housing Act of that year, powers of enforcement against housing discrimination. In spite of President Richard Nixon's 1973 imposition of limits on housing and other forms of assistance associated with the agency, in the next year it consolidated its position with the development of Section 8 housing programs, with which Sursum Corda, among very many other projects and communities, became associated. Though often attacked and frequently reformed, the agency's investment in low- and moderate-income housing was not seriously threatened until 1995, when the "Blueprint for the Re-Invention of HUD" proposed massive changes in public housing. In 1998, according to its HUD.GOV web site, the agency opened its "Enforcement Center" which sought to "take action" against HUD recipients "who violate laws and regulations." The same year, the site reports, Congress approved "reforms" which sought "to reduce segregation by race and income, encourage and reward work, bring more working (as opposed to welfare) families into public housing, and increase the availability of subsidized housing for very poor families," a description which, in theory if not always in practice, represents all that is best about the agency and its history.

On March 31 of last year (2004) Alphonso Jackson, formerly Deputy Secretary of HUD, was confirmed by the U.S. Senate as its Secretary, and it is under his administration that Sursum Corda has had to face its present difficulties, ones in which the policy to "reduce segregation by race and income" has had particular effect. HUD, I am told, seems to be moving away even from supporting Section 8 housing projects that already exist because they believe them to incubate poverty and crime, a policy that has had the effect of giving particular weight to articles in the press that identify and attack individual projects. In the past the policy had the effect of maintaining property values elsewhere by keeping the poor contained where they are. But it is not difficult to believe that the Section 8 housing projects most at risk are those which stand on land that has become suddenly valuable, and on which a developer may have cast his eye. It is not so much that the government has lost interest in such projects and is now willing to hand them over to any who apply, as that the both the moral belief systems, and the more secular world of social policy, which have in the past protected such communities, have now been revised, so that the communities themselves suddenly stand naked to their enemies.

The difficulty with this well intentioned but particularly destructive new policy may be the effect it can have on projects like Sursum Corda, a cooperative, owned by its residents, and not by a slum landlord who is failing to keep his housing up to code. With the latter, a HUD inspection and even a foreclosure makes a certain amount of sense, once, as always, local circumstances are taken into account. But with a co-op the situation is more complicated. The residents own their home, or at least a part of the co-op, subject to regulations. In fact at Sursum Corda the (legally untested) powers of the Board in general, and the President of the Board in particular, are considerable, but they are tempered, if only by DC law, by the rights of the residents. Still, the residents have, over the years, come to treat their sturdy, well-built units as their homes, as their property. In a way it is no more reasonable for HUD to sweep into Sursum Corda and issue collective responsibility and blame, than to do the same on a street in Georgetown. Ah, but at Sursum Corda, they will argue, our investment gives us the legal right to do so.

The respect the poor garner in America comes largely from each other, but to receive it most easily they often come into association as communities, such as the one that thrives in Sursum Corda. No doubt there is crime there, drugs most of all, but is it really convincing that eliminating Section 8 housing will also eliminate drugs in urban America? The policy now seems to be that such depredations may be undertaken, with only the most limited reference to the persons who actually reside in the places being thus attacked, since their residences have been found substandard, and so almost any other place should be preferred. What nonsense. In a place like Sursum Corda, a cooperative residence, many of the residents enjoy a measure of stability and respect available to them nowhere else -- and one for which they have worked and paid for years. The easy identification of residents and drug dealers may hold water in Washington's white suburbs, but anyone who knows the place knows how false a representation it offers of the place itself, where condemnation of the dealers – and concern for their influence – is all but universal, and desire for improvement flourishes. Alas there is little sense, at least in recent years, that such improvement will be supplied by HUD, though as administrations change, who can say what will follow?

Thus, although it was HUD that effectively came to the community's rescue in the mid-1980's when the then-owner wanted to level the project and reclaim the land, it did so, it was then believed, by assuming the community's debt, with the result that, in spite of expressions of gratitude at the time, a certain amount of residual suspicion of owners became attached to the agency itself. "It's the Federal Government," one resident told me when I asked if she thought HUD could be brought around or resisted. "They can do whatever they want." But what HUD actually wants done is hard to say. In a letter sent to the then President of the Board shortly after the November election, HUD listed the apparently objective criteria for its decision effectively to abandon the property. In the formal, legal language in which such documents are couched, it noted that in April HUD's Secretary had notified the Board (legally, the "Sursum Corda Cooperative Association, Inc.") that it had failed to keep the Cooperative in good repair, and had 60 days to address the charges. At the end of August the HUD inspector had returned, "to determine if the owner had taken the required corrective action," but that Sursum Corda had failed its second inspection too. A list of certain (not all) of the "cited deficiencies" followed, and nowhere is HUD's intention more clear.

The inspector had noted paint peeling from some of the walls, and stains on some others. [He's not getting into my house, that man.] He had paid particular attention to electrical sockets and switches, and had noted some of the cover plates were missing, some outlets broken [the actual description read: "missing/broken outlets/switches/cover plates"]. He had noted "damaged/ obstructed storm drain," "torn gutters," "damaged/inoperative stove" [singular for some reason among the 199 units]; "inoperative range hood/exhaust" [again singular: is this some sort of code?]. He also noted other things that he described as "broken/missing," and these included handrails [where? in public places, in houses, both?], and also shower controls; he saw too what he called "damaged door hardware/locks." He noted "insect infestation" [it was August when he made his inspection, so legally the charge could be sustained by either flies or mosquitoes], and a "damaged GFI." He found an "inoperative smoke detector" [singular], missing "electric lights" [did he perhaps mean "light bulbs"?], a leaking "supply line" somewhere, and not less than of any of these, "standing water." This is the legal justification then for turning almost 200 families out of the houses in which they reside, and which, to some degree, they own. The moral and ethical reasons, except for those apparently supplied by those *Washington Post* articles of last winter, are a good deal less clear, and very many of the residents continue to believe that the driving force behind the foreclosure is really the sudden rise in property and land values following the construction of the nearby Civic Center.

In all of this remember that Sursum Corda consists of 199 separate town houses, or units, each one the home of a family that would hardly welcome, indeed that would resist, intrusive oversight. These residents have reason to resent, much as I would, being told that their drains need unclogging. There is no reference in the HUD report to collapsed or weakened walls or roofs, and even the references to electrical connections, that seem designed to imply some unspecified threat of immanent destruction, contain no suggestion that the wiring is either old or substandard. In fact, all of these "deficiencies" could very easily be addressed, and if the residents, rather than the Cooperative, were legally responsible for the upkeep of the property many of them would be. The document responds rather to the requirements of legal power than to realities of the situation it purports to address, and shows all too clearly why residents of Sursum Corda – and no doubt elsewhere – are disinclined to place their confidence in an agency that has, after all, done them signal service in the past.

Talking all this over with Shiv supplied a different insight. Part of the problem is the way HUD holds the Board accountable for things that are not only out of its control, but which its members cannot possibly know. Yet the residents have become accustomed to think that such repairs are the duty of the Management, and specifically whatever management company is then involved, even though that company is often seen as an adversary, whose only real duty is to collect the rent. This function has stripped the residents of any real sense of ownership, the more so since they can be relocated in the interests of a larger family when theirs becomes smaller. One way to deal with this circumstance would be to make the residents the owner in fact as well as in name, and that, of course, is what we have been proposing.

There is the possibility as well, or perhaps, in spite of what I have just said, it is more than that, that once the residents have become the owners they will not attend to the upkeep of their property with equal diligence. Equal diligence no more exists at Sursum Corda than it does in Georgetown. The interior decoration of Sursum Corda houses have always differed greatly, and I remember hearing two of the children in our program discussing what happens to the homes, both inside and out, of those who have succumbed to drugs. Of course such things happen everywhere, and I remember once, visiting a colleague who lived in Silver Spring, being invited to walk a block or two to inspect the home of a neighbor whose tolerance for long grass, abandoned vehicles, and peeling paint, exceeded that of anyone around. Finally calls were made, a visit from an appropriate officer came about, and changes went into effect. But not all, and not soon. We have now the Supreme Court to remind us how property rights must curtsey to the state, though interventions for the common good are made more often against the poor than the rich, who come armed with lawyers and talk of the next election. But if not the Supreme Court, then who will guard the guards?

No doubt HUD is not itself the real antagonist, and would have offered a different response to the question I posed at the beginning of this entry – that it can indeed be brought round, and even work for the community, changes having been made. Strictly speaking, HUD's only real interest is in the millions of dollars they are owed, which only amounts to chump change when the total value of the property is taken into account, not in the care and well being of Washington area developers, who as a general rule can look after themselves. In this telling, however, they do retain an interest in seeing to it that the disadvantaged are not actually defrauded, particularly when government funds are, and have been, deeply invested. We can, after all, accommodate their wishes, at least as they have been expressed, and we should do so in everybody's best interests.

Tuesday February 22, 2005

Partly because a journal is, by its very nature, a disclaimer of omniscience, partly because I have been trying to write with an eye to understanding the way this whole business is seen by those involved in it, and as it is unfolding, I have not focused on what the residents, universally interested and concerned with what is going on, have been told. Some weeks ago, however, the Board, supported and informed by management and perhaps others, drew up a list of "options," which could help to "avoid foreclosure." "There are no good choices," the document warned, "but choices must be made... All of the above [options] involve at least temporary relocation of some or all members. Time is of the essence," it added.

The sheet summarized seven plans, five of which required developers, two (at the bottom) which did not, and itemized "pro and con" for each. The first suggested selling part of the property, but warned of the length of time, and added, as a con, "Still have to finance own building or at least a portion of it." The second option involved partnering with a nonprofit developer, but warned that such organizations usually lack "financial capacity to control project." The third was to partner with a "for-profit developer," and here the "pro" list included "Probably easiest access to investment funds," "Co-op gets partial ownership," and "usually fastest track," among others. It did make clear, however, that "Profit motive is usually paramount," and "Could be difficult to meet members' housing needs," a deal breaker as far as many residents were concerned. Finally this part of the document indicated partnering with both a for-profit and a nonprofit, but warned about disagreement, and what it seemed to imply was the least of these, partnering with the city, which it described as "Probably slowest track... always administrative hassles. City has greater interests."

The options without developers were only two, to sell the property outright and to declare bankruptcy. The first of these was said to produce "Too many unanswered questions for prospective buyers," and a "high risk for others," the first of which "could take too long," while the second, "Pisses off HUD." Thus far I have spoken to only two residents about the options, and both were, I thought, rightly wary of everything. They seemed to have no confidence in a private "for-profit" developer, whose interests they understand as running quite counter to their own, and for all of its faults, as one of them said, want to see the community improved, not destroyed. The only line which seems to have gone home from the document I have been quoting was the one which warned that "There are no good choices," but those I have spoken to, at least, have no intention of moving, and want to hold on as long as they can – not unreasonably thinking that if the community does come to an end, the greatest financial rewards may come to those who do not leave it.

Wednesday February 23, 2005

It has been just over a year since Jahkema Princess Hansen's dreadful murder on January 23, 2004, began the series of events that, for better or, more probably, for worse, will issue in a final chapter in the life of the community at Sursum Corda. Marc Fisher's cliched and sententious column yesterday ("Girl's Family Stumbles Along Road of Grief") commemorated the event, focusing on Princess' family ("periods of rebuilding – classes taken, a new home, the mercy of daily routine – alternating with valleys of despair"), and noting that Princess' mother "has been diligent" about providing the Greater Washington Urban League, which administers the donated funds "receipts for all qualifying expenses," while also recording, really for no good reason, that Mrs. Hansen's partner and son have been reimprisoned for substance abuse ("With all that grief, I fell back, started smoking marijuana, using drugs," the partner is quoted as saying). The column praised the "hundreds of readers" who "responded generously a year ago" by "contributing

$15,000 to pay for Princess' funeral and help the Hansens get out of Sursum Corda."

Marc Fisher was much involved in the *Post's* attack upon Sursum Corda last winter, so it is not surprising that he would write in these terms, implicitly holding the community responsible for the evil which was committed within it, yet another example, as if any was needed, of the rich blaming the poor and exonerating itself. The idea that the community was itself the victim is nowhere considered, nor are Princess' own associations there, which, understood in their complexity, might compel a different reading of events. But this sort of contemptuous, by no means offhand, and only apparently knowing reference to the community of Sursum Corda and, by extension, to those who live there, is one of the engines which has encouraged, perhaps even precipitated, the current crisis. A note at the end of the column promises the next effort will concern itself with Sursum Corda itself.

In class tonight we were discussing the connections between literacy and community, and also the ways in which some parents, who can not themselves read, can feel ambivalent about their children's ability to do so, since some will feel that they will, in time or quickly, thus lose their children to a world that is closed to them. I tell the story of one Sursum Corda mother who saw what was happening, and, not wanting to inhibit her daughter's growth, found a place for herself as a teacher's aide in the local elementary school classroom, so that she could thus learn to read alongside her child. But we agree too that this is one of the properties of literacy that cannot be denied. It introduces its followers into a larger community than any they have thus far known before; it frees them from necessarily observing boundaries that have thus far seemed absolute. With this freedom, with these new communities, can come a feeling, even a nostalgia for the past, a time when truths seemed to be certain, or at least absolute. But with the light which understanding brings they are these things no longer, so that every act of knowing is an act not only of opening but also of disintegration. Let it be the lesser of the two.

Thursday February 24, 2005

I suppose that Marc Fisher's column in today's *Washington Post* ("D.C.'s Plan To Take Back A Neighborhood") is in its way a classic, and, as promised, it certainly continues his attack on the Sursum Corda community. It employs terms that suggest the place is quite beyond salvation, being notorious for drug dealers and crime, and that really, there is no more that needs to be said. I hate to sound at all appreciative of a piece so finally poisonous, but it is not difficult to see why those who have never set foot in Sursum Corda, and know it only through the pages of the *Washington Post*, might respond to Fisher's rhetorical strategy, which will have the effect of confirming their fears and prejudices, be they ever so latent. He begins by describing Sursum Corda as "the scary place where the 14-year-old girl was murdered last year," and adds that the "people who still live there may talk about getting out, but where would they go?," which is a good question.

He then quotes Police Chief Ramsay: "That place is designed for criminals," and describes Sursum Corda as having "lots of isolated corners, a center-city location with lots of office workers nearby but totally invisible from the main drag." The implication seems to be that office workers slip in to buy their drugs there – When? On lunch breaks? – so that nobody can see them do it? But this image of unconstrained lawlessness does not end there: "For years even police were afraid to enter Sursum Corda. The residents are mostly people who couldn't find anyplace else to live – more than half the households earn less than a third of the average U.S. income. The dealers ruled."

Last year, Fisher allows, saw improvements: "City Administrator Robert Bobb decided the city had to regain control. Sursum Corda became the first of 14 'hot spots,' crime-saturated places where the District launched an all-agencies effort to change the rules. A year later crime is down more than 40% and there hasn't been a murder since Princess died." And the effort did not end there. The police understood that most of the dealers did not actually live in Sursum, but simply plied their trade there, and so drew up a list of "the top 50 criminals," 45 of whom they proceeded to arrest. Although most were soon released, the police were able to obtain a court order barring them from entering Sursum Corda again. But at this point the article reaches an impasse. If the drug dealers have been thus removed, and if the police are in charge again, then why is it necessary to shut the community down, which is the implicit argument of the column? There are, of course, two reasons: the HUD loan which is being called in, and the associated increase in property values following the construction of the new Convention Center. It is hard to believe that Fisher is unaware of either circumstance, though he addresses neither directly.

First he quotes "a longtime resident who is leading an effort to rebuild Sursum Corda," Jane Walters, a well-known city activist who had been much involved (with others) in preventing Sursum Corda's destruction in the 1980s, but who moved out of the community some years ago, and has had a somewhat ambiguous relationship with the place since. She is now represented as implicitly denying that there has been any substantive change at all. The action of the police "only mows the weeds," she is said to have insisted, "leaving the roots behind." "How come we can do everything in another country," she asks, "but we can't figure out our own community?" But that question is what Fisher has been leading toward.

In an interesting quote which Fisher may not entirely have understood, City Administrator Bobb echoes much recent thinking about the destruction of inner-city communities and is quoted as saying: "We cannot continue to loose and displace residents to development....We've damaged a lot of communities by parachuting in with our plans. .... This is going to be a slow process of winning trust, but it would be a shameful act if we just sat back and let the wave of gentrification wash over them."

Yes, quite right, but what actually is being proposed? "Details are hazy," Fisher intones, "but the idea is to replace the existing 500 units with 1,500 units, guaranteeing residents the right to return to subsidized housing. The rest of the units would be split between moderate-income families and those that can afford the market rate. With a mixed-income neighborhood, the city hopes to attract developers, create stability and prevent displacement." Fisher puts the cost of a new Sursum Corda at "about $400 million," with the private sector bearing the costs. Bobb thinks it could be built in 5 years, and Walters is quoted as saying, in effect, that "an economically mixed community would have better schools and services than a poor neighborhood could ever muster." The most poisonous remark comes toward the end of the column, and seems to be Fisher's own: "This place is so dangerous that few residents oppose tearing it down." But this is hardly to be believed! Whoever told him that? Anyone at all? Alternatively, he simply invented the implied exchange to deprecate the community further.

The theme throughout, which no doubt will be repeated in days to come, seems to be that in order to save the community it is necessary first of all to destroy it. Or perhaps the argument is that the police have saved the place, so the best thing now would be to tear it down and build something better. I apologize to any who are offended by this, but as I was reading the first part of Fisher's column I was reminded of the sort of propaganda the Nazis used against Jews, seeking to reduce them, in the eyes of the ignorant and gullible, to the point where their destruction would seem not only necessary but praiseworthy. Sursum Corda, by this account, is a very scary place, one almost wholly given over to crime and murder, which frightened even the police. The crime of the "other" residents, and the reason they cannot be trusted to attend to their own best interests, is their poverty, the charge being that "more than half the households earn less than a third of the average U.S. income." The only way finally to save the community is to dilute it with many others, who will not suffer from this impairment, a process made even easier given the rules which both HUD and the economy are likely to impose on the reconstructed units, which will no doubt prevent many of the present residents from returning.

Unsurprisingly, given his antipathy to the place, Fisher has his numbers wrong, even where the correct number would better suit his case. There are only 199 residential units at Sursum Corda, not 500, and, putatively at least, the lower number would make it easier to accommodate all of the current residents in a development of 1,500, since they would be well under the 20% now designated for moderate-income residents in HUD-supported projects. But the sense of community, which Fisher has completely ignored, and which now exists in Sursum Corda, would not survive such an increment, and it is hard to see how such a development would provide home ownership to the current residents, most of whom, in spite of what Fisher has written, are not murderers or drug dealers, and who currently own an interest in the cooperative. The projected plan which City Administrator Bobb offers, which is of course only one of many which the residents are now considering, seems to imply that, if only for reasons of policy, arrangements will be made for them to do so, though the details "are hazy."

As much as anything, I found myself intrigued (if appalled) by what Fisher's source may have been for the remark which came toward the end of his column: "This place is so dangerous that few residents would oppose tearing it down." What's this now – "few of the residents would oppose tearing it down." Really? Took a large sample, did he? It does at least appear from his quite demeaning description of Sursum Corda that he actually has seen it – did he then ask some (many?) residents if they would object to having their homes torn down? Unlikely. Was it an impression he received from Jane Walters, as the order of his sentence might just imply? But if it was, he almost certainly would have said so. Or did he simply invent the sentence out of whole cloth, whether in self defense ("I'm not really against the poor, they agree with me"), or as a way of excusing the depredations being prepared by others? Apparently his desk editor found no reason to question such an extraordinary representation. I myself certainly have observed no such sentiment. Those residents to whom I have spoken would indeed object – though they are much concerned too that the wolf is at their door, and that their objections are simply going to be ridden over by the combined authority of HUD, the City, the developers, and greed. The children in our program have not yet begun to tell their tutors what they know, but last week one little girl whispered to her tutor that her family was going to move, and seemed afraid that they would meet no more.

Nor do I really understand the journalistic ethics involved in Fisher's column. At a particularly vulnerable moment it takes aim at those whom Fisher himself insists are the poorest among us, and while presenting himself as their champion, effectively strikes at the community itself. It offers not only withering commentary, but also what the majority of its readers would undoubtedly regard as news, though in matters of interpretation the column is deeply inflected. I understand that newspaper columns (at least in theory) differ from the news, and that the columnist's views are (again, in theory) his or her own. But by implication and by assertion Fisher's column muddies these distinctions, and since the author's views are not elsewhere balanced in the newspaper, their effect is to speak with the voice of the *Washington Post* itself, and thus substantially help to deprive the present Sursum Corda residents of what is for many of them their only real resource.

No doubt on the city pages of some or many American newspapers these distinctions are not always strictly observed, if only because columnists who write on urban matters must in the course of their presentation detail matters not covered elsewhere. But my anecdotal observation has been that when they do so their usual practice is to write with some circumspection, and only rarely to attack a whole community, as happened here. There is too the larger issue that Fisher is not describing the several proposals that the Sursum Corda Board is now considering, but such an objection may be rather an issue of competence than of ethics, and one the author might dismiss by saying that a full report belongs with the news. Not a very convincing rejoinder, to be sure, and what it really shows is how tenuous Fisher's connections are with the community he is writing about, since a word with almost anyone on the Board could have told him that there was more in play than the destruction he was championing. But the real answer is probably that these matters are complex, not simple, and Fisher writes for those whose attention span is limited, who love surfaces. Not for them any consideration which would challenge what they believe they know, that the poor are untrustworthy and given to drugs and violence, that everybody means well, that money, if there is enough of it, washes away all sin.

Rereading Fisher, I am struck again by how vividly his apprehension of the community, judgmental and destructive as it is, contrasts with the more open, inquisitive, if sometimes apprehensive attitudes I discover among my students, who see it better. To be quite fair to Mr. Fisher, they also see it longer. What sets our little program apart from many another is its oft-repeated twice-weekly, and one-on-one encounter of learner and tutor; its attachment to a community into which the tutor, depending upon his or her sensitivity and insight, inevitably gains some insight; and a communal regard for our program, often enough born, it seems to me, of little else than its longevity. But one result of these circumstances is that the students do not descend to their work, and, unlike Mr. Fisher, assume no precedence. The tendency among us is rather to defer to community than to assume a priority of any kind, and though nothing is invariable in life, such usually, I believe, is finally our practice.

Nietzsche says that anyone who attacks monsters must take care not to become one, and that when I look into the abyss, the abyss also looks into me. Probably a good text for both Mr. Fisher and myself to reflect upon, him for thus seeking to slay the drug monsters that apparently roam and graze freely in inner city America, me for becoming so frustrated with the evident hypocrisy of the present intervention as to play down the lasting problems that live here. But even with such a caveat it is difficult to see in Fisher's column anything but a crude reprise of last winter's coverage, part of an apparently sustained assault on the community which may in time, who knows, bring it down. And if Nietzsche does not answer the moment then perhaps Meg Greenfield does, who wrote in *Washington*: "A paper like the *Post* is a two-ton truck, and we run over a lot of people without even knowing it, and then we just roll on without even the most casual glance in the rearview mirror."

Monday February 28, 2005

Recently (and sadly) Shiv tells me, Boon has been pressing the Board for a signed commitment to become involved in the process, indicating that it wished to be compensated for its good work and support, but it was possible to believe that this was no coincidence, and that it was at least possible that Boon's representative to Sursum Corda, present at our earlier lunch, had given her colleagues a head's up. The Board has decided to defer any action until their March 7th meeting. HUD also had been in touch with the law firm acting for the Board, but it became apparent that the firm was actually employed by Boon, not the Board, and that may have been one reason HUD's reply was as candid as it was. The time period necessary to affect the transfer, which the firm had asked about, could be discharged within six months, the letter said, but it also seemed to indicate that HUD was inclined to offer the city the right of first refusal on paying off the loan and so acquiring the property itself. This was of course an important consideration. In the early days the city had seemed too supportive of the community, evidently aware of the difficulties which residents currently in four, five and six bedroom units would have finding like accommodation in the city. Now, however, the profit motive seemed to have triumphed, and the City's interests certainly seemed to me, to many of us, to have been placed above those of the community, though no doubt those would not be the words City administrators would choose to describe their actions. But whatever the language, as long as the residents can be offered, if only in theory, like accommodation in the new project, HUD and the city seem to have become agreed.

These considerations of course suggested that the Board required its own legal representation with some urgency. This raised one other matter, namely the sort of support we could garner from the City or elsewhere, which seemed particularly important since the City, as far as I could tell, has redefined its position. Shiv believes strongly that what will finally move the project forward is for the community to opt for self determination, not for dependence on anyone else, and to seek for its salvation from its own internal resources. He hopes that home ownership will initiate this process and contribute to it, but that in the end it will take a mixture of self-reliance, good leadership and luck in order to succeed – and no doubt a little help from whatever friends we have left.

Later in the day I talk to a colleague about what has been going on and find him more or less indifferent, and willing to resign the community to its fate. They have not, he thinks, been as willing to take hold of the programs available to them as they should, and a new development could offer the present residents new quarters, encourage the city to better the schools, and perhaps add other services as well. He allows that this has yet to happen, at least in Washington, but that's not to say it couldn't. Yet a former resident manager, a Catholic nun, wrote a *Washington Post* column now 20 years ago that addressed, among other things, that attitude. "If the tenants had fewer children," she wrote, reflecting the attitudes of those with whom she had to contend, "if more of them had jobs, if fewer of them were mentally ill – in other words – if they were just middle-class tenants and not poor, everything would be fine."

She did not hesitate to refer to the residents as poor, a word which in the recent past seemed to be slipping from our vocabulary, presumably because it can condescend, or endorse class, or be too imprecise in an age when disadvantaged persons move in and out of poverty, some economists seem to say, at will. America has indeed developed many ways of being poor, some more long lasting than others, but it is no illusion that there are poor in Washington, and I have used the word, which seems to be gaining currency again, throughout. It perhaps is true that the urban poor are deprived less of food – though that circumstance certainly has existed at Sursum Corda – than of meaningful opportunity and social advantage. Poverty has as much to do with social opening as with money, and though education works for some, for others, not at all. But it is a bad mistake to assume envy or imitation is what governs. The disadvantaged may share with everyone the desire for more money and for the greater autonomy it brings, but often at least, their values, their attitudes, their assumptions, are their own.

Still, one result of that independence is that, depending upon who is counting, and why, and how, the poor, in matters of housing, can sometimes be bought off, or if that doesn't work, then explained away. But not at Sursum Corda. For more than forty years the residents have, sometimes precariously, held this place; and more often than you would think, their writ runs here. Have you really prepared a better place for them? And for their children? Do you promise to respect them, once they leave this place? Will they be richer? Happier? Will their children really have a better chance at things (at least their schools will finally improve). Some will, no doubt. And the rest? At some level of mentation it is when the poor refuse to acknowledge their disadvantage that they become other, and make us want to wash our hands of them. We acknowledge, and we say we understand, their love of their children, and the rough independence which, elected or not, many embrace. But it is hard to forgive them for their evident regard for fairness, and their distrust of rules.

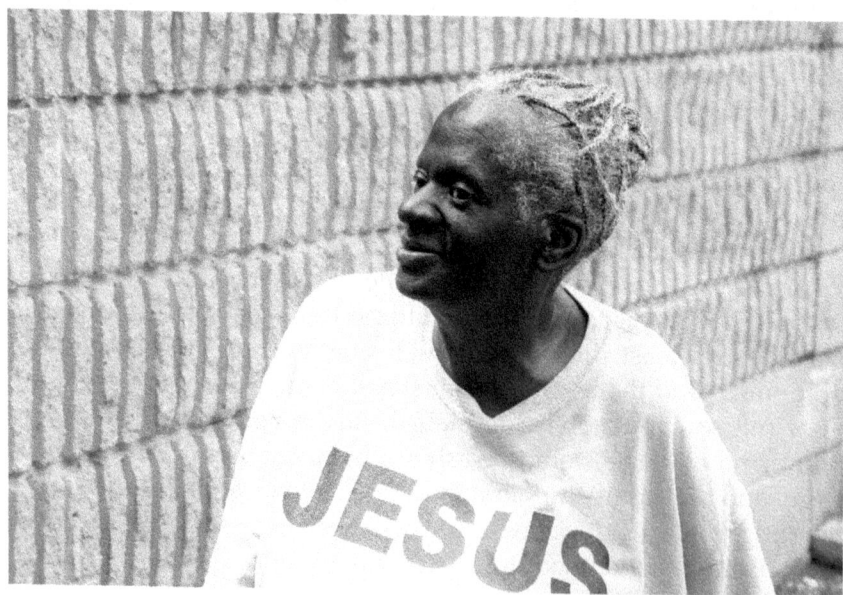

2

Sursum Corda If You Can

Dream delivers us to dream and there is no end to illusion
– Ralph Waldo Emerson

This chapter focuses on the early days of our attempt to preserve the Community of Sursum Corda, a period replete with confusion and blunder, when everything seemed possible and nothing probable. Our early efforts were nothing if not naive, even though we were aware that we were confronting what seemed all but inevitable. It concerns as well the tutoring program I directed, in which Georgetown undergraduates, twice weekly, meet for an hour one-on-one with a K-6 child who lived at Sursum Corda in order to work on the language arts together, in what we call a "tutorial," a meeting and an exchange from which both benefit, more or less equally.

It was through this program that I came to know members of the community, many of them children, and to esteem and to value our association. But at this point everything seemed possible, and my former student and present friend Shiv Newaldass and I set about to see if there was any way through which we could preserve what seemed to us an eminently viable community, one esteemed by its residents, and that attended to the requirements, particularly that of housing, for disadvantaged families with small children. It was during this period that we began to understand what a struggle for power amounted to, but also to receive expressions of support, not all intended, from as far afield as Kentucky.

Wednesday March 2, 2005

We have been having mostly good, on task, tutoring this semester, and last night was no exception, although I am concerned about three children, members of the same family, who have now missed three times. When I raise the issue, however, their tutors spring to their defense, and insist (what is only just true) that we missed once because of a snowstorm and another time for a holiday, so that we must not be too quick to judge, since our absences may have confused them. But with us there is no rush in such matters, and the relationships that have developed among tutors and children generally have been excellent, and led to very strong work all around. So I agree, but not enthusiastically, and say we will wait and see what develops.

At my request, Shiv agrees to come to the second hour of our Wednesday seminar, mostly to discuss the community with the students, but as he is agreeing to come he mentions that the Board is now considering selling off the units which lie along First Place, the so-called Sursum Corda horseshoe, after having moved those now living there into the 30 vacant units which have opened up elsewhere within the community. Under the circumstances I say, Hmmm, and Yes, I see, and even though a partial sale was one of the options which the Board had under consideration, I wonder, once the process has begun, how easy it would be to control it. But I must stop writing this now and prepare a sheet I want to give the tutors at our meeting this afternoon, which I will quote here so as to indicate some at least of the intentions of our program.

Sursum Corda Tutoring Program
March 2005

This is the time in the semester when it is easy to get comfortable, too comfortable. By now you and your young learner know each other well, understand what each will give and get, and most nights at least, the tutorial hour passes quickly. This is therefore the time to raise your expectations, not only of your learner, but also of yourself.

1. For one thing, spend part of each hour on **Writing**. We have discussed in the past "**portfolios**," notebooks in which your learner (and sometimes you) write, but which you retain, since your learner may well forget to bring it as regularly (ahem) as you will. Ideally, these can encourage *re*writing as well as writing – so that at the end you have produced a good piece of writing (from both of you) which we can publish in the literary magazine at the end of the semester (which is coming soon). Remember the concept of "**ownership**," as well, which means that it's ok, even good, for you to help with your learner's writing, but it's not ok to take it over. It's his or hers, not yours. This is sometimes a fine line, but important. Sometimes you'll be able to tell you've crossed it when your learner loses interest.

Also, don't forget about **dictated stories**, and even writing stories in which your learner, and his or her friends, figure prominently. But dictated stories are usually best.

2. For another thing, please do rededicate yourself to **Reading Comprehension**. As you know, I very respectfully eavesdrop whenever I can, and I am beginning to become a little bit concerned that, in a very few cases (perhaps) familiarity may have bred a certain disinclination to press your young learner as you should. But such familiarity should lead you to a greater investment in comprehension, not less! Remember the usual teaching strategies we have been employing to develop comprehension among our learners:

a.) **Previewing and Predicting Strategies.** Both before you begin to read a text together, and at certain stopping points in the narrative, be sure to do what you can to engage your learner's higher thinking faculties. If he or she is disinclined to predict, offer to write down the predictions in that excellent portfolio which you have suddenly begun to bring again. But don't give up on your search for mental engagement of the text you are reading and negotiating together! Every act of reading is an act of interpretation.

b.) **Rereading**. This is a most important reading strategy, with particular importance for comprehension, though also for fluency. Sometimes it's a good idea to take it in small bites – reread a page, for example, and just after you've read it, don't wait for the very end of the text. It's important of course to combine rereading with comprehension, asking what a phrase or sentence actually means, and seeing to it (or trying to!) that your learner actually understands its importance in the story itself. If your learner resists rereading, that may be because the text you are reading is too easy; so try another.

c.) **Applicative and Transactive Questioning.** In brief, these of course are questions which draw upon prior knowledge (applicative: "Have you ever...") or values (transactive: "What do you think s/he should have done when..."). Important because they cause your learner to engage higher thinking and to understand the text, their only danger (particularly when used at a stopping point) is that they may also cause the text to be left behind and so forgotten in a rush to other things – avoid that, to be sure, but focus on comprehension first of all!

Thursday March 3, 2005

In class last night we hardly had time to discuss my sheet, reminding and enjoining a new engagement, for the time we spent on Marc Fisher's article. An African American student asked, with evident implication, about the tenor of Fisher's attitude toward the community as a whole, and though we explored the issue, her questions suggested clearly that she believed it to be plainly racist, though she did not use the word, which probably was just as well.

One point on which two students took me up was the sentence, "This place is so dangerous that few residents would oppose tearing it down." From their own experience at Sursum Corda, most seemed to understand that the statement was simply untrue, and many were inclined to object. "And where did this come from?," asked one, seeking its source.

After this and more I asked certain of the tutors who seemed to me most able (the first of them alerted by me in advance) to tell the class what they have been about. Having been chosen not at all at random, they were certainly very good, but I was most moved by Tom, who spoke for the "older learners" program, a very small number of learners aged 12-14 who work with their tutors on special projects. The group had been founded, over mild objection, by Shiv, while he was a student at Georgetown, and taking the class. But Tom and Chris, friends and now colleagues, had enlisted their learners to help them write their course paper, which is to treat the early history of Sursum Corda. For that they had brought them to Georgetown's Lauinger Library, and to the Special Collections reading room, which sometimes seems to students a church-like sort of place, and where together they had consulted box 8 of the Father Horace McKenna papers, which deal with the founding and the early days of the community. Awed in the first place by the setting, the boys were, in Tom's word, shocked by the aging papers, maps, minutes and photographs which they excavated from the folders, all alive with the passions of those early years, and testifying to a past which is no more. The aging contents of the cardboard box offered them an opening on their community's past, and perhaps their own as well. Tom's sense was that the Sursum Corda they found reflected there, painted with all the hope that gave it birth, may have seemed to offer a promise of what's to come.

Saturday March 5, 2005

I have dinner with a present Georgetown student who was raised in Sursum Corda, and we discuss events. He had not seen Marc Fisher's column, and is shocked when I show it to him. He describes why he thinks some people who don't know Sursum Corda have such a visceral reaction against it – they can't really control the place, which anyway lies well outside their own experience – but thinks that drugs are less to blame than class. It's not that it's perfect, he says, not even, or especially, if you live there and know it well. But living there you do know everybody, quite literally, and you know that somebody's always got your back. You know that you're respected for what you do and who you are. When all is said and done everybody knows everything, and they know that, too. The drugs people are not really a part of the place, though some of them want to be. But they're not. He asks what he can do to help.

Saturday March 12, 2005

I was in Kentucky last week to work on some ballad texts of John Jacob Niles in the University of Kentucky library, and stayed while I was there with a most hospitable former colleague and close friend and his wife, whose now grown-up daughter had been a Sursum Corda tutor in the 1980's, shortly before I became involved with the program. She now has three gentle young children, a boy, aged eight, and the twins, girls, aged five. But even so, some twenty years later, she remembers her time at Sursum Corda clearly and warmly – two years, working with the same young boy throughout – and reports that she had experienced none of the distractions and occasional difficulties other tutors encountered. The boy's mother was always there to welcome her into her house, and her time there was invariably (well, almost invariably) happy and productive. I have no doubt she was not alone in that experience, and it is good for me to be reminded that however important I believe the initial training, the continuing support, and the place for reflection may be, it all starts with the tutor. In fact, continuing support was what registered with this former tutor most of all (though I tend not to think of Sursum Corda tutors as former, even when they graduate: temporarily inactive, perhaps). She adds that she wished the Wednesday seminar I now give ("Community Tutoring: Sursum Corda") had been on offer when she was at Georgetown, and was taken too with our field trips – to the Smithsonian, to the movies, to the zoo – that we now encourage our tutors to engage, both in order to extend our learners' schemata, and to deepen their relationships with their tutors.

I asked her, not entirely disingenuously, if her work at Sursum Corda affected her even now, two decades later, and she thought it probably did. She pointed out that she regularly takes her son with her when she delivers "meals-on-wheels," reminding me again that the primary determinant of social and personal values is often a parent, whose values and instructions are first understood in childhood, renegotiated in college years, or with an effort rejected, or both. But in one way or another, they remain of lasting influence. The question I was asking had too a "chicken-or-the-egg" quality to it, though it seemed to me the fact that this former tutor was about to begin K-6 teacher training partly answered it too. Tutoring itself encourages but hardly produces such commitment, and maintaining after graduation such values as we honor in our work takes an effort not only of the heart and the mind, but also, and very much, of the will. There is nothing inevitable involved in it, and it is the product of many sources, not one.

The family is Catholic (the children attend a Catholic school in Lexington), and understands the church's social teachings in some detail. It is also politically progressive, a circumstance that both informs and is informed by its religious values. The family's values endured long after the mother's commitment to Sursum Corda ended, but it may be that when a student is relatively young and asking somewhat unformed questions, the experience of tutoring can be particularly useful, and able to supply not so much answers – the issues here are education and disadvantage – as motive and context for asking them. Given the context, I was concerned with such considered attitudes as are related to our work, though the larger point may be that the most meaningful values are those that attach the individual to the world of others, strangers among them, so that for tutoring to enjoy a meaningful role in anything like value formation, it must first of all be pedagogically effective, and that is what, as I have explained, we work to achieve in our program.

Initial instruction and sustained support for the tutors is not at all a detail, somehow apart from the values they may or may not engage. They are integral to the process, themselves the way through which the tutor reaches his or her learner, and except they be done well, not much is achievable – though cases differ, and even the poorest intervention can contribute to the tutor's (though not necessarily to the learner's) understanding. I stress to students what hardly needs it, that, in spite of our name, our program is by no means limited to Catholics or indeed to religious persons, and what possibly does, that neither is it confined to Democrats or to those who identify with the Left – indeed I very much welcome the reverse when it appears. In one way or other, education, poverty, literacy, affluence, and the links between and among them, engage all of us, and the values and attitudes that we take from our work, whether secular or religious or both, are likely to inform what we assume, and so whom we become. The experience of tutoring can make these things real, and so create a hard measuring stick by which to encourage the tutor's effectiveness, and the tutor's hope.

It has seemed to me for some time that some of our tutors move through two distinct stages as they come, perhaps not exactly to understand, but certainly to engage, the complex community that is Sursum Corda. First comes what a medieval mystic, in quite another context, called a process of unknowing, in which many of the attitudes towards the disadvantaged, absorbed through the usual American ways, are first of all diluted, and then quite drained away. What comes next is less easy to define, and varies from one person to the next, though it seems to me to spring from virtue, and to involve that part of us that, as Thoreau almost says, sleeps for much of the day. In my early years with the program I remember a student asking, perhaps a little selfishly, if tutoring at Sursum Corda would make him a "good person." Of course the answer was no, but neither would it, I joked, make him a "bad person." Becoming any kind of person is a complex process, I said, and not so easily resolved. But I have wondered since what, if any, the long-term effects of a young person tutoring at Sursum Corda may be, even granting that they will differ from one to another. Perhaps some of the tutors who leave us for other realities will return to the values they have encountered at Sursum Corda when those they have adopted elsewhere prove incomplete. No doubt such values as we adopt and acknowledge will need themselves to be adapted, sometimes or often, to other places and other conditions, though perhaps not entirely left behind.

Back in Washington, I call Shiv, who reports that the Sursum Corda Board posed certain questions to him at their Monday meeting. What about a family, they asked, who for whatever reason (perhaps drugs among them) simply wants to accept $20,000 for their home? We agree to meet on Sunday evening to talk things through.

Sunday March 13, 2005

A much delayed meeting in my living room, which in the end proves revealing. Shiv arrives shortly before 7pm (we had arranged to meet at 6), and we talk for more than an hour. I come away with a fairly clear idea of what the Board – and from what I can tell that means primarily Wilma – has in mind. For one thing, the idea about building a new luxury apartment complex on part of the property has strengthened, though it now wants to dedicate the area behind the community center, and including some of the units on First Street NW and (if necessary) the back alley, to the project, but to leave the rest intact. If I understood Shiv rightly, the Board would remain in charge of the project throughout, though it is hoped that such a project might both supply funds to support the community, and also to appease the City, which would realize some tax revenues, etc. Shiv himself is now trying to find a developer. Somehow it all doesn't feel right, and I can't help wondering if the present Board – not all of whose members regularly attend the meetings – really thinks itself able both to accept liability for all the decisions which would have to be made, and also to direct a building project of such evident complexity.

We consider that constructing a project like the one described is no simple task, and that it is also very expensive – Shiv says the computed construction costs in the District are about $300 a square foot, and it is unclear that projected sales would cover what would be needed, as the Board now expects. He reprises my song, and points out that the drugs problem at Sursum Corda could undermine the value of the project, and leave the Board deeper in debt than ever. This seems to me a major point, but not one, according to Shiv, that much concerns the Board. Neither is he entirely convinced that the City would cooperate with the new plan, so that permits might not be approved in time, and other obstacles might appear in the way. He is concerned too that the project might be seen as enriching individual Board members, and points out that that circumstance could have repercussions which would be hard (or perhaps easy) to gauge.

He answers fairly easily the question the Board posed – What about the family which simply wants to accept quickly an offer of $20,000 for their $100,000 (?) property? – by pointing out that the new Condominium Board could regulate sales through a designated realtor and a designated banker, who could enforce fair market value. He adds that if the units were designated a condominium it would probably be two years before any sales would be accomplished. But there is a larger issue here we cannot deny: that some – many? – residents do not fully understand what "cooperative" means, and have the sense that they are simply paying rent on their homes, so that a large check could look like free money – they only have to agree to move elsewhere, and with a HUD voucher at that.

Shiv is also concerned that such sales are part of a larger pattern, and that whatever transpires at Sursum Corda the development of the surrounding area will continue apace, and that new projects will appear along K Street, across from Gonzaga High School. He notes too that the City has had almost no contact with the Board itself, and when Mr. Bobb met Wilma some time ago her impression was that he more or less dismissed her. Even so, it is widely thought that he consulted with certain developers, as he has with Ms. Jane Walters, the head of a group known as "Northwest 1." This is a neighborhood group that claims a somewhat problematic oversight role for the area around Sursum Corda, though the inclusion of Sursum Corda itself in its remit is somewhat problematic. Taken as a whole, the area contains about 28 acres; Sursum Corda, including the roads that run through it, comes to about 5.8 of that, but it is situated more or less in the middle of Northwest 1, so is central to any proposed development of a larger project. The other properties in the area are not cooperatives, however, and so enjoy a different legal status vis-a-vis the City than Sursum Corda does. Wilma is perhaps not as concerned with this circumstance as she might be, since she still is said to have Ms. Walters's ear, though I somewhat doubt that there is much mutual trust between them. Recently, however, she communicated to Shiv, what she may herself have imperfectly understood, that Jane is enlisting the help of "the Jesuits" (at Gonzaga?) in the project, though Shiv thinks she may simply be reaching out to some of the more affluent Catholics whom she knows. But it certainly seems that the Board may not fully appreciate the City's interest in what is to happen, or the means it has at its disposal to put its own case forward.

We decide that we must simply wait for the Board to develop its plan more fully, but agree to talk again in a week's time to see where things stand. Shiv also points out that at one point Sursum Corda was entirely free and unencumbered by debt, and that the millions of dollars currently owed HUD came from a loan taken to improve the property under a former management company. But the improvement actually effected seemed to many of the residents to be very minimal – new windows, doors, and some new cabinets – and neither top of the line nor the top to bottom improvements that had, some thought, been promised. And now that possibly misspent, and, some say, quite unnecessary HUD loan seems poised to destroy the very community it was meant to serve.

Tuesday March 15, 2005

Going to tutoring tonight means that I shall miss our Annual Faculty Convocation, where three friends are having their twenty years of teaching deservedly acknowledged. Once arrived, I break away from our session in order to call on Shiv and discover what transpired at the Board meeting last night: apparently quite a lot. The Board seems set on a split development, with a phased development of the property, moving residents from one unit to another as the homes are leveled and rebuilt, and as a new more luxurious complex is constructed for sale. But Shiv himself seems now less certain that dependency can be broken by imposing or generating self-reliance, and thinks that some of the residents will probably never be able to take on the responsibilities of home ownership, but will continue to need ongoing support. What has brought on this change of heart is access to some of the Board's documents, which he does not share with me, except to say that he was surprised to find how many residents were paying less than $100 a month for their town houses (utilities included), and how in some cases the payment, primarily for older residents, some without income, was as low as $15.

He agrees, as we said on Sunday, that construction costs could indeed reach $350 a square foot, but reckons (from his experience in real estate) that the new units could be sold for $450 a square foot, and that in relatively short order. Many of those who live here, Shiv has reluctantly concluded, cannot reasonably be expected at this stage in their lives to take over the responsibilities of home ownership, and it would be naive to ask them to do so. The result of turning their homes into condominiums would simply be to defer the sale for two or so years, and then to thrust their new owners into the city, better compensated to be sure, but still rootless. One of the reasons for preserving Sursum Corda, Shiv rightly thinks, is that, for all its faults, the place clearly enjoys a sense of community which is only infrequently present elsewhere, and which its residents, many of them aging, are unlikely to find in the city beyond their gates.

The answer, he now thinks (swimming in seas unknown to me), is to get a Commercial Loan from (say) some reputable investor like the Bank of Boston, using the property as collateral, to pay off a suddenly rapacious HUD and then to rebuild the property in stages, while also leasing some part of the 5.8 acres to a private developer. The Board would thus effectively remain in control of the present community, while the condo fees of the attached community would pay to maintain the present arrangements. Ideally, he would like Magic Johnson to become involved in this project as he has in others elsewhere, though he notes too that, whatever happens, Sursum Corda as we have known it, will probably cease to exist. Big plans indeed. He asks what I think and I say that there are probably legal implications here which neither of us understand, and ask about getting a lawyer committed to the Board alone, to comment on these new ideas. We reflect that the City's opposition may discourage some of them. But the Board seems not to be greatly concerned – or as greatly concerned as I think they might be – with the City's ability to make difficulties, should it be disposed to do so. I ask Shiv's mother what she thinks, and she echoes what I suspect many others may think too. She goes from one extreme to another, she says. One moment very excited and hopeful, another really worried that it all may not work out after all, and they will be left with nothing. We agree to meet again on Sunday, to discuss things further.

Shiv also revealed that, although he had been sent as a delegate of the Board and is himself a Sursum Corda resident, he had been ordered out of a Northwest 1 Council meeting yesterday by Ms. Walters, who is seeking to regain some of the ground she evidently lost in the community from the references to her (all favorable) in recent newspaper articles. There are copies of her call to Sursum Corda residents lying about in the community center, and in them she seems, though decorously and politely, now to oppose the City, insisting that the City believes that it will have only 500 families to relocate when in fact there are closer to 1500 if all the affected projects (that is, in Northwest 1) are counted together. She has been trying to take a survey in the community, and that too is alluded to in the flyer, which offers "three dollars [for] a completed survey," but it seems to me that within Sursum Corda at least, she is no longer as widely trusted as she once was. Increasingly, she has seemed to want it both ways, to run with the hare and to hunt with the hounds – as which of us doesn't? This all but acknowledged split – between Jane Walters and the Board which, from all reports, in the old days she used to control – seems to me a great pity, and one which is already working against the community's best interests. The present Board certainly lacks both her experience and her City connections, but she seems repeatedly to communicate, if indirectly, that her intention is, at least in part, to regain lost power. No doubt she believes that she knows a good deal more about what's going on than anyone else, and so she may, but she is now so championed by the newspapers, and so bracketed with the City, that her reputation stands in need of repair. She remains, however, a most perceptive, acute thinker, and at some level of mentation must surely understand that she herself is at least part-author of her difficulties. But she retains too an utter confidence in her own judgment and her own rectitude – and she has never suffered fools gladly.

Meanwhile the Board has announced another meeting for the residents for tomorrow night at 6pm in the Community Center, and the poster enjoins the residents "Take a closer look at your house. What do you see wrong? The time has come for you to step up. Find out what the Board is doing. The house you save will be your own. It is your obligation to make decisions for yourself. If you are not at the meeting, you will never know."

Friday March 18, 2005

Tutoring last night went well enough, though we were confined to the upstairs room since a meeting, I have no doubt on what subject, was underway below. There is no talk in our tutorials of possibly impending events by anyone, but it is impossible not to believe that they are having their effect in one way or another. Nothing has changed, but some things have, and what might have blown away a month or two ago now stamps its foot and threatens to remain. I spent a fair amount of time with Linwood and his fine tutor, since the five-year-old had been acting up in recent meetings, doubtlessly in reaction to his tutor of last semester, who sadly decided not to come back to the program after Christmas. Over the years I have been doing this I have been repeatedly impressed by the maturity and good judgment of the undergraduate tutors, and this young man, who excused himself saying (what in some cases is true) that his commitments conflicted with a course he needed to take, was an exception. There seemed, however, to be other things involved as well, and when I emailed back to him saying I understood his decision not to continue, I quite untypically asked if he was sure. He never answered, though he did have the grace to enlist a friend of his to take his place in the new semester. But the first tutor, who had an easy and agreeable manner to him and was well liked by most of his fellow students, had proved an excellent tutor, and had not only made very good progress with Linwood, but had also had come to know his mother, who was understandably taken aback to find him leaving.

Talking with another smart tutor about her work, Linwood came into our conversation, and I was surprised to find that she both understood the difficulties and the reasons for them which his new tutor was facing, and also shared my reactions to his former tutor's behavior. But the young man in question, who is now working most assiduously with Linwood, has proved to be an excellent tutor. Careful and scrupulous in a way that his predecessor was not, he has yet to achieved the same working relationship with Linwood (or his mother), but he has that dedication which is at the heart of good tutoring. Linwood can now read, if with some hesitation, the first of our "Phonics First" booklets, and though his fluency and his comprehension need more attention, there is every reason to believe that he has been very well served.

On the way out I also have a few words with a markedly able tutor who (at the request of his learner's mother) has begun working with the very young boy on arithmetic. He had been intending to see what he could accomplish with coins, but had come to Sursum without any, and the collection I had in my pocket proved to have too many quarters, not enough pennies, so his progress was limited. This tutor is a particularly able student who will have to miss next Tuesday for a final interview connected with a seven-year graduate school offer in California (full tuition and $20K a year, as I understand it), and the following Thursday we will all miss because of Easter. He will effectively have to begin his arithmetic lesson all over again the week following (with more pennies, nickels and perhaps one or two dimes), but the exercise is perhaps a good counterbalance for a young man whose own academic life has gone almost too swimmingly.

In the middle of working with Linwood, I pause to represent to a pouting and angry nine-year-old that he should not leave the program (and his excellent African American tutor, who has already taken him to a Georgetown basketball game) simply because he is forbidden to bounce his basketball on the floor while a meeting is going on downstairs (in fact he would not be allowed to do so in any case, but it seems none too smart to tell him that just now, and so add insult to injury). In the end he decides to remain, and I have no doubt that it was the memory of the basketball expedition with his tutor which helped him banish (or at least mitigate) his fit of pique. But his tutor is (understandably) aggrieved at his behavior, and I reflect that bad behavior of one sort or another seems almost to be a leitmotif tonight. Finally, one of our learners has moved out of Sursum Corda, and though living nearby, has not been as faithful in attendance as she was before. Her tutor wants to be sure that she will not be coming at all regularly before agreeing to a change, and I of course agree to delay, but really think that the writing is on the wall, and consider when I can ask Christine Nicholson for a new learner, even this late in the semester.

Sunday March 20, 2005

Justin gave a birthday party for Lewis and Mark Williams in the Community Center yesterday afternoon, but when I stopped by (later than I'd hoped) I found the party – which cannot have run for much more than forty minutes -- all but over, and the tutors and children, now old friends, playing basketball in the court behind the Center.   By good luck Maria Hernandez is helping with the clean-up in the room where we tutor, and explains that someone had produced a *pinata*, but when the children started bashing at it with the bat things began to get out of hand, so Justin broke it open with one sweep, and then, once its contents had been distributed, wisely adjourned the party to the basketball court. We laugh about it, though it crosses my mind that there may have been more to the children's blows than met the eye. I ask Maria if she is ok with seeing if we can arrange for a new learner for her, and she agrees. We walk over to talk to Mrs. Nicholson, who luckily is at home and welcomes us kindly, and adds that the mother of a seven-year-old just last week asked about getting a tutor for her child. We arrange for him to begin as soon as possible.

This is all to the good, and my sense is that we have done this soon-to-be-dear child a real service. Maria, a friend of Justin's, is simply an excellent tutor, bright, experienced, sensitive and perceptive, and with a quick sense of humor, and we certainly do have enough weeks left in the semester for someone that good to have a real effect on a willing young child, even under the present circumstances. Such changes, however uncommon, have long been a part of our program, though they are sometimes a little painful to bring about. Often the best tutors need time to adjust to the idea that their young learner is theirs no longer, and will want to delay the formal separation as long as possible. But as we walk back to the Center I feel a little tug at my heart, and wonder how many more such changes I will be helping to expedite.

Monday March 21, 2005

Shiv came to me at home last night, and we talked the whole thing through again. The question seems to remain Who will do what with whom? The key may be Wilma, who seems to know better than anyone what's actually in play. Shiv believes her to be focused on development, though she may not see all of the difficulties that are emerging, believing that by development alone the Board can secure the current units and keep the community intact. But there remains the danger, observed before, that she may be underestimating the power of the City, and it is not clear that she fully understands that the residents have rights which either HUD or the City can step forward to enforce. It also emerges that none of us, and who else God knows, actually knows how much (or what percentage) of the mortgage HUD still may hold.

Jane Walters comes again into the discussion, since Shiv thinks that she is still listened to by many of the residents who have thus far not come to any of the meetings which have been called, and that if push came to shove they might flock to her banner, or at least act as she directs. In this connection he narrates that when her friend and associate Phil, a friend of the community and a very decent man, came to a residents' meeting last Thursday, he was politely asked to leave. After he had left, Shiv, himself the victim of a like banishment, said that he felt badly about the expulsion, and that he likes Phil a lot. We agree and he was told, what's not to like? The difficulty is that he is widely seen as Jane's eyes and ears, and for now at least, neither one enjoys the Board's confidence.

That may, I suppose, be the heart of the matter: a struggle for control worthy of a board room conflict in General Motors. What Jane wants is complicated by the perception that even though she may (well, perhaps) know better than anyone what should be done, her no doubt genuine attachment to the community is all but negated by a perception of her determined attachment to personal authority, an easy contempt for others that she all too often shows, and the closeness she now appears to enjoy with the City, an attachment now reported so publically and so often that she is generally assumed to be at one with them. But my own sense increasingly has been that if Wilma and Jane come together the community could more easily prevail. But increasingly, I somewhat doubt they will.

Wednesday March 23, 2005

Good tutoring last night in spite of the fact that Georgetown's basketball team was playing in the National Invitational Tournament on campus (in the event Georgetown won, but by such a lopsided score, 74-57, that it cannot have been a very interesting game, except perhaps to the young). In any case, we're close enough to Easter break that a few of the students have already begun to take flight, alas. That our tutors are not indifferent to basketball became clear on the ride back to campus, when the easy conversation of the ride down gave way to a silent attention directed toward the radio. But the hour in between was a good one, though my artful eavesdropping again suggests to me that not all of the tutors of very young children, say five and six-year-olds, are fully convinced that their learners enjoy higher learning facilities, and so are disinclined to engage them in comprehension strategies as fully as they should. I shall attend to this, and shortly. Meanwhile Mrs. Nicholson has been as good as her word, and the promised seven-year-old arrives to be tutored by Maria, one of our very best tutors. Later Maria reports herself much impressed by the girl's reading skills, and we agree to meet after the break to discuss useful strategies.

We were again confined to the upstairs room, since he downstairs room was given over to another meeting, and so I consented, if reluctantly, to the proposition that the tutors in the older learners' program might adjourn, just for today, to a nearby McDonald's, rather than crowd in with the rest. As they were going off they showed me that their lesson for the night was the library copy of my little book on tutoring at Sursum Corda, and which was evidently intended as a follow up to the group's visit to the Horace McKenna papers in Georgetown's Special Collections, and to their documenting of the early history of the place. One of their younger learners checks to be sure I am the same John Hirsh whose name appears on the front cover. After they leave I talk for a while with Bob, who was in our program some years ago and, on the basis of a short story he showed me last week, remains one of the best young writers I know. In his recent work he has been moving away from plots he had observed in movies and on TV, and basing his writing more on his own reading and experience. I know he has been working in Georgetown (the place, not the university), and he tells me that he has a girlfriend, also a writer and an artist, who lives in Columbus, whom he visited last weekend. He is considering moving there himself in the fall. I congratulate and encourage him, but also quote the old saw, "childhood is a writer's capital." I say that, since he was born and raised here, we are talking in the middle of his estate, but add that it may be only when he has left Sursum Corda that he finally will be able to write about it. He agrees, and though we laugh about it, I am struck by how much he has matured.

I go back inside, and from all appearances tutoring has been going well, with the tutors generally on task and the children (for the most part) responding to them. I am reminded by something Father Royden Davis, S.J., a former, late and very excellent Dean of Georgetown College once said to a small group of us, that the

College is operating at its best when nothing special seems to be happening, so that learning is taking place smoothly, and without interruption.

Thursday March 24, 2005

Today Shiv, Wilma, Paula Knox, the Board's Secretary, another friend and I meet for lunch, this time in the Tombs. Shiv explains the Texas Plan which involves converting the residences from a co-op to condominiums, and the reason he thinks the Board should consider it. That reason has to do with the legal power which we now understand HUD to enjoy, a power which permits it to approve or disapprove any development plan that the Board may advance, at least as long as their HUD loan has not been repaid (or been "retired," as I used to say, though now Shiv, who is working in real estate, has taught me to say "cured" instead, a word which to a medievalist has distinctly religious overtones). Once the HUD debt is cured, we (perhaps naively) agree, the Board will gain such authority that City will have to take account of it, listen to it even, which is more than it has been doing thus far. But the City apparently believes the Board to be really quite helpless, since it cannot pay off the HUD loan without money from developers, money to which it cannot get access without HUD's approval. Quite a vicious circle.

Or so it seems. As I think about the situation before our meeting I am as ever hopeful, but perhaps not entirely so. We are all so green at what we are trying to do, and though our goals reach out to each other, they are hardly identical. My sense is, though I quite understand that this will sound unbearably sentimental, that what we want most of all to support are the mothers of Sursum Corda, who will otherwise be turned out of their homes with only a Section 8 voucher and may well prove to be a token payment, and will not easily find like accommodation in this most rapacious of cities (though no worse than others, I suppose). Shiv, who began by thinking that breaking the putative chain of dependency was the best way forward, has now deepened (as it seems to me) his position to embrace an understanding of those who have, for age or for some other reason, become so dependent on the Sursum Corda office that they will probably not be able to assume the responsibility of home ownership. Without quite abandoning his belief in the necessity of increased self-reliance, he now wants the needs of these persons attended to as well. My own position is no doubt conflicted, since my sense is that although condominium conversions, or some like project, might possibly be the only alternative to the developers' wrecking ball, after years spent here I also believe that not all of the residents are going to want to become property owners. But my position really rests upon a foundation of outrage at the way the poor are not only being driven from their homes so that the rich can continue to prosper on their land, but also at the way they are being deprecated and demeaned in the process.

The lunch itself goes very well, and my sense is that both women, and Shiv too, have had their responsibilities born in upon them since last we met, and were feeling the heat. By far the most powerful moment came when Wilma interrupted Shiv to explain why she felt so strongly about preserving the residents' homes as part of a larger community, and did not want to turn them into condominiums. She knows a woman who still lives in Sursum Corda under section 8, Wilma said, who in her younger days had young children to look after; and was helped, somewhat at least, by welfare payments. Finding her feet at last, she looked for and finally found a job in the federal government. But doing so ended much of the support she was already receiving, so much so that both she and her children sometimes went hungry to bed. If the residents actually owned their own homes, Wilma, perhaps rightly, thinks that would certainly limit the amount of welfare support residents like that woman could expect to receive, and she wants to do nothing, nothing, as President of the Board, that might cause other children to go to bed hungry, too.

We discuss the issue at some length, and consider who else could be approached to help cure the HUD debt, since that has now become the albatross about the Board's neck and stands in danger of allowing the City and the developers to break the community. For reasons I do not fully understand, it seems not possible to divide the community, making some units private while leaving the rest public. But thus to divide the community would effectively address this most important problem, and in some ways at least, it seems quite a logical way to proceed. Together we come to an understanding that the Condominium Board, if and when it comes into being, might then be able to acquire and so effectively rent certain of the units to those among the present residents who for age or for some other reason are unable to assume the burden of home ownership. We talk too about the need, which seems urgent, for the Board to get both a lawyer and an accountant who will be responsible to it alone. Only such persons, we all agree, will be able to help them when the time arrives to face the City, and perhaps the press too.

Towards the end, Wilma and Paula both speak briefly and warmly, and not for the first time, of the hope and trust they put in God to guide them. I have been reading Mary Ann Glendon's *A World Made New*, about Eleanor Roosevelt and the Universal Declaration of Human Rights, and am reminded of one of Roosevelt's associates, a Canadian socialist named John Humphrey. Glendon reports the circumstances of his hard childhood, one not unlike those that obtain at Sursum Corda. Humphrey reacted against all of the pious obstructions, many of them posed by the Left, which the Universal Declaration encountered as it was being written, saying in effect that, though he remained a socialist himself, Socialism was not finally the way the world should be organized after the War, and that "What we need is Christian morality, but without the tommyrot." Here in Washington, as it happens, we have much praise of Christianity, but quite a lot of tommyrot too, and it honestly doesn't matter whether it comes from the cons, neo and other, of the Christian Right, or from those on the putative Left who will line their pockets as they piously destroy the community. But for all of that, surely Wilma and Paula are quite right. Stripped of the shibboleths of Left or Right, there is no better measure and goad in the ethical miasma that is everywhere about us than an understanding of the ways in which many religious traditions view the relationship that should exist between the rich and the poor. But these constructions are not much honored here.

(Easter) Sunday March 27, 2005

A friend tells me that he knows former Redskins football player, Dan Black let's call him, now retired, and associated with a group that supports inner-city mortgages. He is said to have expressed an interest in Sursum Corda. We'll see. Thanks to the repeated attacks the community has suffered in the *Washington Post* it is clearly going to be necessary to have support of many kinds, and that includes a measure of simply political support as well. In such circumstances the backing of known names, whether Magic Johnson or Dan Black, seems quite essential. But we shall have to see what develops, and it is no good counting our chickens too early.

Meanwhile I am reminded again of the pressure which Wilma and Paula have so evidently been feeling, and also of the support they seek, as both those who seek their land, and those who earlier had volunteered to help, approach with threats and promises in almost equal measure. One of the Easter tide readings is from Psalm 31, "I am the scorn of all my adversaries, a horror to my neighbors, an object of dread to my acquaintances; those who see me in the street flee from me. I have passed out of mind like one who is dead; I have become like a broken dish." The liturgical reading stops there, but the biblical text continues: "But I trust in thee, O LORD. I say, 'Thou art my God.' My times are in thy hand; deliver me from the hand of my enemies and persecutors! Let thy face shine on thy servant; save me in thy steadfast love."

Tuesday March 29, 2005

We discuss the two groups Wilma and Shiv had been most concerned about: The young mother who very simply needs welfare support to carry on, and older persons, who have been living for years – decades even – paying perhaps $15 (or in other cases less than $100) a month to live in a two or three bedroom town house in what is more or less the middle of Washington. Put in these terms I find myself beginning to equivocate, and ask again why a public-private partnership is impossible, since it seems so obvious a way of dealing with an evident social inequity. The issues present here are not Sursum Corda's alone. Over the past decades the government has developed a large number of Section 8 housing projects, and many of the residents, hardly among the most fortunate in this country, have enjoyed a measure of security thereby. I understand, I sympathize with, I do in part believe, Shiv's now-qualified sense that if government support is to change at all (and my sense is that given the politics of the hour, it is), self-sufficiency should replace dependency in the administration of state supported housing, but that is a general principal, not a mandate for displacing the old, the poor, and the disadvantaged.

At the same time, and sitting in my warm house in Georgetown I hesitate to write this most un-Christian sentence: I cannot escape the sense that, now at least, $15 (or even $99) is really quite a low per-month payment for accommodation of the kind I have described, and I cannot but wonder how long it can be sustained. It is not that I want to change this only apparent discrepancy. Most economic systems can tolerate any number of financial irregularities, and in our country they seem mostly to favor corporations, certain members of the middle class (like myself), the rich and, perhaps most of all, the super-rich. Thus the fact that a certain number (speaking nationally for a moment) of the poor get a deal on what amounts to rent is, by any measure, quite a good thing. And of course it goes without saying that when a public or private body undertakes to supply housing for the disadvantaged, it should provide the best it can. So for all its challenges and evident difficulties, Viva section 8. Particularly in a place like Sursum Corda, where such things were arranged years ago, low rents (for some at least) have enabled some residents to maintain themselves on a very limited income, and so to contend with those other prices which have been rising around all of us.

But there must come a point when the disparity between what is paid for and what is received is so evident that the coincidence needs to be considered and addressed, though I have no objection to postponing such a consideration for as long as possible, and recognize no moral imperative to rush into it now. In any case, it seems quite wrong to do as seems to be happening here, saying, in effect: Well, we've let things go on as they have for quite a few years, but now we're going to catch up with them all at once, cost what it may. Surely, and particularly when such an exigency is upon us, the only reasonable resolution is one that acts in favor of the disadvantaged. By which I hardly mean such practices as handing those who are about to lose their homes an only apparently generous payment, while saying to them, Best of Luck! We might just let you back in here when we're done with the place. No promises, but maybe. If not the law, then shame itself should prevent grown men (for men they usually are) from doing these things. We share, when all is said and done, a common thread of life, and if nothing else will move you, consider that.

The old, of whom there seem to be more in Sursum Corda than I had appreciated, working with the children as I do, might afford a condo fee, if it was low enough, but, as Shiv points out, probably not a mortgage. And in the world outside of Section 8 we do not expect such payments of the old, so that among the middle class, among the rich, age can expect that demands will decrease, and some things at least will finish. But when the old are turned out of their Section 8 housing, they really have no defense at all. A little money perhaps, and a HUD voucher, but that's largely be-cause Sursum Corda is a co-op. Is there not some way for the pro-jected Condominium Board to assume ownership of those proper-ties whose residents are of a certain age and wish it, collecting a peppercorn rent to be sure, but maintaining them for many years to come? What financing would be necessary to make this work? Could vacant properties be pressed into service? I understand now and sympathize with the idea that when it is not necessary to change, then it is necessary not to change. Shiv thinks about 50 families, of the 160 now in place, would be able to maintain home ownership. No more.

For those who are able to do so, the only real solution may be to become invested in one or more of the social programs which are projected to attend upon the renewed community. The complica-tion here is that there are already such programs in profusion near-by, in the Perry School, for example, which houses a fair number of such programs, but of which, as Shiv points out, not all the Sursum Corda residents currently take advantage. This is particularly im-portant for the young families whose plight concerns Wilma, since they too will need increased support to equip themselves to find a place in a society which in many respects cares for them not at all, and this at a time when the engine of government seems to be moving in quite the opposite direction. In other words, getting self-sufficiency will itself require both a substantial investment and also kinds of personal support in which our culture is quite unpracticed, so much so that traditionally it has assigned such roles exclusively to the state. But if a semi-public project is to become private, it is obviously important that the new, private entity take on a fair measure of these putatively public responsibilities too. It must offer such opportunities as it possibly can, and also, as far as is decent, follow through in individual cases. I say must, but who must? And how can it be done? I understand that there are cases when such scrutiny has been helpful – but always? And if not, what then?

But even such programs as these will not answer Wilma's questions, and what we are really providing for is for those left in a lurch as Section 8 housing is withdrawn, and even then, at least largely, for those who can adapt. As a nation we seem to be concluding that the poor do not actually exist. So, that is where we are now, standing between hope and the developers, between the City and those at Sursum Corda for whom the best thing would be to have the community continue as it is. This is a hard place, since to do nothing, or to present a plan that wouldn't work, will hand the poor and disadvantaged over to the rich and powerful, but to act even as best we can will draw us inescapably into a wilderness of pain, one that we may be able to moderate, but probably not dispel, and to which we would contribute change and difficulty, along with, let us hope, some better things as well.

Meanwhile the friend who knows of a property group formed around the former Redskins Dan Black and (as it turns out) Joe Friar, expects to follow up with them this week. Shiv says that he can then report whatever progress there may be at the Thursday Board meeting. Apart from that, we will write letters seeking support elsewhere, but my own sense is that time is getting short, with the HUD foreclosure already two months old. But Shiv think that the danger is less great than it seems, and could always be curtailed (if it was suddenly pushed up for some reason) by declaring bankruptcy, a thought which cheers me not at all. But I remind myself, a little doubtfully, that Shiv (and probably others) know more about all this than I do.

Thursday March 31, 2005

I call Christine Nicholson to check on a new learner for our tutoring program, but she cannot come to the phone because Washington Mayor Anthony Williams and others in his entourage are this morning visiting Sursum Corda, looking it over, appearing very concerned to do the right thing. Pronouncements will no doubt follow, but as I learn later when I talk to Christine during tutoring, the Mayor said all the right things, and she is convinced that most of the residents, she thinks about 80 per cent, will be able to return to a rebuilt (and improved) project, which will combine both subsidized and market price units. She thinks too that the rebuilding is important because the infrastructure seems to be failing. They had to spend $300,000 on the dynamo recently when it gave out, and she thinks some of the pipes have not long to go. She understands that the new community will not work for some residents, either because of their involvement in the drug trade or because, even with the subsidized apartments the Mayor has promised, the expected monthly payment will be too great. Christine also spoke with him about constructing a building expressly for older residents, with level floors to allow for wheel chair access and apartments so arranged as to allow family members to live near each other. From what I can tell, he Mayor seems to have expressed interest, and said in effect, Good Idea. I simply am not sure how much of this will come to pass, but it is good to see Christine again hopeful, as she now describes herself, and as not many of us have been recently.

As I go back to tutoring I run into Shiv entering the Community Center, and he asks if we can have a lunch or dinner tomorrow, as Luke Gratian, the new Chief Operating Officer of the Board, wants to hear about Condominium conversion. Although not a member of the Board (currently, he lives in Baltimore) Mr. Gratian has taken an active role in directing its actions, and represents himself as well connected, and one who knows some at least of the "power players" involved. He also wants to line up a lawyer he knows, and is quite committed to building market price units, Shiv thinks. Later in the evening I call Shiv and agree to meet in the Georgetown faculty lunchroom about noon, together with Luke Gratian, Wilma and Paula. I know this is important, but it's getting expensive too.

3

Sursum Corda in the Spring

We will reach the goal of freedom in Birmingham and all over the nation, because the goal of America is freedom. Abused and scorned though we may be, our destiny is tied up with America's destiny.
–Dr. Martin Luther King, Jr.

Unlike what has come before, this chapter (and changes having been made, the one following as well) turns unmistakably to what I have found myself calling the "local politics" of our project, the internal exigencies thanks to which we managed to sail on. Its focus thus directed, it will largely concern itself with the part played by the group of former Redskins players, who were announced in the last chapter, but whose role here grows apace, at least for a while, until it vanishes.

But while they were on board, the group certainly had its uses. These had less to do with whatever the financial arrangements may have been – those I never really understood – as with a sense that the Community as a whole, and the Board in particular, were not irredeemable. The group brought with it a certain celebrity, and did so at a time when our reputation was at rock bottom, thanks largely to the *Washington Post* and certain of its columnists, editorials and news articles. Part of my thesis, after all, is that what matters here is not only what happened, but what was thought to have happened, who could be trusted, who not, and when.

The Redskins group was drawn into those considerations, indeed their presence mat have helped formulate what came about, not only with their putative contribution, but also with the challenge they came to present to the Board. There was good will all around in the beginning, but as events proceeded a certain irreconcilability emerged, born of money issues, as so often. What their role was to be was never entirely clear and while differences in personalities also played their part; whatever the outcome, their intervention was not unimportant, and lent a kind of focus to what soon became our work. In any case, things take shape in this chapter; they are accomplished in the next.

Saturday April 2, 2005

My sense is that the lunch yesterday with Shiv, Wilma, Paula and Luke Gratian, the Board's new Chief Operating Officer, went about as well as it could have, though like me they seem to be very much in doubt about more or less everything. The proposal of trying to get mortgages for everyone would allow the Board and the community to clear such pressing debts as the managerial mismanagement of the past decade has brought about, and to address some of the apparently endemic social problems, but without, hopefully, destroying the community as such. We also considered the dangers the Board might face without its own lawyer, which seem to me considerable and unnecessary. Apparently the Board has already decided on some kind of tear-down, build-up development project, probably in that large open area with the swimming pool and basketball court, which would eliminate some houses along First Street as well. But there at least seemed to be a sense too that perhaps some of the houses might be turned into condominiums, depending upon who, if anyone, actually wanted to buy them. The idea is both preserve the community as such and also to supply funds for its putative renewal (or at least to pay the bills which seem to have been piling up). Still, it was not easy to believe that the Board actually knew what it was doing. I wonder if the same might be true of Shiv and I.

Those present seemed at least not less concerned than I about who would be able to stay, who would be forced out, but tended to be fairly specific about the way they expected those who stayed to carry their own weight. Luke Gratian, a large man who speaks with a not quite credible conviction, seemed to me to be very much leading the charge, and I thought I heard as well from Shiv a sense of self-sufficiency which I somewhat hoped might save the day. I was conflicted by the demands which the plan seemed to imply, and concerned too, if also somewhat impressed, by this certain confidence that the Board members newly manifest. It is not just the families whose members are involved in the drug trade that they want to be rid of, but also other families, whom they think simply too dependent on what is provided for them. The new apartments, if new they be, will of course cost more, they almost rush to say, so residents will have to pay more, too. They hope for, or at least talk about, what seems to me a somewhat improbable jobs program so that those unemployed will have a chance to support themselves, and though there is an employment office in Perry School already, they seem to believe that for many the opportunity would indeed present itself, could they but grasp it. Almost all of this seemed to come from Luke.

Well, maybe. I myself am still concerned that it is the sense of community that gives life to Sursum Corda, and it is that which is most at risk. I see small hope for it in what I hear, but I am concerned too that I may know too little, be partly deaf and largely blind, if not to facts, then to other things. These are slippery slopes, and too much speed or confidence could pull us down. But I hesitate to dismiss, even in my own mind, what may have sprung from earnestness and hope. Perhaps I am lingering in winter, as Thoreau says, when already it is spring. But is it really?

Friday April 6, 2005

The ride down and back to tutoring was more than usually engaging last night, with the students' gently snide banter, mixed with reasonably witty persiflage, often being directed either at each other, or occasionally at absent friends. It is a discourse to which, appropriately I hope, I hardly ever contribute, though a few weeks ago when David O'Brien broke a pause in the conversation by asking me who I thought the next Pope would be, I said that I had no idea, only adding that if it came down to a choice between Justin (who was in New York that night) and himself, my money was on

Justin. But the tone last night was even more than usually relaxed. Several of the tutors had been to an address which Dr. Lawrence (as they respectfully call him), a Georgetown administrator who teaches some very good and popular courses in education, gives annually to the graduating class, in which he seems to have encouraged close but not fully committed couples not to separate too quickly after graduation, now 45 days away. One particularly bright student, Sean Morris, a smart College sophomore who has moved rather quickly into a leadership position in our program, reflected wittily on the effect of the talk on two senior friends who had heard it, but who were only now trying to "hook up," and for whose relationship the lecture probably spelled disaster.

The session itself went well, partly due to the rain, partly to the nervous energy I have been sensing during the last few weeks. That energy now seems to be lessening, though in the case of some of our learners that would be hard to prove. In one case a particularly difficult 7 year-old has been resisting all bounds, so much so that, even given the circumstances that may be motivating his behavior, I was steeling myself to disinvite him from the program, but now suddenly a change of attitude seems to have taken hold. And we have begun to identify, somewhat painfully, those who will take over, from the graduating seniors, the young learners to whom they have become so attached.

Meanwhile, great events have been happening. The City, in the person of the City Administrator, has met with the Board as he promised to, and seems to have displayed greater candor than the Mayor and the Chief of Police did the week before, though the message intended may not have been so very different. The City intends to absorb Sursum Corda into its plan for Northwest 1, and there is precious little the Board or anyone else can do about it, or so he says. But one result has been that the Board is beginning to take stock of its options, and understand that it must come to a decision, soon, and assisted by its own lawyer. Shiv says that it is moving towards a mixed plan, which would involve home ownership for those able to contend with a mortgage, rental units for those who would prefer them, and some new construction to support the foregoing (and the community). The result, Shiv says, is that the Board's meetings have taken on a new urgency.

One surprising result of the meeting was the reaction reported at a recent Northwest 1 meeting where, if the reports are true, Jane Walters's spoke strongly, even angrily, about the City's having opened a dialogue with the Sursum Corda Board. When I heard the report I felt a little pang for her, even though I still believe that her representations over the last year have by no means helped the community in its time of need. To many residents and others, it has seemed that she has cast her lot with the City, perhaps crediting too easily whatever representations its representative (rumored to be the City Administrator) made to her. Not one to underestimate her own authority, she seems now publically to have burnt whatever bridges once linked her to those who seek still to defend the place she once called home. It is said too that the Board, whose invitation to the meeting with the City she ignored, is now insisting on its due.

Monday April 11, 2005

A brilliant Washington spring day. Shiv and I meet with a Mr. Matt Wilson, who with former Redskins players Dan Black, Joe Friar and Chris Vir has a company (probably not the right word) which may be able to help with the development project on which the Board is resolved. Mr. Wilson is forthright and to the point, and we explain ourselves, including the details of the legal relationship between Sursum Corda residents and the Board, and arrange for a follow up meeting with one or two others. He attaches particular importance to the relationship his group would develop with the Sursum Corda Board, which expects to be one of shared values, purposes and goals. They are an intriguing group, and even I, whose knowledge of things athletic hardly counts, had heard of all of them. From the first, I found Chris Vir the most attractive, articulate and alert, with what seemed at least a genuine interest not only in our difficulties, but also in the larger ethical issues we are concerned with. In the course of things he asked about the name, Sursum Corda, and when I translated it for him, and said that it came from the Preface of the Catholic mass, he seemed genuinely interested. What came next, he asked? After the phrase "Lift up your hearts" was uttered. Joe Friar was harder to read. He was silent and focused, and less at-

tuned, at least in the context in which we met, to the presence, perhaps even to the existence, of other human beings in the room. A
hard man, perhaps, and one who, with him mind made up, did not
easily change course. Dan Black, the youngest and most recently
retired of the three, seemed to be still finding his way, perhaps with
an eye for the main chance (Joe Friar too); a bit green those two, but
far from innocent. Time will tell, I suppose.

In the course of our discussion Chris Vir tells the story of how
the group (they are close friends, all attend the same church, etc.)
came into being. After one of his games in RFK Stadium, Dan Black
was caught in traffic on the way home, and while thus stranded was
approached, as he sat in his car, by a very young boy, who tapped
on his window and asked for some money. Dan rolled down the
window and was shocked at what he saw – a very young African-
American boy, poor and weak and obviously hungry, asking for
money for food. Tears in his eyes, he pulled his car over to the curb.
He obliged the child. He began to think about what he had seen.

There are like stories, I cannot help remembering, in many early
saints' lives, Bede's life of St. Cuthbert among them. There, as any
medievalist can tell you, the boy is not a boy at all but an angel,
sent to inform and illuminate, to awaken the heart of the usually
young saint to what will prove to be his (and many other people's)
salvation. Understandably, I suppose, modern scholars are often
skeptical of such stories, and even Bede admits that he wrote his
Life of Saint Cuthbert with a simple faith, not asking the hard question he brought to his great *History*. But God exists otherwise than
in thunder storms. Who knows if either story is true?

Afterwards I go to dinner with Shiv, who has been encouraged
by the discussions which have been taking place in the Board, and
now seems convinced, or almost so, that the development will be
able both to cure the HUD loan, and also to cover the residents,
who, if I understand it rightly, are actually in the legal position of
renting their homes from the Board, even though some at least may
also own two percent of the cooperative, the situation being further
complicated by arrangements made (or not made) when the cooperative itself was established. We are both hopeful that the association with this new group will come to something, and, Shiv thinks,
one indication that it will is the consideration that, all being well,
the group itself will be well rewarded for its participation.

Tuesday April 12, 2005

I talk to Shiv about our lunch with Matt Wilson's group which is still in the process of being arranged (there is some talk among the Board members of having it at Sursum Corda rather than George-town), having been told last night that Shiv had discovered a document which seemed to indicate that the Board's indebtedness to HUD was only $871,000, not the millions which we had been given to understand. But the document may not be current, and Shiv is going to try to obtain a payment history from HUD to be sure. None to soon, I suppose, but if this new number proves correct than it indicates as well quite an extraordinary depth of duplicity on the part of some of those who have been involved. Shiv says that he was dumbfounded when he understood how duplicitous some of these people may well have been. The Board is meeting with the management company tonight, to confront them with some exces-sive charges that have emerged, and with other irregularities.

In the course of our conversation he also says that Wilma has the sense that, as far as Sursum Corda mortgages go, the residents seem to fall into four groups: those who are capable and willing to shoulder the burden of home ownership; those who are capable of doing so, but not willing; those who are willing, but perhaps not capable; and those who are neither. The Board has been consider-ing a two year lease with an option to buy for those (quite possibly many) who are reluctant to assume a mortgage when first offered. We talk too about the projected development, which, now that Matt Wilson's group may be involved, has become a pressing issue, but Shiv says the Board is still divided, and that last night's meeting, which went on until 11pm, couldn't agree on the matter, since Luke sees the development as far off, whereas he and Wilma think it is all of a piece, and should be presented together with the cured HUD debt, when the time comes. I side with him and Wilma, and say again that the usefulness of the new group lies in part in the profile that people like Dan Black and Chris Vir will bring to the table, and that their concern will be with what Matt Wilson kept calling its "synergy" at our last meeting. Without that, the group probably will not engage, and if the Sursum Corda Board is divided then there will likely be no "synergy" at all. Shiv agrees, and says they will probably talk about all that at their meeting tonight.

Wednesday April 13, 2005

Another beautiful spring evening. Drat. Or so I thought on the ride to Sursum last night, since Washington's spring, particularly after daylight savings time has begun, does not invariably improve our young learners' concentration – or attendance. The first minutes were, as usual, a little crazy, but soon gave way to a finally negotiated, not an imposed, order, and attendance was fine. But as we were coming in Stewart tells me that "a man in a tie" had been looking for me, and when I went upstairs to the third floor I found Luke and Wilma about to begin a Board meeting, but waiting to ask me if I would like to join them on the Board. I agreed I would, and we talked about it – they have decided to expand the Board to some outside Sursum Corda who share their sympathies, and considered, for reasons I thought best not to explore, that a Georgetown professor might be a good addition. As we are talking Shiv came in, and I am uncomfortably aware that the sound echoing up from the second floor is somewhat greater than it should be. Worse still, three of the children suddenly appear, sent by their tutors to see if, tonight at least, they can work on the third floor. I excuse myself and attend to duties.

During the session I spent some time with 5 year-old Linwood and his tutor Andrew, and am happy at the very clear advances in reading that Linwood has made, and not less so with the closeness of the relationship that has finally developed between them, so that Linwood's last tutor now seems to the boy well and truly of the past, and he is now attentive to, if demanding, only of Andrew. I have had the sense that this change of heart is not unattached to his increased reading ability and the independence that has come with it, as if the liberation that literacy brings has freed his heart as well.

On the Wednesday night following, a young man whom I had myself tutored at Sursum Corda as a boy and is now on leave from Georgetown, comes in to speak to my class. He tells the students what I already have, but in a way I never could, and afterwards the ones who seem to me most sympathetic with the place are the ones who tell me how much they liked it, how moved they were by what he had to say, and that he made them, in that old cliché, "think again." His themes were broad enough – a stubborn sense of community throughout, the violence he remembers from his childhood, the tutoring program, and what its uses were – but to some at least, they evidently went home.

Friday April 15, 2005

A little problem last night. Betty O'Connell, one of our tutors new this semester, has been working with Christine Nicholson's 7 year-old granddaughter, a shy girl with whom she has struck up a warm and academically productive relationship. But now that girl has had an asthma attack, one that her frightened mother witnessed, and she now keeps the girl home whenever possible, and has effectively stopped sending her to tutoring. Her grandmother understands but, if I read her reaction aright, thinks that her daughter is being a little over protective (the community center where we work is not many minutes from her front door), though the girl herself welcomes the new maternal attention her malady has brought, and doesn't object. Catherine thinks she may know another child who would welcome even two weeks tutoring – all the time we have left this semester, though my sense – and my hope – is that she may want to give her granddaughter one more chance.

I was drinking coffee on one of the benches in front of Copley Hall en route to tutoring, having come tired from a sparsely attended Faculty Senate meeting, when Betty comes along, and we talk about developments. She will skip tonight when there will be no one for her to tutor, but will return on Tuesday, to find her former learner, begin with a new learner, or otherwise do what she can. And indeed her present learner fails again to appear at tutoring, which in general goes very well, though I notice that one of a pair of twins is missing, and while his older brother is at his books, the younger is said to be enjoying the evening air. This is a great bore because the older boy should have put an oar in, and by the time I see what has happened it is too late to enlist the boys' supportive father, a rather draconian measure in any case. Next Tuesday, though.

Later that day I am in front of the community center at Sursum, talking to Bill Harris about his learner, when I see Wilma and Luke on the other side of the drive that runs down the hill in front of the community center, talking to a woman I don't know. Luke calls me over and introduces me to Mary Hume, another (and long-time) Board member, and the mother of a girl who has gone to Holy Trinity School in Georgetown. We chat about Matt Wilson's group, each of us expressing both hope, and in varying degrees, conditioned optimism.

Saturday April 16, 2005

Half of April has now followed February and March, and though much has changed, at least as much has yet to do so, and the final end is, for me at least, still somewhat in doubt. Shiv in the meantime has been active, first in helping Wilma and Luke, but also in making discoveries himself, the amount owed to HUD, a fraction of what he believes the management team represented, being only the most recent and important. Meanwhile, Shiv's own understanding of the complications in what we are about has grown apace, and his sympathy for the residents as well. Still attracted to a new-found sense of "self-sufficiency" with which to replace the old and dated "dependency" of the past, he has added to this understanding, in a way Emerson above all would have understood, one of limitation, whether of money, law or human capacity, and a sense of obligation. In many ways Shiv is for me the best that we can do, a Sursum Corda resident who graduated from Georgetown, and now returns to save not only his home but his community as well. But he is also a warning against the easy romanticism against which I warn the students, since his own first days in Sursum Corda were hardly untroubled – his family is not African-American, and took no part in the drug trade, so that in his early years the neighborhood children hardly warmed to him. His subsequent understanding and even identification with the place, his passion, as he called it recently, came from a growth of heart as well as mind, and also from a final act of resistance against those who thought him not of the place he now both serves and, in part, leads.

As for me, as so often in my association with Sursum Corda, I have again learned more than I have taught, though like an inattentive student at exam time, I face now the problem of finding out what exactly it is that I have learned. I know that I have contributed far less to the present deliberations than Shiv has, and lack the passionate insight which Wilma's experiences have brought her, or whatever insight it is that fuels Luke's sometimes angry understanding of the best way to proceed. I scrutinize my thinking, that the rich should not be allowed to exploit the poor unchallenged, that might, whether or not sanctioned by law, does not make it right, and that in all things, human motivation somewhat matters. The legal arguments have only just begun, and my secret fear is that, even when the HUD loan is cured, the City will somehow have its way, and get the land another way instead. I am no expert in what might follow next, still, I hardly think that even the semi-aristocratic writers of the Constitution treated the poor as we do now. Washington is awash in private wealth, but here is a place the poor can call their own. If the Law really won't help, then let it stand back. For there is no "need," legal or otherwise, to do this grasping thing, except that Gluttony, pretending Hunger now, declares it all a kind of civic good, and Greed applauds him from a nearby hill, for all the property they stand to gain together. But finally the Law grows up, not down. And if we act as best we can, with thoughtful people helping us perhaps, it may be that the place will yet endure. Well, as Hemingway has it, it's nice to think so.

Still, and close as we are, I sense that in some matters at least, Shiv is going one way, I another. A concern for those who cannot sustain home ownership is certainly now present in the plans, but also expelling those who watch as their children begin to deal in drugs, until it becomes the hard core of their lives. The old arguments don't move me as they once did – that only so can they endure at all – since I see the children whom they hope to guard are thus left unprotected, and fall into a net that holds them fast, or else they lead their parents to it, in their need. But they are still our fellow citizens, as willful and as greedy as we, and so deserve such help as we can give, and education too to help them home.

Thursday April 21, 2005

Yesterday afternoon, after meeting at the Law Center about our course next year, my colleague there drops me off at Sursum Corda not long after 3pm, and I go in to a Board meeting on the third floor of the community center, which is just concluding as I arrive. Shortly thereafter Matt Wilson' group appears, first Matt himself together with Dan Black and Joe Friar, and not long thereafter Chris Vir and others, not all of whose names I catch. Various young persons from the community come up and greet Dan Black in particular (it's a bit hard that they don't recognize Misters Friar and Vir as well), and one in particular, a slightly older youth, has been loudly proclaiming his attachment to the Dallas Cowboys. As we are making our way back into the community center another young man comes up to Dan Black, introduces himself, and offers, there and then, to run a race with him. Dan is polite but understandably unaccommodating, and asks the young man how old he is. "Twenty one," comes the reply, which allows Dan to say, in a very friendly fashion, that he's fourteen years older, so of course the young man would win. Taken aback, the young man continues to wheedle, though in an equally friendly sort of way, as we make our way into the Center.

The meeting that develops is a good one, and, introductions having been made, Luke and Wilma offer their presentations, and Maggie Davis, the Treasurer, is attentively present too. In what follows, Chris Vir in particular directs the discussion, showing again what seems to me a real skill in drawing out his several interlocutors, including his colleagues, too. Joe Friar, somewhat more reserved, is content to defer to him, though he is obviously on top of what is being said, and his relatively few interventions are invariably *ad rem*. For the first part of the meeting Dan Black says relatively little, but then speaks at some length, drawing a response from Chris, somewhat refocusing the discussion so as to make it more practical again. In the course of things, very few past issues are not sounded, and at some length, including the interaction, both present and projected, with city fathers and with federal administrators, and also with those who came to help and stayed, as it were, to prey. But throughout there is a sense, both among the Board and in the group, that the new community will be rebuilt, either somewhat or substantially, that it will aim for a measure of financial and social self-sufficiency which will be possible for perhaps half or more of the current residents, and that there will be some form of new construction as well, the nature and extent of which has yet to be determined. They agree too that they both understand their work together to be rooted in an ethic to serve the community which in turn has its roots in a trust of God, who alone, if finally, directs the choices they must make, and whose will they finally seek to do.

Not long after 5pm I leave for my weekly seminar with the Sursum Corda tutors. Later I learn from Shiv that Matt Wilson's group has made a proposal to the Board, offering to become minority partners in developing the community as the Board wishes, the Board to remain the majority partners. They have in place the support which they believe that the Board most needs – lawyers (the absence of one to advise the Board alone has been a continuing concern) – accountants, and other such advisers as the Board and the community may require. Shiv tells me that the Board reacted with reasonable caution, and the group responded that they did not expect an immediate answer, though as Shiv tells me this I cannot but wonder how the conversation would have developed had the response been immediate. Howbeit, Shiv himself now seems to be all but convinced, and resolved to seek Luke's support before he goes to work tomorrow so that they can move the issue forward at the next Board meeting. I agree with him that seems the best way to proceed, and cross my fingers.

Saturday April 23, 2005

Matt Wilson's group (which the Board now refers to as the "Redskins") asked for a minority 20% interest in the project, an investment which would constitute a considerable sum, and make it possible both to cure the HUD loan and to attend to other things as well. In the course of the conversation talk turned to what those residents who were not among the original residents, and so may not own, either legally or otherwise, any stake in the property. In fact, as noted before, because of the way the first documents governing the Sursum Corda Coop were written, it seems that all residents are, in terms of law, renters (from the Board) rather than owners, so that the only real requirement for those who leave Sursum Corda, voluntarily or not, is to return their original $250 security deposit plus interest. But as Shiv immediately said, simply to hand them that seemed quite unethical, and though some numbers were mooted, in the end nothing was decided. What lent particular strength to Shiv's position was the markedly ethical position that the Redskins group had struck. What struck me then, and then again today, was the easy and even confident way in which all of the Redskins, led by Chris Vir, agreed with the Board that some, that many, present residents, involved in the drug trade, would have to leave Sursum Corda for good, though no one else would have to be displaced. To some extent, I know I have to trust their judgment, who know so much more than I do about this thing, and not my own, which tends to worry about those for whom the project will be too much. In the end, and though areas of grey remain, there may not be a middle way for us. The financial picture, even when terms with the Redskins have been agreed, is far from clear, and this is something that will call again.

But I noticed too how powerfully the positions the Redskins group (as I suppose I now must call it) have already informed the discussion, and how their ethical concerns have secured a place at the table. This consideration could become particularly useful when the time comes to decide who is, and who is not, going to be allowed to remain in the community. Such a choice has to be a legal judgment call, but one which only someone long acquainted with Sursum Corda can make with any confidence, and however made, one almost certain to have its fairness questioned. No doubt some cases are obvious, but others are not, and as in all things human, friendships and animosities are bound to play a part. Drugs are general enough in Sursum Corda so that only a very few, so charged, would be able to contest an order of removal, but other cases could prove less clear, and the fact that an adolescent child uses drugs will be a slender reed with which to effect a family's expulsion, particularly one with many young children, and which otherwise may be reduced to public assistance alone. Mercy will need to temper Justice then, and I foresee a thorny road ahead.

The Board thought that Chris Vir would be a particularly able spokesman for the group when any public announcement was made, and that we should arrange for another meeting with the Redskins group, and move towards a conclusion, as soon as possible. There was too some very reasonable concern at to exactly how far a minority partner's power and influence should extend.

As things stand now, one phase of the Board's actions seem to be moving, really quite quickly, toward a conclusion, even though it will be a conclusion in which, to tell the truth, nothing will be a concluded, and which will come none too soon. Other difficulties – challenges if you prefer – will no doubt follow these, and what Shiv predicted at the beginning, that the Sursum Corda we have known will disappear, seem to me as true now as it was then. Rebuilding will be followed with new building, but at least if all is done as said, and in spite of what I have just written, the displacements of the residents may possibly be fewer than expected. But I wonder too how useful, in the end, this little account will really prove to be. I began writing it partly to come to terms myself with what I felt about the wrongs, both acted and complicit, and partly to record what looked to be a very bitter end. But then things started to improve, and I continued because I thought a record, written and rewritten, might have its uses too. In a way that stands but our circumstances increasingly seem to be exceptional. Still, the contours of our plan, if not the details, may be of interest to some who read and understand, perhaps better than I do, what happened here. When all is said and done, this little text is as American as Campbell Soup. After all, our Section 8 developments, built both to serve the poor and to contain them, are now under an attack both moral and mean-spirited, and need to reinvent what they can be. When the land on which you stand suddenly becomes valuable, then you'll need a bank that cares for other things besides its bottom line, and a partner with deep pockets you can trust. Good luck to you (you'll need that too). All cases are unique and all are one. We live our lives on sliding surfaces.

Friday April 29, 2005

Our last tutoring session of the year took place last night, and during it Justin, assisted by his young learner Lewis, with me helping at the end, packed up the books for transport back to Georgetown, where they will be used in the Sursum Corda summer camp that he and Stewart have arranged again this year. The story of the camp deserves a book by itself (a small one), as initially it was not at all embraced by standing authority at Georgetown which found the children not sufficiently overseen or studious, but when it gained outside financial support the obstacles began to disappear, though sadly its long-term prospects remain in doubt.

I had originally asked a medievalist friend who seemed to me to have a felt interest in social justice, to visit us on our last tutoring session of the semester, thinking that his presence might invoke an appropriately serious attitude towards work on an evening customarily given over to other things. In the end, and thinking there was to be a Board meeting that evening as well as tutoring, I asked him, with many apologies, to defer, which was perhaps just as well. Since this was our last meeting, tutors divided their time between tutoring their young learners one last time, explaining why they would not be coming back in the fall or saying that they would, or simply enjoying the fine spring evening together. Not really on task tutoring, I suppose – Justin teased me about it afterwards, asking if I was pleased with the way tutoring had gone tonight, if it had been academic enough – but not a bad ending either.

At one point, seeing that there was no Board meeting and having a sense as to how things were falling out, I decided that rather than play the spoilsport I would call in on Shiv, and see how things stood with the Board, and if progress had been made with HUD. He met me at the door and turned off the television, and we talked together for about 15 minutes. His news was promising: Luke, as Chief Operating Officer, would discover the final figures which the Redskins group needs as soon as he could, with luck tomorrow, and quickly sent them on; the Board had at last obtained a final payoff figure from HUD, and it was the expected $871,000, not the several millions first foretold to them; he himself was about to move into their own Sursum Corda house on McKenna Walk; and he revealed too that at the last meeting with Matt Wilson (the one I had largely missed by attending to the tutoring instead) the Board had offered the Redskins group a 25% interest in the project for 5 million dollars, not the 2.5 million for 20% that first had been considered, and though not formally accepted, the offer was at very least under active consideration. Shiv thought that a good appraisal would clinch the deal, and, confident as ever, was expecting to deliver one shortly.

He mentioned too that several of the Board members would

probably take up full time paid positions, himself included. Having for sometime entertained the idea that Shiv might do well to think about grad school, I asked what had made him move in that direction, and he said that his work for the community had begun to irritate the very complicated man for whom he now works, who yesterday had told him that he was wasting his time with those not worthy of it, and that he should attend instead to those who better deserved his attention. A not uncommon reaction where Sursum Corda is concerned, alas race-specific. Shiv was repelled by the evident racism of the remark, and had in effect replied that that was not how he saw things. But he is now very much looking to leave, as best and as soon as he can.

Outside, although the sun was already darkening and there was now a little breeze, the tutors and the children were still talking and laughing together, or playing catch with the ever-present small football, so that with the loading of the books and the last farewells we were late away, ending the semester ever more gently than it had begun.

Sunday May 1, 2005

I have been reading the end of semester papers the tutors write about their work at Sursum Corda, and with one exception the standard is reasonably high. One tutor wittily compares meeting her young learner for the first time to going on a blind date, another, one of many over the years who has been accepted into Teach for America, reflects on how she hopes her work this year will help her next, several contrast their sometimes wild initial expectations to the simpler but also more complex realities which slowly they began to understand. Not for the first time, many of what I can only call the most heartfelt papers came from our African American tutors, and it is they who reveal the deepest insight into their young learners, and now as in the past their own backgrounds, though sometimes very different from those of their young learners, seem to offer a kind of common ground. Not all of the stories that came forward were familiar, and one in particular involved two Georgetown tutors, waiting in their car to take the children whom they tutor to a Saturday movie, being approached by a member of the Sursum Corda crew, who warned them that their tags had just expired, and that there were so many police about Sursum Corda now they stood in some danger of getting a ticket. The story was followed by another in which their young learners instructed them about the local crew (SCC graffiti appears here and there about the community) but then insist that they have not been invited to join "because they know we're doing the school thing."

A third story involves a fellow student who, on a like mission, is stopped and questioned rather too aggressively by the police who suspect her of coming into the community to buy drugs, until two young men from the community intervene on her behalf, and vouch for her. I mean to use the story in the fall further to encourage the tutors to wear Georgetown t-shirts or sweatshirts when they come down to visit their young learners on weekends, a simple enough practice, but one that I simply cannot, for love nor money, get these excellent young people to employ. Still, what comes through in two or three of the best papers is the final incommutability of the experience their authors have enjoyed, a sense of crossing boundaries of whose existence previously they had been only dimly aware, and establishing a kind of communication whose qualities they can only partly articulate. But I can do no better, and our mutual linguistic limitations may give some credence to the representations of one of our more happy graduates, who insists that no one who has not tutored at Sursum Corda, or lived there, can finally understand its interest and attraction.

But in some ways the most interesting paper is Adam Smith's, a markedly perceptive young man whose academic success at Georgetown and now elsewhere has become particularly evident. Like some others, he elected to write about the history of Sursum Corda, and so, as directed, plunged into box 8 of the McKenna papers in the Library's Special Collections, which contains some of the best source material to which our students have ready access. Unlike the others, Adam forewent the usual panegyric, focusing instead not only on the early promise, but also on the early difficulties and failures that the community and its founders confronted. He did not fail to document the promise of those early days as well, nor to cite some letters from those who sought a place there, often as an escape from present misery. He quoted an October 1968 letter to Gene Stewart, the founder, from Father Horace McKenna, when construction was already begun: "Sursum Corda rises like a promised section of the new Jerusalem. I hope in many ways it will remind one of St. John's gold-paved Jerusalem describe in the 21st chapter of the Apocalypse. But I hope it will not have walls, and that the Lamb will be its light, and that there will be no 'night time'."

But the realities, Adam thoughtfully insisted, were otherwise. By May 1971 the community, complete less than a year, was suffering the effects of vandalism, to such an extent that the owner was being urged to impose a rent hike. The following July the deficit stood at $123,000, and seemed to be climbing still. In the next paragraph we jump to Princess' murder, the source of all our present complications. Missing from this careful narrative are the years during which the sense of community, still palpable, was taking shape, before drugs and violence had made their presence known, when Sister Roche, in association with those who shared her views, brought hope to many here.

It is a young man's history, and quickly drawn. The past is never prologue to one thing only, what happens next could always have been otherwise. Sursum Corda may rise in spite of you, young man; the past determines nothing. Basta the forum, Caesar will stay at home. Antony may thrash Augustus yet. Not a whit. We defy augury. We have beat them to their beds.

Wednesday May 4, 2005

Our end-of-the-year party last night took place on the Leavey Center Esplanade, having been told we were too many for Montrose Park, our former and usual venue. The usual crise-du-jour notwithstanding, we went down at the appointed hour to collect the children, and Christine Nicholson came out to the vans when we arrived to help with arrangements and to say goodbye. I went in the van Elizabeth was driving, partly to show the flag and also to try and preserve something like order on the way back. Five-year-old Linwood, in the back seat, was the most excited of all, leaving even Danny behind in his joyful anticipation and wild glee. In the event the party went very well, as they tend to at Georgetown, the children pausing from their games and pizza long enough to read the piece they had published in the "Sursum Corda Georgetown University Literary Magazine," which arrived from the printers just in time, having been well edited by Melanie. Only one child had the piece she had written omitted, and sadly that was by the oversight of her tutor. No tears, however. The small, hand-held and battery powered mike I had found at Restoration Hardware worked surprisingly well, so that those who did read could at least be heard by the fit audience who attended to them.

Later that night I called Shiv to see where we are, only to find him concerned. The Board still has yet to engage its own lawyer or auditor, and on the advice of the Boon lawyer who has been intermittently advising it, has called a meeting of the residents for Thursday to discuss and to vote on the Redskins proposal. Shiv is further concerned with the increasingly easy confidence of the Board, whose members now seem to believe that their great task is effectively over. Even with the foreclosure is still in process, there now appears an eight million debt to HUD (long suspected but only recently confirmed) as well as the $871,000 we knew about (the eight million debt is said to be forgivable, whatever that means), but without its own lawyer the Board seems to me to be flying blind.

It may be too, Shiv thinks, that the possibility of confronting the City has induced more than one auditor to shy away, though probably that difficulty may itself be, as everyone now says, cured, and perhaps the Redskins group could be a help in doing so. But be that as it may, much hangs on the residents meeting tomorrow night.

Friday May 6, 2005

I usually take a small number of the students most engaged in help-ing me direct the program out to dinner at the end of the year, but this year Justin Campbell and Elizabeth Hall prevented me from doing so by asking me to dinner with David O'Brien, Stewart Mor-ris (that smart Sophomore who is much interested in education, and who, as the others point out to him, has risen very quickly in the group's informal hierarchy), and Sara S., who, together with her friend Angela (busy elsewhere tonight), certainly have been the most consistently helpful in what has proved a somewhat difficult year. We met last night in Elizabeth's Village A apartment, and I brought copies of my little *Sursum Corda* book along for the graduates, together with two copies of the *Napoleon* essays collection which I had edited with a friend, for those who were staying on next year. In return Justin unexpectedly presents me with a copy of Tim Russert's memoir of his father, *Big Russ and Me,* I hope not too symbolic a choice, and Justin points out that Russert, like him and me, had a Jesuit education. It was signed by all of them.

I was somewhat uncomfortably aware that, while this was going on, the residents' meeting, a gathering which is potentially of real importance, was taking place at Sursum Corda, and not long after I got home Shiv called me to tell me what had transpired. In the event, it could hardly have gone better. One hundred and two of the residents had attended, as had Matt Wilson, and they had voted to partner with the Redskins group. The turnout was as unexpected and as welcome as the unanimity, and certainly resolves any internal doubt as to the legitimacy of the direction that the Board had chosen. The result was strengthened as well by the decision, or the lack of decision, on the part of those who might have opposed the motion, simply to stay home. It has very recently been reported that Jane Walters, who seems not to have any idea of the direction in which the Board has been moving, had convened one or more meetings at the Perry School to discuss what should happen next in the community, and had induced Mr. Bobb to speak at one of them. But the number of residents who attended was tiny, a fraction of those who came last night, so that within the community at least the choice has been made. Shiv remarked too that there was a strong sense of community present at the meeting, and a powerful sense of acting as one. He notes too that the community now apparently has another lawyer at the same law firm which has been advising them, but his understanding is that this lawyer is responsible to the Board alone, and not to Boon.

Afterwards I turn on the television, and happen upon an already underway presentation which took place earlier at Sursum Corda, and which involved Mayor Anthony Williams, Police Chief Williams, and others, who had come together to discuss developments in the community, and the plans they have for it. They point out that Sursum Corda was the first of the "Hot Spots" which the Police Department had identified as needing additional police presence to offset crime, and add that since they began their efforts, crime has declined by 36%. They add that one of their more important discoveries has been that most of those whom they have identified and arrested have not been residents of Sursum Corda, and add that their objective has been to make the area safe for those who live there. What they say seems to be generally compatible with the plans that the Board has made, and, taken at face value, to support what it hopes for in the future.

It would have been more convincing still had they been a little more attentive to those members of the community who were then invited forward to speak, so that the M.C. simply called upon this one as a resident and Board member, apparently not knowing who was the President, or that that one, present as well, was likewise an officer. Those chosen to speak looked none too happy about the confusion, but discussed, if briefly, some of the Board's initiatives, including an idea for issuing I.D cards to community residents over 13 years old, the better to assist the police, but passing over in silence the proposal to engage members of the Nation of Islam to help with security. There was, of course, no mention of any other plans, still less of the impending action by HUD. But all of that hardly seems to matter now, and though I may be indulging in the overconfidence I have been worried about, last night's vote, though not perhaps the realization of all our hopes and dreams, seems to me a victory of sorts.

Monday May 9, 2005

Shiv remains concerned with the delay which seems to be coming from Luke's reluctance to move quickly, a particularly important consideration, he estimates, now that the prospective partnership with the Redskins group has been presented to the residents at last Thursday's meeting (which was videotaped, Shiv now tells me), and is now widely known – he also says that there was a story in last Friday's *Washington Post*, putting forward the City's plan to gain control of the property and to level the buildings. He is also concerned with a possible conflict-of-interest posed by the Board's proposed trip next Thursday, courtesy of Boon.

Shiv and I talk on the phone, and in answer to some questions that I had, told me this story: Some years ago a resident manager had observed that the daughter of one of the present Board members, then only recently moved into Sursum Corda, had struck up a friendship with one of the local drug dealers, one of those who lives elsewhere. Thinking that the woman's house was being used as a place for the dealer to hide his stash, she reported to the police that the house had drugs in it, and the police thereupon obtained a warrant and searched the property, without result. Believing that he had been misled out of petty vindictiveness, one officer then told the woman who had reported her, thereby instilling an injury which is far from healed, and which the woman concerned, now a member of the Board, may one day seek to repay. But was this tip to the police an example of personal spite or of a genuine, if this time mistaken, attentiveness to the needs of the community? The woman's whose house was searched has her answer, though knowing both women it seems to me unlikely that she was quite innocent, but even so, the incident may come back to haunt us. Of course there are unknowns in all of this. Had the two women otherwise clashed? Was the daughter really innocent of any involvement in the drug trade? Whatever the answers, certainly the officer who revealed the source of the tip and so precipitated the now standing animosity, acted very badly.

The general consensus seems to be that Sursum Corda is still invested in the drug trade, and even the now-heavy police presence seems not to have deterred some of the dealers, though it has much reduced their numbers and audacity. But without an even more strenuous effort it is hard to believe that they will surrender their turf, without which there is no particular reason to think that things will improve. No doubt the attention of the Redskins group will encourage them to do so, less from moral pressure than from actual influence, and without their presence, and without the human investment the group means to bring, there would be little reason to hold out hope, especially for the children. But with it there is at least a possibility, or better, a decent chance, that their futures may be brighter than they would be if the worst should happen, and the community is scattered to the winds. Fracturing the community will simply move the problem elsewhere, but there is no easy ending here, and what is finally on offer is a possibility, not Nirvana. But Nirvana is what the drug dealers – and occasionally the *Washington Post* – seem to hold out, and we will have none of it.

In the end ours may be a conclusion in which nothing is concluded, and which will offer no final solution to the questions posed by poverty and property, by social alienation, and by Section 8 housing. Still, if the community is able to maintain that degree of City support which has clearly been held out, an un-conclusion may for a time sustain those whom we mean to serve. No doubt what we do will only mitigate, not change forever, a few of the difficulties attendant upon being poor in America, but our venture still offers an opening for a possibility for our children that our adversaries would deny them.

Tuesday May 10, 2005

Yesterday, like today, was an almost extravagantly beautiful Washington spring day, and I left early a Faculty Senate meeting to go to a 6pm Board meeting at Sursum Corda. I was uncomfortably aware that, given the revelations the Board had made to the community at the Thursday meeting, time now was fleeting, and could not understand, obvious reasons apart, why it was still contemplating taking a trip to Florida, to be paid for by Boon, the one agency from which, given the way things have been developing, its members should avoid. I am not entirely sure that Boon is dealing with the Board with very great candor, and am somewhat concerned that it may thus snatch victory from the jaws of what must seem to them defeat. Matt Wilson was expected at our meeting, but in the event attended only via speaker phone, a circumstance that focused the discussion and made us go straight to the point. But before that happened, and soon after we arrived, Luke talked about the contacts he had been developing with the City, in particular with some of the City Council members, whom he hoped might take the community's part, since, according to that Friday article in the *Washington Post*, the Mayor is now reported to be seeking City Council approval to buy up Sursum Corda in its entirety. We discuss how best to proceed, and Luke, who has now negotiated the really very low price of about $4 million with the Redskins group for their now

25%, wants to use it to cure the smaller HUD debt without any delay at all so as to end that particular threat, whereas the Redskins group wishes to approach HUD directly, apart from the apparently rapacious City, to see what can be done that way. The Redskins also have proposed, as part of their investment, to assume part of our debt, and after some discussion we seem to accept the arrangements they have suggested.

Financially at least, some of our ducks seem to be waddling into what appears to be a row. Shiv has obtained an informal estimate of individual house prices, and the gentrification in the area has gone so far now that the numbers run between $300K and $500K depending on the number of bedrooms involved, and exclusive of common land areas. This valuation very much supports the figure of about (or over) $60 million that we had been estimating for the property as it stands, even before any improvements are introduced. Luke also produced a document we had not seen before, an audited account of the last two years at Sursum Corda, which could certainly pose some hard questions for management, and which shows clearly that the community has within itself the resources necessary to sustain it, if only given proper direction. (But is there no end to these unexpected, misplaced, or hidden documents?) Even so, there is still a strong feeling that partnering with the Redskins group is likely to prove in the best interests of the community, since the group will bring in resources that will powerfully address quality-of-life issues, and add support that will be particularly helpful to the community's children.

All of this is reported to Matt Wilson over the phone, and though his reaction is muted, he asks, reasonably enough, to have the documents faxed over to him, so that he can lay them before his group. To these we add a third, an unbinding Letter of Intent, in which the Board expresses its intention to effect the partnership, and specifies the percentage each group is to control. This would then be followed by a more binding MOU (Memorandum of Understanding), that would specify details. Mr. Wilson says that his group will arrange for a full and formal appraisal made of the property in due course, but such an operation can take 45 days, more time than we now have. Though unbinding, the Letter of Intent would have to be formally withdrawn should the Board decide for any reason to change course, which given both the expressions of approval all have made, and the vote of the residents last Thursday, now seems most likely. Touch wood.

That night I find and read the short unsigned article in the "Metro in Brief" section of last Friday's *Washington Post*, "City Might Buy Troubled Sursum Corda," and am struck again at the flood of half-truths, innuendos, misinformation and outright lies with which the Board and the residents alike have had to contend. This extraordinary little account, which appeared, perhaps coincidentally, the morning after the meeting of the residents on Thursday night, seems designed more than anything to allow the City to stake a claim, and so to warn off any who might feel inclined to take the community's part. In keeping with the *Post*'s practice of vilifying the community, it calls it "long-troubled" in the second line, perhaps for the benefit of any who have forgotten its past articles, and actually insists in the same sentence that the city is acting as it is "to save the homes of 167 low-income families." It goes on to emphasize the April 27 letter in which "HUD notified the city that it was foreclosing on the property," and insists that "HUD rebuffed a request to delay foreclosure proceedings on the development," which it further identifies as lying "at the heart of a neighborhood targeted for redevelopment under Mayor Anthony A. Williams's 'New Communities' initiative." It's all over, the article seems to be warning, so stop trying to save it. "Williams (D) has requested council approval to purchase the property," the article concludes, "which is estimated to cost $12 million."

4

Season of Mists

One fire drives out one fire; one nail, one nail; rights by rights do falter, strengths by strengths do fail.
–Shakespeare

In my headnote to the last chapter I promised that something would be accomplished in this one. Well, yes and no. On the one hand something certainly is, indeed (in a way) the book comes to its first climax here, as the Community, through the Board, seeks to prevent HUD from taking it over. It does so by doing a deal with a developer who, in what some later came to think of as a Faustian agreement, undertook to correct and repair those faults, flaws and depredations that HUD would have cited in order to condemn the property, strip the Section 8 protection from it, and so move all the residents who depended on section 8 (a large number) away.

But the developers knew their business as well as HUD. Was that tree too close to that outer wall? Have it down. Was the condition of that sidewalk a problem? And those concrete steps! The ones with the broken handrail! What of them? Inside, the rules were every bit as bad. I doubt my little Georgetown home would stand HUD's scrutiny. But the developers knew their playbook, knew what needed to be done, and in a hurry. There certainly seemed to be a lot that needed fixing if Sursum Corda was to be saved. And they went to work with a will.

But what were they getting in return! Now there's the rub! The right to pay off the residents (as is almost never done!), and so to

get the property free and clear and cheap?   In an area between
Capitol Hill and the new Convention Center, it stands on a prime
location, and though the property values were low when Sursum
Corda was built, they are no longer, that's for sure. There's money
to be made here, if we can but keep the Feds at bay, and afterwards,
have the whole thing down. Come on then! Let's save the place, if
only for a bit. Only sign here.

Thursday July 7, 2005

I had been working on a project in London since mid-May, coming
back to Washington on June 30th, but during my absence, needless
to say, things had continued on course. When I left Washington all
was flourishing, or so it seemed, with FBV (the Redskins group) at
one with the Board and ready to supply the needed funds, so that
the HUD loan would finally be all but cured. But early in June,
I learn from Shiv, there developed discussions amounting to dis-
agreements among members of the Board, Luke (who, with this
substantial change in direction, has now become the director in
all but name) and FBV, concerning both the amount of money required of FBV, and also the direction of the project as a whole. As I
understand it, the situation seems to be this: FBV was either unable
or unwilling to commit the money required to discharge the HUD
debt (a surprising development that I do not yet understand), and
as a result Joe Friar, acting for FBV, brought in a development firm
called BAR, and through them a like firm, but one better able to
undertake the physical efforts required, called ABC Services, Inc.

ABC asked for and received (not yet formally, but through a
non-binding Memorandum of Understanding, or MOU) a quite extraordinary 85% of the project, and that for a very minimal investment, the Board to have but 15%, FBV, if all the cards are actually
face up on the table, 25% of the Board's 15%, or 3.75%, leaving the
Board with 11.25%. But these figures are not yet fixed, and ABC's
85% may include an undisclosed amount for BAR, which seems
rather to be calling the shots through two of its officers who have
been identified with the project, one the wife of a powerful Vir-
ginia Democratic congressman, said to be a powerful and forceful
woman in her own right, since she is also said to have one or more

other properties in or around Northwest 1, and part of her interest in redeveloping the neighborhood may have sprung from that. The minutes of a planning committee meeting which took place on June 29 report that Sursum Corda Community Inc., and ABC, are "the primary joint venture partners in the venture, while FBV and BAR will provide critical support."

Given the amount of trust some of us at least were prepared to place in FBV in May this is a surprising and not particularly welcomed development, since it also poses a related question concerning FBV itself, namely, what exactly are *its members* now going to bring to the table? Or to put another way: Is FBV's participation now strictly necessary? Apart from these rather stark developments, there are also rumors a-plenty, which seem to have increased exponentially as the number of "advisers" has grown. Things have all of a sudden become even less transparent than they were, and although spoken undertakings are not uncommon in this world, and often are honored, I am reminded of a saying attributed to a movie executive, "oral agreements are not worth the paper they're written on." If there is a bottom to any of this it is hidden in the mud, and, in the interest of satisfying HUD, the whole operation seems to have slipped – or been driven – onto a precipitous declivity.

In one of the many now flourishing rumors, Dan Black is said to be known by, and in contact with, President George W. Bush (he is, according to this by no means credible account, represented as being on some sort of White House committee having to do with athletics), and it is believed by some to be that association, together with a direct request, which induced HUD to relent, and to allow time for the community to "improve" itself. If this unlikely circumstance be so, then Mr. Black certainly has rendered no small service, and the rumor mill has also thrown up this: that when he was in conversation with the President – over lunch? – President Bush himself had urged him to see to it that those who now live at Sursum Corda be attended to, and above all, not left homeless. Full marks to him if this unlikely rumor actually is true. Will any of this keep the community intact? Doubtful. But on the basis of a handshake (and an MOU?) with the Board, ABC has already brought in construction workers and begun to address the "Health and Safety" requirements that HUD had indicated, and others it had not, so as to allow the community to pass the new inspection to which HUD has now agreed. But if things actually are as I have just reported them, the Board accepted ABC's presence only because HUD effectively forced them to do so, allowing (I am informally told) only 5 days for health and safety issues to be corrected, or foreclosure would begin. With a gun thus to its head, the Board felt it had no choice. But even so it seems to have acted too quickly and more or less obviously under duress. We have now fallen into the world of white people, who for the first time will appear in these pages individually, and as major players.

There are developments present in these circumstances which certainly are difficult to understand. First, the percentage which ABC has apparently obtained seems quite extraordinary, even under the circumstances that I have described. They now have, I am told, exactly what the Board had thus far resisted assigning to any other developer, and apparently ABC has given no assurance how it intends to preserve the community in the future, so that should, for example, the City and ABC make common cause, perhaps in association with FBV and BAR, everything we have been working for could easily come crashing down. Apparently too, there was a confrontation of sorts between Joe Friar and the Board, in which he more or less baldly told them that FBV's development plans did not match theirs, thus bringing the breach into full view. This development concerns me, because I had high hopes for the association with FBV, which I still believe to be, I hope not naively, high minded and sincere, concerned for the welfare of the Sursum Corda children first of all, not for turning a profit. May it be so. But it is difficult not to notice and to wonder at how far Luke has embraced the proposed (but not yet final) arrangement, together with one or two members of the Board – but not, as it seems to Shiv and I, Wilma, our Chair.

And now it is late in the afternoon and I am being interviewed, if somewhat deferentially, by Lori Montgomery, a smart and, it seems to me, perceptive *Washington Post* reporter who has been trying to catch up with me for an article about Sursum which she is writing, and that is soon to appear, she says this weekend. (In the event, the piece does not do so. Maybe later.) Given the treatment the *Post* has meted out to Sursum Corda in the past, and its well-known responsiveness to the interests of developers, Shiv and I have informally renamed the esteemed newspaper the *Developer's Times*, at least among ourselves. As a result, I was somewhat reluctant to return her phone calls, but urged by Shiv did so, not knowing what to expect. In the event, it was all a little embarrassing, since she clearly knows far more than I do about what has been going on, though the tenor of our conversation makes me wonder what Luke's agenda may be (she believes Luke to be widely distrusted not only in the community, but elsewhere), and also makes me concerned about ABC, who won't tell her or anyone what their plans are. The residents are therefore assuming the worst, as is she, and also, I begin to realize, am I. But if that be so, what exactly is FBV's role in all of this? What is BAR up to? She says too (what I had gathered from Shiv) that as far as she knows nothing is yet final or in writing, so that everything is more or less still in play. I'm not sure that I'm much use to her, however, except for filling in some rather minor points concerning Sursum Corda's history, and promising to send her a copy of a very high-minded little book I wrote more than a decade ago about our tutoring program there. Dream delivers us to dream, and there is no end to illusion.

Monday July 11, 2005

Shiv comes over last night with a former Sursum Corda tutor and one of his friends from high school, who has just finished an internship at the World Bank, and is now in the process of deciding which graduate school to attend in the fall. Before we go to dinner, we discuss the latest crisis. It was more the players than the game plan that engaged us, since by this point we all seem to be agreed that ABC's and BAR's long term intentions do not seem so very different from those of the developers who preceded them, and if they do in fact acquire an 85% interest in the project, the community is probably at an end. The only real check on such an outcome is Wilma, in whom the Sursum Corda by-laws seem to place very great authority. That being so (if it is) we asked ourselves whom it is that she trusts, and how much confidence she yet has in Luke, and came to the conclusion that the answer is quite a lot. Shiv thinks she has been impressed by the rebuilding work now going on, and sees that as Luke's doing.

We discuss the perception of Luke in the community, and Shiv believes that his reputation is in precipitous decline, largely because there is so much uncertainty about. He insists, what seems to me true, that there is no evidence, as common rumor has it, that Luke and a woman believed to be related to him are having an affair, and whatever it is that people may have seen – the two visiting each other's houses, for example – could be better explained by consanguinity, their being close relatives, brother and sister, for example. There is an obviously important Board meeting at 10am on Tuesday which both ABC and FBV are expected to attend, so if we are going to have any chance at all to talk with Wilma beforehand we'll have to do so on Monday (today), and ask Shiv to try to arrange a lunch or dinner, and get back to me. I also urge that we may need legal representation if we break with ABC, since such a move would probably land us in litigation. We hope that the association with FBV will be able to continue, however, both because of the evident usefulness of their HUD and City connections, and because of what I at least remember from last May – their evident interest in working with the Sursum Corda children, though how that is to come about under the proposed dispensation remains to be seen.

It is increasingly clear that whatever happened over the summer, the community, the Board, and all of its putative "partners" have passed a kind of watershed, and the Board no longer is directing the course of things. Shiv and I discuss this development together some time later, and he wonders if there has not been some unseen collusion between HUD, FBV and ABC, of which most of the members of the Board, including him and me, are not yet informed. It all happened so quickly and dramatically, he points out. Something seems to have pushed HUD into taking action, and giving the Board virtually no time to make up its mind – or seek an alternative. Really, things seem to makes no sense at all. But one of FBV's claims to joining up with the Board was that it was close to HUD – indeed one member was represented as a close friend of the HUD Secretary. Not that much was made of it, and I'm not sure that either Shiv or I believed it at the time, but what if it was true? It was, after all, HUD's sudden action that forced ABC onto the Board: HUD would foreclose unless extensive physical changes were made to the property, and the only group that could make them on time was ABC, suddenly brought in by FBV, and approved by the Board, who believed it had no choice in the matter.

But doing so effectively made the Board, and through it the community, tied and indebted to ABC, so much so that it could cost them their autonomy. It all seems simply preposterous. The Secretary, in person it would have to be, colluded with a group whose connections to the community are recent, shallow and finally unclear (FBV), and with a development firm it has identified (ABC), effectively to cheat the residents out of their homes and their property? If so, where is the City in all this? As ignorant as the Board? It's possible, we speculate. The fewer involved the better. And if HUD had earlier consulted with the City, but didn't this time (HUD simply may have guessed that the City wouldn't object to the plan), than the whole scheme seems quite deliberately twisted! If that actually is what happened, then the community will reap a whirlwind, and FBV and ABC will reap millions of dollars. Literally. After all, any such arrangement must have been private and oral. So where's the evidence? If there is none, then it would take the FBI convincing someone to talk to find them out. But would the FBI ever do so? And of course we don't know what actually happened. We speculate, but we're helpless.

Under such shadows, life goes on. Earlier in the day I call Christine Nicholson to offer friendly greetings and say that I'm back in town. We speak ever so briefly about developments. She puts everything in very positive terms, and I wonder if the fact that I am now on the Board means that we cannot talk as freely as we once did. As one, we praise Justin's summer camp at Georgetown, which apparently has been going very well, and mutually hope that the best may yet to be.

Wednesday July 12, 2005

A most convoluted and confusing but still very interesting day. Shiv and I arrive (a little late) for the 10am Board meeting to find it cancelled, and moved to 9:30am tomorrow morning. Earlier someone had "called HUD on us," as Wilma tells us when we see her downstairs in the Community Canter. What seems to have happened is that someone, perhaps a resident fed up with all the noise and dust of the renovations, and knowledgeable enough to know whom to call, and called HUD and reported that the place was "dirty," which had brought a HUD officer around to the community, who however left (it is said) impressed with the evident diligence and good order that he discovered there. Afterwards Shiv and I climb up to greet Luke on the third floor of the Community Center, and, putting on our friendliest possible faces, have a long conversation in the course of which he confirms everything. The plan is indeed for the present community to be razed, and a thirteen hundred unit apartment building to be built in its place. The great difference between this and the earlier plan (which actually had projected 2,000 units) is that the new one is said to promise a new home for each of the 163 current residents, fewer than 8 of whom are believed to be so deeply invested in the drug trade as to make their retention impossible.

The new plan calls for all the residents to be settled elsewhere (possibly nearby) for however long it takes to build the new 1300 unit building, and then to be "allowed" back in, charged only build-out fees, and supplied with a mortgage to cover whatever may be required of them. They will also continue to own a percentage of the whole development, and though they will not be allowed to sell their new apartment at market value until they lived in it for five years, the equity they will thus acquire will stand them in good stead in the future. The plan, thus described, sounds so attractive that I begin to press down my initial doubts, and when I say that it will be of course the death of the community and of our little tutoring program, Luke asks, reasonably enough, if I am not willing to see myself out of a job, in the best interests of the residents, and I admit his point. Thus far, however, the residents have been told none of this, not even that their newly washed and suddenly attractive community is to be razed to the ground (though there have been complaints of trees being felled, which is said to be done in pursuance of HUD regulations), but in due course "Block Meetings" will explain the situation to them, followed by a general meeting, where the issue will be voted on. Shiv, who has had several run-ins with Luke in the past, now goes out of his way to be supportive and to ingratiate himself, and later tells me that I had been much too forward in the questions I asked, though I thought I had done so in the friendliest possible way, and indeed at the end of our conversation he revealed, thanks to Shiv's questioning but as if among friends, that he was later that day going to meet with a Baltimore representative to see about becoming involve in a project already underway there, perhaps using what he has done at Sursum Corda as leverage, in a way I do not understand.

On the way out we stop by Wilma's house and Shiv invites her to lunch at least in part to see how married she is to the present proposal, and to suggest alternatives. On one hand, Luke and ABC, who seem to us increasingly on the same page, may not be entirely mistaken. Since what we are trying to accomplish is meant to be in the best interests of the residents perhaps we should indeed support it, particularly if we believe that the developers will stand by what we understand them to have agreed, and will do all they can, within reason, to act in the residents' best interests – while understandably looking after their own profits, too. But can we? In the course of our conversation Luke remarked that he is presently engaged in informing residents with five or six bedroom units that they will have to content themselves with three. (When I asked if people with six bedroom units could not have two three-bedrooms he said Yes, but dubiously). No less revealing, the "build out costs" are as unspecified as the terms of the mortgages, and from what we can tell, are unlikely to be so until after the residents have voted, in the run up to actually signing the document which will hand over the land. But how can the vote of the residents be meaningful unless the details are complete? Worst of all, as I understand it, the residents are to be given no meaningful choice. It's our way or the highway, the Board seems to be saying.

ABC's offer is the only one now on the table, and that in itself is a problem, albeit one brought about by the pressure of HUD's quite extraordinary 5 day deadline to the Board, a deadline that effectively hobbles any search for a competing offer. It has the effect of more or less locking in ABC, and so supplying HUD, FBV and ABC exactly what they want, while undermining the position of the residents and the Board. Not to keep on about the unproven, but it smells. The Memorandum of Understanding that the Board and ABC have now signed is more or less being treated by all parties as having created a *fait accompli*. The present offer may not be as bad as what was on the table before (the pre-ABC proposal had held out only the possibility of current residents being allowed back, and then only if their family was without criminal convictions and they were financially able to assume a mortgage), but is the present one that much better? The residents are certainly not being treated as the owners that they are, but rather as marginally interested persons who must be accommodated because a more powerful entity – HUD, FBV, ABC – finds it expedient that they be so. And although we certainly must look very carefully at the offer on the table (though that seems to be ever changing, so that what is agreed upon orally one day is not what appears on paper the next), we need not suspend our best judgment as to what our prospective partners actually have in mind, and what the final package is likely to be. I still hold to my original position – that the community of Sursum Corda is being attacked, and may well be destroyed, in the interests of the affluent, and some accommodation should certainly be made for the residents, even if it means an end to that more amorphous entity called a community.

Needless to say, if the land on which Sursum Corda stands had not become as valuable as it has, none of this would be happening. When wealthy developers decide to act, and particularly when they do so in consort with other authorities, there is little the poor can do to resist them, at least in America. But things are as they are, not as we wish them. If the result of these new circumstances is that we come to lack conviction, then those who do not share our scruples, filled with passionate intensity as they may be, will simply ignore the residents, at least as far as they are able to do so. But if doing nothing is not an ethical option, we must do what we can, even at this stage, neither to be co-opted by, nor simply to acquiesce in, a final solution which hardly represents the best interests of those whom, however imperfectly, we try to serve. Sursum Corda is a private cooperative, after all, not a public project. HUD's authority, and that of the state generally, should know bounds. But this is a marriage of convenience, born of HUD's shotgun, not any moral commitment. And from what Luke and Shiv both say, that is the way ABC and FBV see things too. But Shiv has developed a contact with another development firm, KCH, and thinks it important to have a second offer on hand as well. I agree to go with him to the meeting.

Later in the day...

In the event, the meeting with KCH proved as interesting as it could be. Our contact at KCH was a friend of Shiv's, and he introduced us to his boss, a smart, alert, and from all appearances a very decent youngish man called Ted, who gives every indication both of being aware of the traps success can lay, but still preferring it to its opposite. He has a large number of photos of his young family on a bulletin board behind his desk, a most attractive diversion from what we have been concerned with. He knows of ABC, and the president with whom we have been dealing, but apart from that acknowledgment says nothing more about the man or the company. We explain what has happened, and the speed and the circumstances by which ABC became involved, and when we describe the details of the projected transaction, and particularly the 85% ABC has insisted upon for its really very limited investment, I notice that his eyes raise a little as they move toward his colleague.

We take a break so that he can consult with one of his colleagues, and after he has left I take advantage of the pause to use the men's room. But as I pass the office where Ted is briefing his colleague, who is sitting at his desk while Ted, standing over him, is animatedly explaining what he has just heard. The look on each face is a mixture of incredulity and high amusement. When we regroup Ted has put all humor aside, and now soberly explains that although, in common with all such firms, KCH seeks to generate the best profits it can, it has a policy of never doing so by using to its advantage the ignorance of those with whom it works, who in such a business rarely have the educational or administrative background to understand when they are being cheated. Although nothing is said directly, it seems to all of us later, as we discuss the meeting, that Ted was referring specifically to the extraordinary 85% of the project which ABC is seeking, indeed to which it is trying to lay claim. But that such a judgment would be made by a colleague of ABC, albeit one which is also a competitor, seems to us particularly compelling.

As the discussion proceeds, Ted sympathizes with our concern for the several agencies, apparent and unseen, which have been let loose in the affair, and from what is then said to us it appears that ABC is really using very little of its own money (apart from the $1 or 2 million or so they are said to have dedicated to bringing the community up to code), since the 1300 unit development now being projected is exactly the one which the City also expects built, and for which they mayor set aside $65 million from last year's budget surplus. The unmistakable implication of our discussion is that ABC acted as they did – putting up the money for the HUD- appeasing renovations – because it saw that there was a lot of money to be made with comparatively little risk. It was the mayor, as all know, who directed that all residents would be given the opportunity to return to the rebuilt community, and that humane stipulation, however unlikely of final accomplishment, is no doubt the reason it is included in ABC's offer. Ted asks, among other things, how far the physical details of the apartments to be offered to the residents on their return have been specified, and, more pertinently, if we are quite sure that the residents would prefer to come back into the rebuilt development, particularly if they are now a small minority in a place that resembles in no way the community in which they have been living.

About this point we are joined by two visiting colleagues, not members of KCH as I understand it. We discuss not what has happened but what the options are, and they say, as Ted had before them, that one alternative would be the sale of the community outright, for a large cash payment, one which would allow residents to move wherever they like, and perhaps have money in hand after that as well. But however reasonable this sounds I am uneasy with it, if only because I am not so very confident that (all? most?) of the money will find its way to the residents. Still, the ABC agreement contains a provision for a payment of fifty thousand dollars for any family that decides not to return to the rebuilt development, but Ted points out that if the Board (with the community's agreement) sold the community outright, so that no family had the specified right to return, that payment could rise to over $200K per family – enough to allow residents a greater financial freedom than simply the right of return, and not to require the increasingly onerous limitations required by HUD's no doubt well-meant supervision. To show that he is quite serious, he consults again with certain of his colleagues, checks some studies (and zoning regulations) for the area in which Sursum Corda stands, and then makes (in writing, in a boilerplate letter addressed to Wilma) a serious but not final offer of $40 million for the land on which Sursum Corda stands. I do not mean to overstate the finality of this offer, which is both real and serious, but which leaves room for negotiation either way. "What the hell, it's only paper," Ted remarks light-heartedly, as he draws the document up, but adds that he means it, that he and KCH are interested in pursuing an offer and an arrangement with the Sursum Corda Board, and that this document is a sign of their intention.

In all of this, and as much because of, as in spite of, the amusement that our plight has occasioned, I come away with a very favorable impression of Ted, who seems to me to mix a canny and sharp understanding, with what I can only call unmistakable integrity. The more I see of developers, the more complicated their moral position seems to me to be – not that they lack integrity (no doubt some do, as do some academics), but my experience has been that they are inclined to look straight ahead, not right or left. But for now at least, in Ted, I have a sense of what this powerful, apparently remorseless, home-land-and-soul devouring profession could become, if its practitioners would only listen harder. Ted seems to me as knowing of our circumstances as our brief presentation would allow, but to have as well another quality I have not seen before, a certain almost instinctive sensitivity to the world we would create, and to its residents. Thus far my best protagonists have been (apart from the children and the tutors) Christine and Shiv, but listening to Ted, I wonder if he might not be a third. Certainly I hope so. Whatever the outcome of his offer, it would, make ABC's offer no longer the only one on the table – though the KCH offer is to remain confidential until after the inspection has been passed, or ABC, Shiv thinks, would find a way to rule it out. Our understanding is that we would, in the somewhat unlikely event of the Board accepting it outright, pay ABC outright for work done, and discharge all other debts as well. And I am not sure but that it might be possible for some residents, at least, to return to a rebuilt Sursum Corda under the KCH offer, even though I have no doubt that many would avail themselves of the cash. *Sat bene*, as my old Latin teacher used to say at the end of a bad quiz. It was no compliment.

Wednesday July 13, 2005

Another not quite fun-filled day that begins when Shiv collects me at 9am for our 9:30 Board meeting. We discuss the previous day's events, Shiv reminding me that when we began this whole process, representatives of the City, Boon, and then ABC had all insisted to us that the community was worth, once all the debts had been paid, $4 million at most, and we would be lucky to realize that. In those early days he alone (who after all knew something about real estate) objected to the number, but was all but ignored. What lies men tell. But when we arrive at Sursum Corda Mr. Vir has just arrived too, and is being lionized by those directing the operations. I go and join him while Shiv goes home to make a phone call, and somewhat to my surprise he remembers me. The director of operations is experienced in his work, and explains the many ways in which even an apparently attractive community can fail a HUD inspection – it can lose 27 points on the outside alone, even before any inside is examined – cracks in the pavement, trees too close to foundations, anything that can trip a resident or visitor (reasonably called "trip-ups," there are several which had been built into the original Sursum Corda construction) – any or all of these, untreated, can lead to a failure. The man insists that his workers have found only the highest level of cooperation among the residents he has ever enjoyed, and predicts final success. There is an interesting moment when he describes the roofing problems he has been dealing with: some of the houses have as many as three layers of cover on top, though only two are legally permitted, since roofing nails are generally too short to guarantee that they will hold through three. But they have not replaced any of the roofs, he notes, which would be an expensive process, and Chris Vir agrees that this is good, "since anyway they all may have to come down," he says.

The meeting, which consisted in 19 of us sitting around a large square made up of the tables on which we tutor (the irony strikes me) on the second floor, proved at once uneventful and revealing. There were four groups represented there as "partners," two having been added since I was last present. We are told that the first group Joe Friar had introduced, BAR, was one mainly concerned with commercial ventures, and it was BAR that had in turn introduced ABC. Certainly those three groups, ABC, BAR and FBV, all sat together and spoke with one voice at the meeting, and it was not a voice that seemed to me attentive to the interests of the residents. The meeting was chaired by one of ABC's vice-presidents, and it was hard to miss the tension in the room, as between the meeting of adversaries, united only in a general agreement that the HUD inspection had to be managed effectively. It began with a report from ABC, which revealed that to the initial 1200 points to be addressed in order to pass the inspection, ABC had added more than 700 more, and was 80% through that list. Final success was confidently expected, though it was explained that for HUD to stay away for 3 years the community would have to score 90, for 2 years 80, and for 1 year 60 on the final HUD evaluation. All health and Safety violations would be in place by July 15 (Friday) as required, and between that date and August 15 ABC would notify HUD that it is ready for a final inspection, which would probably (or might possibly) be completed by August 31 (or soon thereafter, if that date proves impossible for HUD), since after that date HUD could move to foreclosure.

It seemed to me that, evident tension notwithstanding, the Chair had conducted the meeting effectively, moving everything towards what was, after all, a common objective, and doing so by stressing cooperation first of all. Emphasizing that we had to press on with our work whatever the obstacles, he quoted, perhaps too often, what he called "an Arab proverb": "The dog barks, but the caravan moves on." Not the sort of saying, perhaps, calculated to encourage dialogue or reflection. In any case, the sense of the meeting was that success was assured, but when Shiv asked what would happen if we failed, one of the ABC representatives pointed out that there were various strategies which could be employed to delay foreclosure, such as the Board declaring the community bankrupt, which would immediately bring about the protection of the courts, so freezing further HUD actions. We discussed July 27 as a date for the community voting for a formal link with ABC (who would hold an 80% interest, not 85% as had previously been proffered), and a subsequent signing by the Board which ABC wants on the same day, though later in a Board meeting held after this one, we realized that the date is unrealistic, and that if we pressed ahead the community would probably vote No, yet until the HUD inspection has been passed, and by whatever score, we must keep all things sweet.

ABC's president seems a nice enough man, and stressed that all of us, and particularly ABC and the Board, were working together as a team, though he and ABC dominated the meeting, and gave every impression of having assumed authority not only over the proceedings, but, to a degree at least, over the community too. Or so it seemed to me. In spite of an apparent deference to Luke and to Wilma, it was hard to believe that ABC was placing all of its cards face up on the table, but no more were we. In the course of the meeting a Baltimore community planner (her field was described as "Strategic Management Consulting;" Luke had hired her shortly before I left for England) spoke up and showed that, to a degree at least, she really did understand the community and its aspirations, and after having then formally identified herself, was accepted into the group, and asked (by ABC) to prepare a report for our next meeting in two weeks time, but now moved back a day to Tuesday.

But throughout this meeting and others two groups dominated, the Board, for whom Luke spoke almost exclusively, and ABC. An appearance of 'partnership' hardly disguised evident differences, though my sense was that the real purpose of the meeting was to keep the ship on course, and to confront and deal with any problems that might arise. But it was difficult to escape the impression too that the residents were, not to say more, somewhat under represented. The power vested in the Board from its beginning was considerable, and seemed to rest on such familial relationships as may indeed have been present, for better or worse, in the early days of the community. But those relationships had altered dramatically in the light of present events, and what was evident now was a lack of transparency, no longer mitigated by informal relationships and open conversations as of old. (The sense in those early co-op years was not only that the Board knew better, but that it cared more as well.) This Board, certainly, was not known for its transparency, though that stand-alone quality may at least have given it a certain legitimacy in the eyes of ABC, who could reasonably regard its members as capable of speaking of, if not perhaps for, the larger community of residents, and to be reasonably confident, at least for now, that the Board would do nothing to impede the progress on which all depended. Partners, in this sense, they may have been, but loving partners not. Even so, the apparent confrontations that developed seemed to me largely cosmetic, and nothing I saw ever threatened to derail the cooperation that both sides saw as necessary. Real discussions, particularly those that addressed the interests of the residents, perhaps took place elsewhere. But even so, these meetings were in their own way revealing, and in the beginning at least, gave a sense of what the powers that governed believed to be going on.

This general (and apparently now bi-weekly) partners meeting was followed by a lesser but perhaps not less important Board meeting in which I finally got to meet our bright young lawyer, Tim Weigert. He has a graduate degree from Georgetown Law Center, where he worked in the Harrison Institute. In a short conversation before the meeting was called to order, I asked him about the circumstances of our partnering with ABC, and we agree that HUD's imposing the 5 day limit played a key role, and constituted as clear an example of duress as one could want. In the meeting, we discuss more things than I can now recall, and among them, though very briefly, the depth of our commitment to ABC, and the circumstances under which we might need or want to seek, in the event of failed inspection, another partner. We also agree that the July 27 date is unworkable and will have to be moved, though probably we will have to have it before, rather than after, the inspection, which is not our preference.

After all of this, and in a quick, private conversation, Shiv explains the $40 million KCH offered to Wilma, and how she had seemed genuinely delighted to have the offer in hand. They discuss another visit to KCH, this time with Wilma, to explain things further. She entrusts the document containing the KCH offer to Shiv for safekeeping, and agrees that it supplies the Board with some leverage to use against ABC – at least it does if Luke will agree to employ it.

Sunday July 17, 2005

Shiv calls about 10am to say that Lori Montgomery's article is in today's *Post*, and to ask what I made of it, but I have not seen it, having bought my *Sunday Post* on Saturday morning, expecting to find it there; but it missed the early edition, and only went in this morning. Shiv knows about it because Luke has called him and described it as a "smear," which it certainly proves to be from Luke's point of view, since it details aspects of his past career of which I at least was unaware, but it is certainly more accurate than anything the *Post* has published about the community thus far. I obtain a copy and call Shiv back, and Shiv declares himself concerned by "backlash," not from the residents, as I understand him, but within the Board itself. I am struck by several points, and ask Shiv to clarify them: Yes, initially HUD did allow only 5 days, but then added 30 more after being made aware that both FBV and ABC were now involved. Contrary to what Luke is reported as having said, the Board did not "interview several developers," thus arriving at ABC, though the previous and much distrusted former management company, which also acts as a developer, may have been called to mind, but there was certainly no effective search, and as far as I can see ABC was simply agreed upon by Luke, with the Board nodding a hasty agreement, in fear of HUD. The story also speaks of "replacing the shabby apartments and townhouses with more than 300 mixed-income units." This seems to be the key. What ABC wants is not the 300 unit community which would effectively preserve and develop the community that now exists, but a 1300 unit development, which, even with some or many of the residents allowed back in, would all but extinguish it.

Lori's story certainly makes the Board seem quite incompetent, both by quoting Wilma's somewhat unconsidered remark about getting as many as possible of the residents off the site on Inspection Day as possible by offering a free trip to Six Flags ("Load 'em up on a bus and cart 'em away"), and by stressing that Luke was "working as a trash collector when he impressed the Sursum board with his ability to talk to developers and government people." It does not take up some really important points (how many units does ABC intend to build? What of the zoning regulations, whatever they are? Will they sink the community or to preserve it?). According to what is known, the City seems to have the same number of units in mind for the new development as ABC does, 1300, which may have been chosen with zoning regulations in mind (I assume zoning was the reason that the larger number of 2,000 units, mooted earlier, has been dropped, but who knows? Besides, zoning regulations can be changed). Indeed the City's role in the present difficulties, which is of course crucial, hardly appears at all. Jane comes off very well indeed, demanding answers to questions about the development plan that Wilma and Luke "refused to answer," and describing what is going on (not entirely inaccurately, from what I can see) as a "flimflam" – but, *pace* Jane – if that be so, at least it is not the Board's flimflam. The article does make the point however, that Sursum Corda is "one of the very few" low income housing cooperatives in the United States owned and operated by its residents.

In yet another article in the Outlook section of today's *Post* Charlotte Allen which describes "How Renewal Ruined SW [Washington]" – where she now lives, however. The account seems to me accurate enough – patrons of the Arena Theater have now become the most frequent visitors there – though many a developer would list her very reasonable complaints of blighted landscapes, unused parking lots, few stores, restaurants or amenities of any sort, under the heading "lessons learned, and no longer of concern." "Our" developers, for example, could argue that such objections simply won't apply to Sursum Corda, since the reason for its putative redevelopment is that it stands surrounded by places so much more interesting – and currently so much more valuable – than it is. But the lead-in Allen used to her article was last month's Supreme Court decision allowing New London, Connecticut, the right of eminent domain, so as to seize and then raze a working class neighborhood, the better to construct "a waterfront office, residential and hotel complex." Property, money, power -- not ethics. Poor New London, poor Sursum Corda, poor everyone. Elsewhere, a story in the Book Review alludes to a speech given by that sick, evil, tyrant Josef Stalin in 1931, explaining that his country needed to industrialize quickly so as to ward off those who had previously invaded and pillaged it – Mongols, Turks, Poles, Swedes, the British and the

French, among others. "They beat her because to do so was profitable and could be done with impunity," he averred.

Monday July 18, 2005

I had a good if somewhat difficult discussion with Shiv last night, but this morning can remember only a part of what we said. The single most important issue remains the HUD inspection, now less than 30 days away, and (this in answer to me) that we simply don't know what the "final" plan is likely to be. Jane Walters had pressed this point, and when she got no good answer had declared the operation a flimflam. But this only sounds right, and Wilma was probably more correct in saying that the charge was intended to frighten the residents, and so prevent them from supporting the Board – in fact, until the very final contract is signed, much simply is undecided. But that's not what people want to hear, or are inclined, particularly in this somewhat paranoid situation, to believe. We have to proceed step by step, he insisted, with a certain confidence that in the end we may prevail.

Shiv was concerned for the damage done to Luke by the *Washington Post* article, and (even more) for the direction he was taking the project. The real authority remains with Wilma, he pointed out, and his sense is that the *Post's* attack is likely to deepen her inclination to defend him, not weaken it. He thought that the basic metaphor operating here was that of the family, and the families he knew and respected around Sursum Corda never cut off a family member because he (as it usually was) had messed up, had stolen something, for example, or was in jail. The details about Luke's apparently failed work in Baltimore were entirely new to us, as were the facts that he had been charged with mismanaging funds, and had been working as a trash collector when the Sursum Board hired him as its Chief Operating Officer, or COO. We all understand, I think, why Lori Montgomery took the approach she did, and the revelation was probably effective in undermining his position at Sursum – earlier in the day Shiv's mother had heard some of the residents laughing about it – but it rested a little too easily on a concept of class which is neither particularly modern nor particularly American. No doubt the developers and their colleagues were a little taken aback too.

He had a point, which I wondered about afterwards. I had come to think, almost certainly wrongly it now appears, that the men with whom we are dealing have all but set aside any ethical considerations about the work they are engaged in, and that for them it was simply business as usual. Custom had made in them an easy property of it. But as I watched them at work last Wednesday they appeared to have their own code, ethical in its way, I suppose, one that allows for individual accomplishment, but emphasizes "team" responsibility and getting the job done first of all. Its notion of responsibility is attached more or less exclusively to the task at hand, and not to any consideration, personal or otherwise, for the ends or the means of project itself, still less for any of its implications, putative or actual. In effect, whatever the moral implication, no one's to blame.

But even granting that ends do not justify means, ethical judgment, at least as the phrase is usually understood, must contend with both. What was unmistakable at our meetings was the sense that this organized group of intelligent, well-educated, purposeful and affluent persons were engaged in a project calculated to take from another group of equally intelligent but less well-educated, less certain and largely disadvantaged persons their most valuable asset, and to do so, under the color of necessity, as cheaply as possible. They do not seek to do so illegally, though the virtues of justice and equity encoded in law are perhaps not their much loved guide, and though they would probably insist that their practices are fair, they might just allow that in this dog-eat-dog world of ours, it's finally every man for himself. These able and industrious persons no doubt have a considered understanding both of the world and of their role in it, and the Board having apparently set aside any other consideration, it is with that understanding that we have now to deal. Or so it seems. As for me, I have been perhaps too concerned with what seem to me the residents' more or less obviously neglected rights, including those of ownership, Sursum Corda being a co-op, and also their moral right to maintain their imperfect community against the depredations of the powerful. But remaining unconvinced that any rights are absolute, and conscious, if dimly, of the power of those we confront, I have been inclined to believe that the most effective way to defend these rights was in dialogue.

But dialogue is all but silenced now. No doubt I wasn't entirely mistaken, and for some of "them" the only judgments that matter are those encoded on the bottom line. But for now at least, I still want to believe that there finally is a relation, if not perhaps a relationship, between power and probity. But is probity, in twenty-first century America, anything other than law? And too often, when the weak confront the powerful, can that suffice?

Occasionally Shiv and I have discussed, both indirectly but also directly, the ethics and even the morality that we have seen revealed as the usual standards for right and wrong seemed to dissolve and then to reform in front of us. Influenced by those more reflective Board members who pray that God will inform their judgments, we have wondered what else may be influencing Shiv's judgment and mine, and how far we could publically employ those religious teachings that seek to defend the widow and the orphan against what looks like nothing else than well bred rapaciousness. Not very far, we reluctantly conclude, though we hope that the one virtue that may not be entirely mocked is justice. But for ourselves, we consider that although we may indeed trust in God, we had better tie our camel too.

After having written this entry I go to a Tombs lunch with a conservative (no longer neo-) friend of some years standing, and though neither of us really wants to, we fall into conversation about Sursum Corda. Ed, who has a doctorate both in law and in religion, has usually a warm heart, and is an excellent father. Over the years he has been particularly generous to a hospital in one of the poorest cities in India – which in gratitude named an ambulance after him. Partly as a result, he is, as a general rule at least, less ideologically driven on issues that impinge upon the poor, but when we turn to what is happening he asks whether the best thing might be to tear the community down. Doing so, he suggests, might result in a higher payment to those who live there than any a developer might pay. Initially he says "Yes, yes," to my concern about destroying the community, but then, like the child of the media that I falsely tell him he is, actually asks if the community is really worth saving. But in all of this I want a middle way, and not to absolve myself or anyone of responsibility for those with whom we have to do. The legal fiction is that under the law we are equal – but in this our

talking America, we all know better. And if so then, when you construct your ethical constraints, remember that you have no moral
right to take, for a legal peppercorn, what's theirs, not yours. The
law's an ass, or can be. Whatever the life requirements of the present situation – or the present century – we can not finally pretend
ignorance of the changes that result from what we do, but must account for them, if only somehow, neither dictating ends and means
as we prefer, nor behaving as if communities can be dispensed with
in favor of a larger group than theirs. As I am writing this Ed calls
up and says he hopes we didn't get off Sursum too quickly. I insist
we didn't, but he presses on, and says that I must believe that he
has no sympathy at all for the developer who simply wants to have
homes down and the poor gone, so he can build his fortune on their
past.

Before I met Ed for lunch I stopped by the Sursum Corda camp
which Justin, Stewart and their friends are holding, now for a second year, at Georgetown, having converted the coffee room in the
library to a morning classroom (the children play and swim in the
afternoon, and go on day trips too), and it is going very well indeed.
When I come in Stewart is leading the children through a text, prob-
ing with questions and enticing with rewards. Two young women,
who will be Georgetown students next year, come up to talk, and
as we do so the attractiveness of Sursum Corda comes back to me.
Lewis and Mark, aged 6 and 7, both old friends, notice me too, and
I promise to return.

Friday July 22, 2005

Shiv can't get a read on the Monday meeting with residents that
he had not been able to attend, but which sounds to have been a
disaster. One Board member told him that it had in the end become
very personal, and Wilma left at midpoint, but Luke thought it a
triumph. I wonder. Earlier Luke told Shiv that Lori Montgomery
had telephoned him to ask, apparently with a straight face, if he
had liked the article in the *Post*, but he had not risen to the bait,
and said, in effect, that it was all fair content; that he didn't mind.
Shiv thinks the article may have been written in the first place because Luke had called the *Post* and suggested it, no doubt expect-

ing something other than what appeared. He also remarks that Wilma has been greatly angered by the discovery that ABC had approached the Board's lawyer without reference to her, and means to call them on it at our next meeting together. But everyone now counsels moderation, as everything now turns on the inspection, which should not be jeopardized for any reason. But Wilma means to tell Joe Austen with ABC that if he ever again approaches the Board's lawyer she will move at once to seek another partner, a representation that would no doubt cause some concern. No doubt Joe was trying, a little too hard under the circumstances, to be sure all his ducks are all in a row (his conversation with Shiv after our last meeting no doubt falls under the same heading). Or perhaps he is concerned about what will follow the inspection, and needs the sort reassurance only a lawyer can give (but he has his own). Whatever the motivation, it was evidently a mistake, probably not a serious one, however. In any case, it's now a waiting game.

I have been reading Jared Diamond's *Collapse*, published earlier this year, a study, as the subtitle explains, of *How Societies Choose to Fail or Succeed*, and musing on its several propositions, my thoughts turned, of course, to Sursum Corda too. Among other things, Diamond identifies five factors that he believes people inflict on their environment that can lead to systemic failure. These focus upon the fragility of any eco-system, climactic change, hostile neighbors, decreased support from putatively friendly neighbors, and society's response to its difficulties. Changes having been made (and extending the use of the word "climate"), it would not be difficult to identify all of them as virtually present here, from the withdrawal of City and other support, the attacks from Northwest 1 and the *Washington Post*, and the evident fragility of social and human relationships which the new land valuation brought about. But the most obviously relevant concerns are the social ones, and the extent to which a failure to adapt to new conditions has condemned many a system to extinction. Even with our several attacks, we have not yet had the breakdown of authority which Diamond has observed in many collapsing societies, and which could play havoc here. But the Board's response to the way things are is still somewhat uncertain, though conditioned by the pressure of events it seems to me often acting more quickly than it should.

Wednesday July 27, 2005

More heat than light at the meeting yesterday, though a certain amount of light too. Collette, the Strategic Management Consultant, in the chair if not always in charge, calls order but begins with Wilma's objection that ABC had arranged a meeting with the City without the Board being informed or present; Joe Austen was (appropriately but carefully) temporizing, blaming it an error that did not bear repeating. Wilma was insistent, and a ABC member intervened saying, disingenuously as it seemed to me, Well, since we're partners now, of course we'll have to attend meetings at which not all are present, etc. She was at once taken up on her not very convincing representation, and among other things the tentative and early nature of the partnership were held out as reasons for not assuming too much, too soon. In fact, ABC had been set back by the meeting (though they reported that it had gone very well), since the City apparently had insisted that they build 5 and 6 bedroom units for those who have them now. Bravo City. When this was pointed out, Luke sought to ingratiate himself with both Wilma and ABC by saying, in effect, Yes, you should have consulted us, because I've been getting residents to agree to three or four bedroom units, irrespective of however many they have now. But throughout this particular exchange, it seemed to me that both Wilma and Joe Austen, though perhaps not Luke Gratian, had acquitted themselves well.

The meeting ran on into many other issues. Carl, who had been leading the improvements for ABC, reported that all 1,700 deficiencies on the initial (and augmented) to-do list had now been addressed, and that at a cost of $817K. We took up the process of inspection, and were given to understand that once we report to HUD that the community is ready for inspection, HUD will have to wait two weeks in order to inform the residents of the date, and, since they have said that they are going to inspect 80% of the units (a higher percentage than usual, Carl believes) they may need many inspectors, which could further delay things (or not). But if 85 % of the units are occupied, HUD will not then inspect the unoccupied ones. Meanwhile nearby Temple Courts, which had (it was reported) passed an earlier inspection has failed a follow-up one, and had done so with a score of only 35. Some concern is expressed, but Carl, who has gone by for a look, says that he can understand why.

Wilma also represented reasons for slowing the process of community approval, objecting at one point that "We can't flood our membership with a lot of information all at one time." At one point Joe Friar, today replacing Chris Vir, intervened to support her, saying, in effect, we should put off our professional hats and listen to what Wilma has to say about the community, which she knows it better than we do. If we present the proposal as it is right now, Wilma rightly insisted, they [the residents] are going to say No. As a result of this and other representations, Joe Austen called for a meeting in a week's time, in which what was on offer from ABC would be made explicitly clear to the Board members – so that they could better represent it to the residents, he says, but perhaps also to confirm us in our purposes as well. I shall be away next week, however, which is a pity, since I expect that other issues will appear at that meeting too.

At one point in the meeting, however, a representative of BAR, seemed to me to supply a particularly unsettling edge, displaying an attitude that was, for no apparent reason, utterly contemptuous of the community, which she simply wanted removed as quickly and as cheaply as possible. Against this, Wilma represented the importance of Block meetings, countering another suggestion that such meetings be more formally structured by pointing out that these smaller, more informal meetings, attracted residents who never came out to the bigger meetings.

Towards the end, discussion turned to Northwest 1, the group said to represent all the residents and communities in the area around Sursum Corda, and which has been Jane Walters's power base in recent years. The general perception has been that the organization has worked vigorously (if ineffectively) against the community here, and that it has disseminated misinformation and, if truth be told, representations that some at our meeting thought slanderous. On the other hand, because the City consults Jane at least semi-regularly, and because she speaks for the area around Sursum Corda which would be part of any larger plan the City either is evolving or has in hand, ABC wants to approach the group, even attach themselves in some way to it. To this Wilma objected with vigor, and loudly. Her focus was on the inspection, she said, and she was *not*, NOT going to become involved with Northwest

1, which had, consistently misrepresented what has been going on at our meetings and elsewhere, and been nothing but a distraction and a drain. Luke agreed with her, and insisted that one of the problems the Board had in dealing with residents, is that the City and Northwest 1 are forever whispering in their ear. Discussion continued, and it was at this point that someone made an intervention on Wilma's behalf, which caused ABC rather to tack its sails, and suggest sending a representative to offer corrections as needed, and collect information, but not to supply such information as would probably be distorted. But their larger purpose for the suggestion was palpable.

The meeting ended almost three quarters of an hour late, and after it a group of ABC managers suddenly come in to get autographs from Joe Friar, and to have their photographs taken with him, further evidence of their usefulness to our enterprise. Not long thereafter Luke buttonholed both Joe Friar and Charles Wilson to ask about the investment the Board had been expecting from FBV, but since he had no details in hand the request fell flat, though Joe Friar said he would take the matter up with his colleagues. Afterwards, when they had left, Luke asked Tim Weigert, our lawyer (also at the meeting) what we should be looking for from FBV. Tim suggested something in the region of $800K, for their 25% of our 15%, which is what we have, thus far at least, been discussing. It doesn't seem much. Luke insists that the Board is now very short of money, and that he has not been collecting a portion of his own salary so as to keep the place afloat. Tim also gives us a draft of the ABC agreement document, but it all seems to Shiv and me something of a giveaway.

Tim's draft makes us want to meet again with Wilma before I leave for Berkeley, and there are evident deficiencies in the document, not least of all that the Board would dissolve and loose the standing necessary to contest any departure from the agreement which ABC might undertake. Nor could it continue with the lawsuit against the earlier management, an action in which the Board would probably seek two or three million dollars. This second matter in particular is good reason for the Board to remain intact. But as I am writing this Shiv calls to say that Wilma is out of town until tomorrow, adding that Carl has told him that ABC has in fact spent almost two million thus far, and will probably spend more. Carl has added that although he knows it is not his department, he thinks ABC is quite right to want a contract a.s.a.p. But Shiv points out to me that ABC has half a million dollars in escrow with HUD, and that in order to recover it, the inspection must be passed by August 30. But my own sense is that HUD could work around that date, and not deny ABC its escrow, if they wanted to.

Thinking about everything again, I reflect how quickly and (apparently at least) how far we have come, and I am not comforted. But in spite of what has transpired, it seems to me that the most important thing is to resist a growing sense of inevitability, a sense that all of the operational details are in place, and that the only real choice concerns the number of units to be constructed. But so much has happened: the new Washington Convention Center and the chaos it has caused, Princess' appalling murder, the subsequent and related attacks by the *Washington Post,* by all of our old adversaries now embolden, the perhaps not unrelated HUD inspections which ended in failure, the opening which FBV supplied and the sudden possibility of hope, but all tied to a perception of a community which must be transmuted, not reborn, and resting on the proposition that all this new White power is working to the good. I do not know whether the lifeline which has so far sustained the community has now been severed, but it may have been. At any rate, though we cannot escape our history, it may be that we can prosper in spite of it, if we but keep our wits about us now.

Sunday August 7, 2005

I was away for a week in Berkeley, and among other things read an editorial in the August 3 *San Francisco Bay Guardian* (a free paper) objecting to the "rapid gentrification of SoMa," the area south of Market Street in San Francisco which is now awash in development. "San Francisco is in real danger of becoming a place that drives out the poor and others who give this city its vibrancy and diversity," the editorial runs, adding this: "If greedy developers are allowed to build whatever type of housing they want in exchange for what amounts to multi-million dollar extortion by a cash-strapped city, then even well-intentioned officials will become unwitting accomplices to a drastic remaking of San Francisco." But is there any American city without a like problem? And what would it take to make the *Washington Post* consider that a community of the poor and disadvantaged should not be the wealthy's to dispose of, and to think in these terms?

Monday August 8, 2005

In the event the lunch proved less decisive than we had anticipated, largely because of Tim's artful dodging of Shiv's email (he didn't answer it), but we decide that Shiv and Wilma will meet him later in the week when I am visiting a friend in Connecticut. Later, Wilma reveals that in a recent conversation Tim had remarked, unprompted, that it was time for him to use some delay tactics to slow things down. Viva Tim. Wilma herself now seems to have taken against ABC, at least somewhat, whom she apparently believes untrustworthy and even duplicitous, remarking at one point "they're robbing us without a gun." She has further concluded that Joe Austen is simply unconcerned with the human cost of what he is seeking to do, and when I asked where her doubts had begun, she said months earlier, when she and Luke had gone to ABC's main office one Friday to iron out details of the arrangement. There they had established, she thought, that the Board was going to receive 170 units of the new project free and clear, but when they read the description of what had been agreed upon the next Monday, it turned out that there were going to be mortgages for all of them. Bait and switch tactics, I inquired? No, she replied. Lying.

Monday August 15, 2005

I visited a friend in Kent, Connecticut last week, and have not been able to write about recent developments, of which there were several, until now. Our Tuesday meeting, which I had to leave early in order to catch a train, proved more than usually important. Joe Austen revealed a discussion with the City, that he, Luke Gratian, Hans Johnson of BAR, and James Nathans, a young architect brought on by Luke, had on August 5 with the Deputy Mayor for Development, and an associate of his, also connected with the City.

It had, incontestably, yielded important results: the City had reject-ed ABC's plan for high density development (1,500 units, its price for warding off HUD's foreclosure, but one to which the Board has never actually acceded), and insisted on a low density plan instead, one that would involve four to five hundred new units in Sursum Corda itself, a third dedicated to low, a third to moderate, and a third to market rate housing. Such an arrangement would not al-low us our profit, ABC had insisted, but then the City sprang its surprise, and said, in effect, Yes it will, because we're going to throw in two or three properties on North Capitol Street where you can build about 1000 luxury high-rise units, and so realize your profit there. Other affordable units would have to be constructed else-where, so as to allow 528 affordable units throughout Northwest 1. As he revealed this at least apparent breakthrough, Joe noted, what was not strictly true, that the offer had come about because the Board had "signed on" for a high density development at Sur-sum. He said he was proud of it for having done so.

A map was produced and consulted which showed the location on North Capitol Street of the proposed lots, and the question was raised as to why the City had been so forthcoming. The general sense seemed to be that the difficulties with Northwest 1 were such as to make too great reliance on that body inadvisable; that a devel-oper was going to be needed to construct the luxury high rises from which the City expected to generate income anyway, and linking both to ABC had the effect of killing two birds with one stone; and that doing so was in accord with the charette which the City had both organized and effectively managed not long since, and whose dictates they can thus be seen as respecting. That meeting, after all, in which Northwest 1 had assumed an important role, had very usefully and quite rightly specified low density – and town houses – in Sursum Corda, and high density in such places as the vacant lots with which ABC had now, apparently at least, been presented, though no doubt elsewhere too. I say apparently because these are sliding surfaces upon which we skate, and I should be very much surprised if the final arrangements are as they were represented that morning. Is any of this in writing? And how much is simply game?

The following day, a Wednesday, Luke took the Board to a dinner in Georgetown, apparently to give 30 days' notice of his intention to resign but in actuality to press for the completion of the arrangement with ABC. He is said to have represented that he has brought the community along this far, and he did not mean to stand by while all his good work went for naught. The ABC arrangement, he insisted, was the best by far of any we could achieve, and what he wanted most of all was the Board to agree with him and, after due consultation with the residents, to sign it forthwith. Shiv did not intervene in his usual way, but Wilma remained unmoved, and in a conversation they had together later, both thought that Luke had tipped his hand. I doubt it. Although the Board members present said the right things – at least from Luke's point of view – at the time, Shiv believes that Wilma later spoke with most or all of them, and undid the damage.

Shiv and I meet again yesterday for what has become our usual chat and Sunday dinner, and decide that one reason Luke and ABC are so concerned with finalizing the agreement is that someone from the City has approached Luke, and mooted yet another plan, one which, in spite of what has been said, might or might not include ABC. We need to know more about this meeting, including if it actually happened. But the result is that Collette is now pressing ahead on that front, and reports as well that HUD has now suspended its foreclosure plan, which, if true, would buy us more time, particularly if the inspection goes ahead as expected. Much is still in play, but whatever now happens, recent events have written *finis* to the old plan of implementing the foreclosure this summer, and starting the putative redevelopment soon thereafter. Meanwhile Shiv thinks we should meet with Wilma again, and I much agree if only to support her in what she is up against. Wilma has been insisting on acting alone, on being responsible to no one, on being free to come to her own conclusions, but that stance has had the effect of imposing a certain isolation upon her, which our lunch-time talks together have not done much to alter. We consider too how far KCH may go along with the new arrangements, and suggest that Shiv should ask them, so that we can have some idea. We consider that it may be time to explore some other options too, if we can do so with reasonable speed and discretion.

Tuesday August 16, 2005

Shiv kindly gives me a ride to our meeting this morning, and on the way tells me of a rather sudden meeting Wilma had called with the Board members last night. Luke was not present, and Shiv thought had not been asked to attend. In the course of it, she posed this conundrum: You have just finished baking three apple pies, and have taken them from the oven. You turn your back on them, but in doing so you knock one of them off the counter, and it begins to fall, face down, toward the floor. Just before it strikes, however, someone reaches forward and catches it. To whom does the pie belong?

She went around those present, asking each his (Shiv) or her opinion: and each one said that it was hers, since the resources which had gone into the pie were hers, and hers was the labor of its creation. They also got the point. In the course of what followed, however, one member asked with evident pointedness who Luke works for. Us or ABC? But Wilma had his back, and insisted that he was a businessman, doing what it is that businessmen do. But this may have been because one of Luke's allies was present. So in a way, Luke may have been too. All those present, Shiv reported, felt strongly that it was no coincidence that HUD had put pressure on the community, and so on the Board, just when ABC appeared on the scene, and that their connection to ABC had been anything but freely given.

The meeting itself took place as usual on the second floor of the Community Center, but without Wilma, and perhaps as a result went forward swimmingly, with Luke indicating, yet again and very clearly, his support of the ABC arrangement. Just as we are about to begin Shiv comes in with Dion, his learner when he was tutoring in the program, now grown into a fine young man of sixteen years. He has brought him in to introduce him to Chris Vir, who seems to me to treat him with the greatest kindness and consideration, not grandstanding or playing a role, but talking to Dion, if briefly, with directness and respect, like the good man he has so often showed himself to be. Dion, Shiv and I have a word on the way out, and I am pleased with the encounter, brief though it was. The meeting itself began – after a prayer and introductions – with Carl's usual report, in which he remarked that the time between completion of work and the announcement of the inspection was "the worst time for a person in my business," and that we were now very much in Phase 2, with 1.1 million dollars having been spent. Carl, another good man, then goes out of his way to praise some of those who have been working with and for him, saying, what is hardly true, that he has simply been showing off in his reports to us, but that they have been the unsung heroes. Chris Vir, representing FBV, then asked about the unsightly trash he had seen blowing about (but not in) the community, and we discussed the matter at some length, concluding that, since the trash belonged rather to our neighbors, it could work for the inspection, by showing the evident difference between Sursum Corda, where the trash was now attended to and collected, and elsewhere, where it was not. But Chris Vir very honorably wanted our efforts to radiate beyond Sursum Corda, and to include, as he said, "some sort of plan for the people around."

We discussed the budget, not yet ready for presentation, and the extent to which some bills from the previous management group may not have come to light. From that came a discussion of HUD's attitude toward Sursum Corda itself, said at the last inspection to be the worst that the inspectors had ever experienced. Luke insisted that "HUD is not playing," that he expected them to come back to "the management piece," and not to be less attentive to it than they are to the property's physical condition. Lisa T., who has long seemed to me one of the most knowledgeable and perceptive members of the group and the only one with real insight into what HUD is about, remarked that it was her sense that there was a "lot of politics going on in HUD about this inspection," effectively reminding me at least how little we really know about how others see us, whether the others be HUD, the City, or ABC itself. I have been wondering throughout how deeply HUD may see into this whole affair, and cannot think it likely that its attitude is unambiguous, either with regards to the community or ABC. In the course of this part of the discussion Luke objected that residents have a right only to the size unit which is right for them – not to the size that they have now.

It was in this somewhat mixed conversation that Luke suddenly brought up a major point, namely that very recently he had been again approached by the City, and asked that it be allowed to make its own proposal to the residents, one far different than ABC's. The City's plan, at least as last presented, included only 150 units at Sursum Corda, fewer than are there now, and as Luke dropped his revelation he added too that of course we should not consider the proposition, but it should make us hasten to complete the ABC agreement. Shiv intervened to say that there was nothing surprising in the offer, that it had been all but made before, and Chris Vir took the matter up too, insisting, what was quite true, that the City had ignored the community and assumed that the HUD foreclosure would succeed, and that they could then ignore the people here. We should be loyal to those who stood up for us in hard times, he averred, sounding what will in all likelihood become the charge and complaint when and if ABC is shown the door. Finally the discussion turned to how best to present the ABC plan to the residents, but Shiv and I then left, both for another meeting.

If the whole ABC business has taught us anything, it must be what a complex and demanding process we have in hand, and how naive it would be simply to dump all of it on Wilma and the Board. I say that it seems to me that we should consider, and meet with, the City, though I agree that their behavior toward the community and the Board has been more than a little condescending, and that Chris Vir was obviously right when he said they were expecting a foreclosure. But that circumstance places us in a stronger position, it seemed to me, and furthermore they, perhaps alone, have the authority necessary to change partners without undue difficulty – if only because, in consideration of future ventures, ABC may prove somewhat reluctant to go toe-to-toe with the City even in a circumstance like this one, though it will undoubtedly result in hard feelings. It strikes me too that what may interest ABC more are those land parcels on North Capitol Street, and its concern for Sursum Corda may not be unconnected with that. So there may be an opening possible that would yet please them. Even so, if time allows, I think that we should see what other developers have to say, and hope to raise some or all of this tomorrow.

Friday August 19, 2005

I am working at home when Shiv calls to tell me about a meeting of the Board that Luke had called last night. Its main business seems to have been to allow Luke to press the Board to approve the ABC agreement just as it stands, and from what Shiv now says his fire was directed primarily at Wilma and himself. This is not unexpected, to be sure, and Shiv remarks that he must be coming under a lot of pressure from ABC, but still somehow it seems to be revealing. Shiv says again to me, as he later did to Wilma, that he has in the past been disappointed in Luke, but now he simply distrusts him. We hope to meet with lawyer Tim sometime over the weekend.

Tuesday August 23, 2005

I was working in my office yesterday when an email appears saying that the HUD inspection will be conducted September 12-16, beginning at 2pm on the 12th. It will be conducted by only one HUD inspector, one John L., and who will inspect, as we had expected, 80% of the units, and no doubt the public areas as well. Small wonder five days will be needed. But may not the fact that only one man is being assigned to carry out the inspection indicate that HUD is expecting us to pass?

Subsequently I talk with Shiv about yesterday's Board meeting which Tim's senior partner had attended. He had been involved in making the original agreement with ABC, and insisted that it was a "good deal." After all, he had reasoned, ABC had taken all the risk, and so merited a really quite extraordinary profit. But a possible if projected 60-80 million dollar profit on a 1.1 to 2 million dollar investment seems to us a little too extraordinary, even by the standards of Washington developers, and we are somewhat concerned that there may be more going on than we have set our hand to. A day or two earlier Shiv had emailed Tim to arrange a lunch in which we hoped to put him more fully in the picture, and thus far had not heard back, but on the way out Tim, who was also at the meeting, mentioned it to him, though the circumstances prevented them from fixing a day. Toward the end of our conversation we decide, for different reasons, not to attend the usual Tuesday meeting of the putative partners.

Later I call an acquaintance at the Georgetown Law Center to see what is known about Tim's firm, and I wonder too whether the changing circumstances could induce the Harrison Institute finally to become involved. After all, everything ABC seeks to accomplish is linked to the interests of the City, not to those of the community, which has thus far only been consulted (and voted) on the association with FBV, an association which had seemed to offer them the assurance of continued residence at Sursum Corda, their home, and the possibility of home ownership. The new ABC deal, even as modified by its putative agreement with the City, was conducted entirely over their head, and without any reference to them, even though they are, in law and in fact, the owners of the property which is under discussion. I understand that property rights, like all rights these days, are not absolute. Rights by rights may indeed falter, as Shakespeare and the Supreme Court have it. But at Sursum Corda they seem rather to have been assumed away, lost in a subclause, treated as if it was in the worst possible taste to mention them. Well, it may be that we cannot expect better from the developers, but we damn well can from our own lawyers. At least that's the theory.

Wednesday August 24, 2005

I hear good things back about Tim's firm, which has a reputation as a defender of tenants' rights, and that further confirms our good opinion of Tim. I neglected to ask about getting the Harrison Institute involved, but my sense is that we are perhaps too far along in the game to expect such a blessing, and besides, they have showed no particular appetite to take on the City when approached before (though the reason also had to do with Sursum Corda already having secured council, which was true enough as far as it went). We met in the faculty lunchroom at Georgetown, with Shiv, Wilma and Tim coming in half an hour late. As we talked, however, he warmed, if at first reluctantly, to these new perspectives, though he pointed out that the Board has after all a signed agreement with ABC, not simply a memorandum of understanding, and even if that document is not final, it is certainly more than a detail. He brought up again the issue of ABC's risk in jumping in as it had, but knowing perhaps better than most what behind-the-scenes machinations went into that putative risk, he did not delay long on that particular point. While accepting what he said about the nature of the agreement, we also thought that it was an arrangement was replete with unknowns, all of which at some point or other would need to be addressed. It was also more or less obviously the product of duress. Shiv then produced the memorandum of understanding offered by KCH, and Tim saw at once what was afoot, and began to think through the possibilities. After a quick read he indicated that the KCH understanding seemed to him less good – and certainly less finished – than the one with ABC (a new one is said to be in the works), but took the point that its existence complicated matters and made delay necessary, if only so that the Board could understand what else might be – or come onto – the table.

Of course we discussed Luke, who seems to us to have become increasingly difficult, as he appropriates more and more responsibilities to himself, and whose attitude toward the Board has become ever more directive. We discussed past history, deeds done before I had returned from London. Wilma had been much disappointed at what certainly sounded to be a classic bait-and-switch tactic, in the course of which ABC certainly seemed to have promised 170 units free and clear to the Board on Friday, but when the document arrived on Monday the promise had not been honored. Luke had insisted that it be signed anyway, since time was short, as it indeed was, but the timing had prevented the Board from looking further, and (what I had not known), initially the Board had rejected a ABC's proposal (they had wanted too much for too little; they still do), and were forced into accepting it only because of IIUD's actions. And how much coordination of these action (and others) took place, God only knows. Tim had not seen his closeness to ABC (which, to be fair, is clearest in Board meetings and in those partner meetings that he does not attend), but thought him increasingly difficult, and believed that the City and perhaps even ABC thought so too. There was of course one way to deal with the situation, he pointed out, and subsequently Wilma indicated that she had someone else in mind to take his place, when and if that need should arise.

The extraordinary thing is that there seems to us simply no

way the residents would accept the present agreement (our judgment remains that they shouldn't), but if they don't, then the whole
agreement falls apart, and we have to start over. This is a problem
for which we really don't have an answer. We are, as the cliché
has it, between a rock and a hard place, brought there by the mal-
administration (if not more) of a previous management firm, but
quite possibly by the coordinated machinations of HUD and the
City too. ABC and Luke no doubt understand this, and, true his
own construction of the only thing that actually will work (ABC),
Luke keeps pressing the vote. Wilma now is less inclined to credit
his earlier and private representation to her that he often acts as he
does, strongly urging one position or another, simply to help edu-
cate members of the Board who are new to their responsibilities.
We say again to Tim that ABC is not being cut out of the process,
but has to revise its position, if only because of the interest of other
parties, like KCH, who may be expected to show more consistency
than ABC.

But there also seems to me to be a kind of matched naiveté operating here: the Board's, acting under what was clearly duress,
approving the agreement (candidly, without fully understanding
it), and now ABC's, in assuming that the residents will as a matter
of course approve that agreement, just as it had earlier the agreement with FBV. We also discuss the role of FBV in the operation,
which is increasingly hard to discern, though they may have been
instrumental earlier, if (what I still think unlikely) there indeed was
White House pressure on HUD, in postponing the foreclosure. But
little or nothing since, and though I myself think that Mr. Vir in particular would be very good to have associated with the children's
programs, the high profile status of FBV may not now be as important as it once was in warding off the implications which, thanks
to the *Washington Post*, earlier attached to the community, and the
impression at the table seems to be that they have certainly positioned themselves very well from a financial point of view, and at
the Board's expense.

Wilma had an interesting story too about a short meeting she
had a day or two earlier with one of the ABC property managers
now working at Sursum Corda. In a brief aside, while they were
simply chatting, the man had warned her to be very, very careful.

Take baby steps, he had said. Be sure of what you're doing. Don't be rushed. That was as well the leit-motif of our afternoon discussion too, and although I know that particularly these days at Sursum Corda all is not what it seems, I thought the words, at least in Wilma's telling of them, a decent and helpful admonition.

This was the first time I really had a chance to hear Tim speak at length, and I liked what I heard: an evidently smart and thoughtful young man equipped with equal measures of skepticism and good judgment, motivated by what certainly seemed to be an innate sense of justice, and genuinely concerned to act in the best interests of the residents. That he did not jump at out new perspective seems to me a mark in his favor, and my sense is that we are lucky to have him with us.

Friday August 26, 2005

I had one other reflection about what I wrote here on Wednesday, an idea I have been playing with since I returned to the changed circumstances of Sursum Corda at the end of June. I have been concerned throughout with a semi-Emersonian concern for the relationship between power and probity, which seems to me to lie at the bottom of this dark lake. When these issues began to register, I thought that they were best understood against the law, and even, in the beginning, considered that they may have been identical with it, probably because the law alone provided a nearly universal limitation, or so it seemed, applicable to almost everyone in power. But now I hardly think so. If ethical issues present themselves for reflection, they are allowed in only for a time, usually at the work's beginning, and must not overstay their welcome. After a decent interval, willy-nilly, they are resolved, and it's no good looking back. But law has been accorded a special role here. Law is the game's rules to these good people, but nothing more. Rules can of course be broken, but carefully, and not too obviously or often. Morality, such as it is, is encoded elsewhere: I have been struck, during our meetings, that on those very infrequent occasions when the word "risk" is employed, it is understood to be a sort of universal ethical key that undoes all locks. It is quite in order, according to this standard, for ABC officers to arrange things as it suits them, because they have taken a "risk," and for that reason too, its profit may be as large as it may be, and the residents' interest sent to second place.

But there are risks and there are risks. ABC is not a vulnerable nineteenth-century venture capitalist undertaking, risking all and hoping for a break. They're covered. The putative risk they claim in this case was much conditioned – by political connections, by the relative smallness of the sum involved, by the circumstances attached to the redevelopment of Northwest 1 – certainly, and thanks to HUD, no risk of competition was involved. Indeed, when all is said and done, their greater risk would be in pulling out. But what if none of that was so? What if the risk was real and evident – even risky? Would that justify 80 or 85%? Their bait-and-switch tactics? The pressure they so clearly brought to bear when the community was most vulnerable and the Board members least able to understand what was at issue, what to decide?

My own answer is evident in the way I have posed these questions, but they of course have no doubts. It's business. It's legal. Let's go. The human factor fails in this machine. How many divisions have they? How many lawyers? How much money? All look away. As far as the residents go, some, even many, may be allowed back. Or possibly not: of course the City's administration will change between now and then, but even so their chances look ok. They're going to be resettled, after all. So what's the problem? It's not as though it's their land, or even if it is, it isn't really theirs unless they sign it away to them as can defend it. Then it is. Or was. And if they don't it's the City's. The Supreme Court said so.

There is one other issue that might have troubled Emerson. During the 1840's, and explicitly throughout the chapter on Napoleon in *Representative Men*, he considered that the deracinated circumstances of modern life, among other things, may mean that, more and more the concept of the individual mattered less and less, so that its very existence was either threatened or irrelevant. Power does such things, or could do, as he thought. In no real sense was Napoleon a man freed from the contingencies that seemed to follow others. Like Emerson's Apollo, he could take interest in the turmoils of the earth only with difficulty. He himself was born into the politics of the eternal and beautiful – to hell with everyone! Viva Austerlitz! But, in this our talking America, is the idea of the individual anything more than a way for the powerful and the rich to justify their finally impersonal hegemony over the weak and the poor? Or does it constitute one reason that a community of the poor, for all its faults, might have meaning for us? But in Napoleon's case, as in this one, power hardly seems to nod to probity. "The dog barks, but the caravan moves on."

I am going to Washington State this weekend to attend the christening of the daughter of a friend and former student who now teaches at the University of Seattle, where I am to be the godfather of a beautiful baby called, name of all names, Sophia. Before I leave I talk to Shiv about our recent meeting. No developments yet, but he has spoken once or twice with Tim about things. Meanwhile Luke has been most bold – when Wilma left a recent meeting he said in effect to the remaining Board members, you see what I mean. He wants her out. But Shiv thinks Wilma finally understands that her position has been undermined, and is willing now to dismiss Luke. I am less sure, and say that when she finally does decide that she is going to let him go she must do so in a formal letter approved by Tim, and then (at once) notify both ABC and the City that he has been terminated. Shiv agrees. We'll see.

Tuesday August 30, 2005

I talk to Shiv to see what has transpired while I was in Seattle. Quite a lot. Luke has approached a member of the Board to see if she will agree to consider other offers, a circumstance that can only mean he has been informed about our meeting with Ted. Given my reading of Ted's character I am disinclined to believe that it was he who broke what we took to be a confidence, but Shiv reasonably speculates (his word) that he could have spoken to a partner in his firm also involved with our case, and that he in turn might have called Luke to let him in on the secret. If that is what happened, it may well be that Joe Austen and ABC know too, from one or both of them. This seems to me, who is somewhat green in such matter to be sure, a more or less obvious violation of somewhat elementary principals of confidentially, but with so much money involved (depending on what finally happens, the *profits* from the Sursum Corda redevelopment could be in the tens of millions, and possibly more) I suppose that I should not be as surprised as I am. But this is such a season of mists we are moving through, and it is now almost as difficult to penetrate our lawyers' thinking as it is that of HUD, or the City, or ABC.

The first departmental meeting for the new semester is this morning at 10:30, so, for better or worse, I shall miss the partners meeting set for today. But increasingly I have wanted to separate myself from these meetings, since, however revealing they may be, I can neither inform nor move them, and the rapaciousness of some of the participants who seem to me to show a certain muted disdain for the residents of Sursum Corda, I do not wish, by my presence, to seem to legitimize.

Later that day...

Now it is late afternoon, and I have talked to Shiv about the meeting. Wilma did not attend, but he did, and both Luke and the partner in "our" law firm had been in full voice, praising the ABC agreement (perhaps a little defensively), and in one case, lending credence to the speculation that it was he who had violated our confidence. Shiv had spoken out at the meeting, but had found no support from any quarter.

After the meeting an FBV member had, in a smaller meeting, taken up with Luke and Shiv the fact that they have no signed agreement with the Board, and wanted one, perhaps having realized that ABC's support may be less strong than they had been led to believe, or simply from having consulted a lawyer of their own. They also indicated that they were interested in remaining involved, whatever happened to ABC. So they have heard as well. In the course of the conversation Shiv had put this question forward: Did FBV, think it right that, after (in some cases) 30 years of living in very difficult circumstances, the residents of Sursum Corda be left with mortgages while ABC with many millions of dollars in quick and relatively profit? The representative disputed the amount (I suppose, caring less for money than for other things, it is quite possible that we are overestimating values), which Shiv had based upon a projection that Sursum Corda's 15% would amount to $150 million, but that decent man had at last the sense to say No, when all was said and done the agreement did not seem to him to be fair.

Wednesday August 31, 2005

It emerges that Luke is trying to get the Board to dismiss Wilma and that she is going to try to fire him. Again: we'll see. It might not be that easy. Last night, after Wilma had told the Board that there were going to be no more meetings until the inspection was over, Luke called one, and took four of the members available to him out to dinner (less Shiv, of course), where he proposed Wilma's ouster. Wilma heard about it from a sympathetic member soon thereafter, and called Shiv at 11pm last night to tell him what had transpired. Shiv insisted that she now had to take action, even to fire Luke. Shiv says that he will try to get the Board to meet this evening, somewhere off site.

Later in the Day...

About 4:30pm Shiv calls, but the news is not good. One of the four, speaking for and in front of the other three, tells Shiv that they won't attend his meeting if it's to be about firing Luke. Evidently Wilma had mentioned the possibility, reasonably enough, to see what support there was. Not much, at least not in this tricky time, when nobody knows which way to jump. I ask if she is not perhaps losing heart, but Shiv doesn't think so, though he had only spoken to her briefly before leaving Sursum Corda for an appointment. I suggest that he get together with Wilma, and see if she wants to continue, though I ask if Shiv thinks that the others might now want to unseat Wilma and push the agreement through. He didn't, and upon reflection, I don't either. Their attitudes seem sprung from a desire, mistaken or not, to act rightly, to do the right thing, whatever the cost. At the partners meetings, after all, we all sit together, black and white, very rich and very poor, and discuss with evident and mutual respect our one common interest, passing the inspection. If a dissent is raised (usually by Shiv) it is addressed by many voices, and so resolved, effectively if not actually. The overall tone is civil. To cry out that the plan stinks, that it is designed further to empower the already powerful and again to reward the already rich, would be regarded as bad taste. I have already noted the tone of inevitability which also attends upon these meetings.

But when one member remonstrated with Shiv, saying that in his desire to change or break the agreement he was in effect "stringing ABC along," there was an implied charge of bad faith, of behaving with less courtesy than he had himself received, of being young and thoughtless.

If this be so, I have myself have a certain sympathy for such views, if not in the present case. But historically the great progression of African-American rights has come from a confrontation of White power, though I do understand that according to some theories – and some people – that time may now be passing. Still, apart from the greatest of the first generation of Civil Rights leaders, Dr. Martin Luther King, Jr., many of the others made the progress they did with their dukes up, and there are certainly places even today where dukes are much needed. But in other places, they seem to be somewhat counter-productive. Some places, at least, are at last into the second generation of the Civil Rights movement, a place where some, even many forms of cooperation are essential. The great leaders on this second generation are still very much with us, and probably in their 40's and 50's. Some of them, like my admired Representative John Lewis, were very much a part of the first generation and have carried forward Dr. King's powerful if conflicted legacy. Knowledge and education, competence and occasionally even patience, now matter more than ever, and with them the ability to cope and deal.

Still, there are white people and there are white people. Sometimes we have to be cunning as serpents, since it's them that we're in bed with. For those members of the Board who want to continue more or less as we have been, and after the inspection too, the understanding that these apparently honorable and decent white people about them have done them wrong, is not available. After all, the only spokesperson they have attended to regularly is Luke, and their attendance at the partners meetings might well have communicated that sense of inevitability which attends upon us there. Shiv spoke alone at the last meeting, and with Wilma apparently at least opting out of engagement, the other Board members may feel that without Luke they would be left largely unsupported. Wilma, at this moment at least, seems not to have brought the other Board members with her. But Luke has.

I am not sure that this can be resolved. After all, we had hoped not to bring things to a head until after the inspection, and in retrospect probably shouldn't have spoken to our lawyer until then. All of this, after all, is the result of what seems to us a violation of our confidence. No doubt the excuse would be that Luke is our COO so that he did no wrong in alerting him, that and the fact that, potentially at least, there was so much money involved.

About 5pm Shiv calls again. Wilma believes she has five votes, so not to worry, he says. If the Board (or a simple majority of it) will stand by her and agrees to follow her timetable, not Luke's, this could prevent Luke from forcing her out. Shiv will call me at home tonight or tomorrow (I have a class until 8pm) and say where we are. Meanwhile I worry.

Thursday September 1, 2005

I talk this morning to Shiv, on whom the lion's share of the work has now fallen, only to find that relatively little progress has been made. Wilma says that she is going to call a Board meeting shortly, and thinks all is well. But Shiv had another story too: when he returned to Sursum last night he fell into conversation with a group of residents who are appalled by the agreement, and were wondering why Wilma had not been attending the Block Meetings, where the projected arrangements for the redevelopment are placed before the residents. As a result, they have come to surmise that she, like they, was not happy with what was being proposed. But Shiv is concerned, no doubt rightly, that many of the residents are not thinking critically about what is put before them.

Shiv has also been in touch with KCH, which very much wants to develop and extend its initial offer, but need some documents from Shiv (which he already has in hand) in order to do so. In the course of making the arrangements they had said to him directly what a very bad – their word was "insulting" – agreement ABC had extracted. I understand that they are competitors, ABC and KCH, but my sense is that their reaction has a real edge to it, and whether it is or not intentional, it is certainly felt. They say they mostly want to help, and if their offer isn't right for Sursum Corda, they hope that they can help the community find one that is.

(Labor Day) Monday September 1, 2005

Shiv calls about noon to suggest I come to the Labor Day celebrations at Sursum Corda, which I do. He picks me up, and on the way down we talk things over, and I say that they seem to me to be going badly. There was recently a Board meeting in which Luke's termination was discussed, but at which he was present. That meeting apart, Wilma has taken no action on anything, and has had a major falling out with another Board member, who is increasingly rumored to be Luke's brother. The two no longer speak to each other, Shiv says. I assume that the member is firmly in Luke's camp, but Shiv says that she still thinks the agreement a bad deal. I doubt it not. Another Board member will not listen to any explanation from anyone, and simply thinks that the Board must stick to the agreement come what may. The senior lawyer has been using what Shiv calls "scare tactics," saying that the Board will be sued by ABC (probably right) if it finds another developer, and that there will be no end of litigation, much of it directed against Board members, etc.

We arrive to find a high school band that Luke, to whom I speak briefly, has brought in from Baltimore, and the community celebration is popcorn, hotdogs and hamburgers (being made by the police), frozen ice to drink, and finally one of the Redskins, who was there signing miniature green ABC footballs. The area around the new playground is full of residents, and I see many old friends, both children and patents and care givers, and after consulting with Christine Nicholson I say that we hope to start tutoring on the twentieth. Wilma was present too, and although we spoke briefly we hardly communicated, and she seemed to me curiously disconnected from everything that was going on around her. This was Luke's show, but he himself seemed to know few if any of the residents, and seemed rather a kind of Master of Ceremonies, even less connected than Wilma, not happy, as the French say, in his skin.

There were free t-shirts as well, and Board members had their name printed on theirs, but I had come in jeans and a Georgetown t-shirt, so by pleading the interests of our tutoring program I was excused wearing the one prepared for me, which had "Professor Hirsh" printed on it. A Labor Day end-of-summer party has been a tradition at Sursum Corda, usually in the past with a neighbor-hood parade, and it was very odd to see the youngsters brought in from Baltimore. But it showed too that, in spite of everything, the community of Sursum Corda flourishes still, bringing rest and sometimes hope to the adults, and often, let us hope, joy to the children. Long life to it.

Later that evening...

Later that evening I talk to Shiv, who thinks the party went very well. In the course of it he had been approached by Charles Wilson, who represented himself as sympathetic to the Board's interests, even saying that the best thing would have been for Sursum Corda and FBV to have gone it alone. But it is now increasingly difficult to credit his assurances, particularly since he dropped, without realizing its importance, the fact that after the ill-fated meeting the Board had with ABC in June, when 170 units had been promised, FBV had met with a representative of BAR who effectively argued that the offer was not in the community's best interests, explaining that the residents would be better off with mortgages. Charles Wilson said he no longer believes that that is so. The admission, as Shiv pointed out, reveals some at least of Luke's prevarications, particularly his oft-repeated representation that the promise had never been made.

Wednesday September 7, 2005

Shiv calls about 8:45 this morning with an "update" on recent events. Neither he nor Wilma had attended the partners meeting yesterday, but after it was over, about noon, "the Redskins," to-gether with an elder in the church the FBV partners attend who had been to other meetings, together with Wilma and another Board member, met thus informally in front of the Community Center to discuss Wilma's evident non-participation. FBV represented it-self as concerned, and asked what was wrong. Wilma explained ABC's reneging on its original promise of 170 units free and clear, and Shiv now revealed to me that when she had signed the ABC agreement she had not read it, but had taken Luke's word that it contained what had been agreed to at their meeting a few days earlier. Neither she nor Shiv raised the matter of ABC obtaining 85% for themselves because (as I recall Shiv's explanation, perhaps imperfectly) that would have meant addressing HUD's role in the whole business, and Black's personal association with HUD Secretary Jackson suggested that such an approach would probably be unproductive. At one point Black reminded the Board members of his HUD connection.

FBV said it would broach the matter with ABC, but insisted that, possible modifications apart, all of the partners had to support the agreement more or less as it stood. Then one of them asked if the Board had a relationship with any group other than ABC. Wilma and Shiv both said no, which was strictly speaking quite true – KCH is very much in the discussion stage, and there is now certainly no relationship with them, more their pity. The assurance, however, was evidently not credited, and brought forth a representation that we are all on the same side, should follow the same coach, etc. This nettled Shiv so that he said, in effect, So what if we do have another relationship in mind? Look at how bad this so-called agreement is, etc. But then one of them had replied at excessive and unguarded length, saying, again in effect, that "we" had to stick to ABC, that ABC had come forward when HUD was about to pounce, that without ABC the whole business would fall apart and when that happened, he, Shiv, would be personally responsible for the residents losing their homes.

Shiv wondered if he really should have said, So what if we do have, etc., but it was that question which made quite clear, from the response it evoked, that FBV, and no doubt ABC as well, know about KCH, further evidence, if any was needed, of the quite extraordinary behavior of our lawyers. Also, since the KCH offer has not yet appeared (and Shiv admits he has not yet supplied all of the documents they have asked of him), it may be that in the end ABC will carry the day. But even if they do, the threat of KCH may make them, in the final analysis, a little more accommodating -- certainly nothing else will. But Shiv also thinks that many of the residents are far from sold on the agreement, and that there is a good chance that they will reject it outright. Recently he heard Paula (now fully in Luke's camp) representing the agreement to some residents, who were by no means accepting her assurances, and seemed to have a fair if unspecific sense that they were being had.

Saturday September 10, 2005

I returned a call from Shiv last night, and so garnered news of the latest Board meeting, which had gone badly. Nobly seeking to play the peacemaker, Pastor Gray, another non-resident recruited by Luke Gratian to be a part of the advisory Board, had asked the Sursum Corda Board members to meet, but naively had asked Luke to be present too, so that positions hardened, and confrontation became the order of the day. As Shiv tells it, he had a particularly difficult time with one member, the one now strongly supporting both Luke and the agreement, and insisting that she could explain it to anyone, but when Shiv asked her to explain the residents' equity, or why those getting a relatively small amount of money back at the same time that they are incurring major but avoidable debt, was a good thing, she demurred. Thereafter tempers had flared. At one time Shiv found himself being reproved for having shouted, and had at once apologized, only to find himself shouted at a few moments later. God knows what the Pastor, a gentle and good man who had sought only to play the peacemaker, thought of all this, but the meeting had resolved itself in nothing but hard feelings.

What had irritated Shiv mightily was the way the agreement would effectively keep the Sursum Corda residence in the dependency under which they have lived for many years. This is, to him, simply a new kind of bondage, whether to HUD, the Federal Government through HUD, or to ABC. There has been some (much?) interest in what individual residents will get from their payments as cooperative members. Some of those who have lived in Sursum Corda may possibly get a $200 payment a year he guesses (most will get less), but with that will come is such debt that many may not survive it. Others will either become or remain attached to Section 8, whereas they had been promised that they could become homeowners, a promise now impossible to realize. The only hope Shiv held out came from the tenants themselves, some of whom have seen through the smoke and mirrors, and are beginning to organize a petition demanding (or perhaps only asking) that the Board *not* vote on approving the agreement, amended or not, with ABC until after the inspection has been completed. Potentially, at least, this would be an important development, since the Board can (or should) hardly ignore such a petition, and such a delay would offer a remedy to the precipitous haste with which the agreement was placed before it. It remains to be seen how many from the community are clued in enough to sign, but Shiv says that one man in particular who has become the leader of a growing number of residents, seems to have quite a clear sense of things, and to understand as well that if the petition is to be effective it must be completed before (or at least by) Wednesday.

Two other points, followed by a third. Shiv also mentioned to me, what I had not known, that one of the Board members most antagonistic to him pays market rate for her unit, a circumstance that may somewhat limit the sympathy she is likely to feel for those who do not, and may also supply a more personal motive for her position. Also, at some point in all of this I told Shiv that I had been writing this journal, but he evinced only polite interest in that circumstance. Toward the end of our conversation Shiv also revealed that Tim had called him off and on, to ask about this and that (most recently, about the residents' reactions), and that a sense of friendliness and even of cooperation is being maintained by both of them. A practice among lawyers, I say. Not to be taken too seriously, even from as good a man as Tim. Meanwhile the inspection is set to begin on Tuesday afternoon and continue through Friday, the residents' vote of approval is to take place on Wednesday.

Wednesday September 14, 2005

The inspection has been underway since Monday afternoon, and emails have been alerting us to its progress, which seems to be quite ok. We lost a few points for some mouse droppings found in one unit (honestly!), some insects in another, but as of today we are maintaining a score of 93 (out of 100) with 70 units (out of 120) left to be examined. In the end everyone seems sure that we will survive the inspection, if only for a time. But given the amount of money ABC has sunk into the project, HUD is unlikely to fail it, or so the experts continue to believe.

The frequency of emails among the partners has increased greatly of late, and particularly after someone had circulated an account of our dealings with KCH. Tim has produced, with no little effort, a document for each head of household to hold, but unaccountably designed to be signed only by Wilma, not by ABC. Today we have another email, this time from 'our' senior lawyer, saying in effect that ABC would under no circumstances put any more money into the project, but that it would withdraw and leave the field to another, provided only that they be reimbursed for what they had put in this far.

I call Shiv and discuss the latest email with him, and he reasonably thinks it another ABC strategy, aimed only at getting the agreement approved. He pointed out, what is certainly true, that the email had come from the lawyer, not ABC, but even so we agree that ABC could hardly maintain that their offer had been misunderstood, as they had with Wilma and the June 15th agreement. He also revealed that FBV had sought a meeting with the Board two days ago, mainly to communicate an ABC demand for a promissory note to cover their expenditures to date. Shiv and Wilma had wanted to sign the note, thinking that it would thus reduce ABC to the status of a creditor, not a partner, but others, including Luke, had objected, sensing, perhaps, that the end was too near to allow for any variation.

But in the end it really does seem that all of this is strategy. ABC may understand that it no longer stands alone, but that seems only have hardened its resolve. Perhaps it has begun to understand as well that the City's proffer was hardly written on stone. But resolve or no, there seems to me a note of panic in it, a sense that one way or another, this is the end. Personally, I doubt that that is so, but even so I urge Shiv to see what KCH will actually put on the table, so as to have another alternative in hand. But of course I suspect that ABC will give nothing away.

Meanwhile I have come down with a late summer cold, and am now steaming. I hope to start the tutoring program again on Tuesday, directly after the inspection is concluded, and tonight's class is the last time I will see the students before we begin, so I carry on, hopefully not infecting too many of them as I am doing so. *Inter alia*, we discuss the Candy Lady, that great motivator of industry whose presence concerns me for many reasons, not least among them my concern for our learners' diet. I agree only to utilize her services in increased moderation – and with the stipulation that out tutors not bring any other treats, except, that is to say, for birthdays or at Christmas. A student who had been in the class last year recounts that another student, now alas graduated, had developed a good strategy with her impatient young learner, dividing a paper into quadrants, and placing a star in each one ever fifteen minutes, provided her young learner cooperated in the lesson. Four stars merited a trip to the Candy Lady – who late in the semester became the Candy Man, he reminds us. I note that tutors must be strong in their resolve, and that if they give in to last minute promises of future good behavior, or even to tears, they will undermine the usefulness of this venerable if somewhat questionable institution, well known to our learners for years now, and Stewart adds to what I have said, saying that it may be hard sometimes to say No, but really you must, and that ten minutes after your learner has departed, tearfully on not, he or she will have forgotten the incident, though you may still be chewing on it.

Later in the day...

About 8:30pm Shiv calls, and I can tell at once from his tone that things could be better. About 80 residents had come to the meeting, which had not gone well. The resident whom Shiv had been trusting to circulate the petition asking the Board not to decide anything until after the inspection, had, for whatever reason, failed to do so, perhaps put off by Luke's secretary, who now lives at Sursum Corda and so came to the meeting, there warning any who listened to her that if they voted against ABC they all would be given Section 8 vouchers and moved out at once. Absurd, of course, but bad information, false representation and intimidation flourish here. As I have observed, perhaps too often, this account is as much about what all of those involved, misled or not, thought to be true or were mistaken about, as about what actually transpired. Shiv had tried to intervene but found himself alone. Wilma had been there in the beginning, but then simply left the meeting. Shiv is going to try to circulate the petition himself, but is not hopeful, and nor am I. In spite of everything, it is beginning to look like a done deal.

But shortly before 10 Shiv calls back, this time a little more hopeful. A resident now represents that he had not understood the importance of the petition, and has agreed to help circulate it. Wilma, Shiv and one or two residents will do so as well, but Shiv thinks if it had been circulated earlier, almost everyone present would have signed it. But when he approached one group of people they demurred, at least for now, and when he pressed them, "I really need it tonight," they had refused. Mixed with doubt is now, unmistakably, fear, and some are beginning to consider that if they oppose this deal they doubt, they may suffer for it. But Shiv has by no means given up, and hopes as well that tomorrow he may hear something back from KCH.

Thursday September 15, 2005

An extraordinary email from Tim in anticipation of the vote. He notes that things have gotten quite volatile at the Cooperative as we approach tonight's ratification vote, and goes on to say that one member has been pressing for a delay. He had spoken with Joe Austen at ABC and Joe had refused any delay and suggested that an approach "which I and a few others are comfortable with is that the residents need to understand the consequences of a no vote or a non-vote and they also need to understand some of the important concessions the Board has negotiated..."

The "concessions" amount to a 45 day wait period before the vote takes effect, and if a better deal can be struck ABC will back off, though expecting repayment "for its expenses." The consequences, however, are rather more serious: "ABC would withdraw its $480K check being held by HUD, it would stop paying operating costs (meaning no more security or repairs), it would withdraw as management company, it would advise HUD and the city that it was no longer the Cooperative's partner, and it would seek to collect the money it has spent."

A more obvious example of intimidation is difficult even to imagine. The residents of Sursum Corda, the great majority not highly educated or even appraised (except in terms entirely favorable to ABC) as to what has been going on, are going to be further instructed that these rich, powerful white people, who have been represented to them as their last best hope, will pull the rug out from under them, except they vote the way they are told. Shame on all of us.

Friday September 16, 2005

Shiv calls me in my office late in the afternoon to ask that I alert Lori Montgomery of the *Washington Post* to the meeting tonight, but when I do so she calls back, and we have a longish chat. She knows that her last piece had not gone down well, because Luke had called her (not she, him, as he had previously represented) afterwards, and they had discussed matters. She answers (not entirely convincingly, perhaps) my objection that she should not have focused on Luke's employment as a trash collector after he had been laid off his last job, and reveals that when she last talked to the Board they all defended Luke warmly; but I tell her that such is no longer the case. She had heard about tonight's meeting before I called (though mistaking the time), and already had decided to attend.

But in the event this meeting, like the one before it, did not go well. Luke had spoken first, Joe Austen after. Thereafter the usual three members of the Board had warmly defended ABC's offer, issuing dire warnings of what would happen else. One had gone out of her way to attack Wilma ("Shiv's the only one who's got your back"), and Shiv believes that they are now more intent than ever on forcing Wilma off the Board. But at the meeting Shiv insists that she acquitted herself well, patiently explaining the circumstances of her doubts about ABC – and though perhaps not attacking the agreement as forcefully she might, fending off a very sharp attack from Paula with evident dignity. I suppose other interpretations might be possible. Because of the petition, as I understand it, residents were given until Monday to turn in the paper ballots they had been issued, but the meeting had not gone well, and my sense, after having spoken to Shiv, is that he expects a vote, even a strong vote, for the ABC offer – which carries with it, however, a 45 day waiting period during which other offers can be explored. But the question, of course, is this one: Who will determine which offer is the best? If the Board, then ABC can relax, but if the residents, or even if the residents can advise the Board, all may not be lost.

Later in the day...

But now it is early evening and Shiv calls again, in surprisingly good form. He has spoken to Lori Montgomery for an hour who revealed, among other things, that Tim is now calling the agreement historic, a partnership, perhaps for the first time ever, between a developer and inner-city residents. Rich developers have often extracted land from the poor without paying a penny: I expect that that is meant to be the difference here. But without a change in the law, who will defend the interests of the poor? ABC can represent that it is simply following good corporate policy when it effectively eats Sursum Corda, availing itself of HUD's strangle hold to set a derisory price, and also of the evident ignorance of many of the residents and the rapaciousness of some members of the Board. Down with justice, up with the law. All is corporate practice. The evident requirements of social justice are frustrated here by the dictates of the state. There is a quote from Augustine buzzing in my head, but I cannot place it. I email Georgetown's resident Augustine expert, our Provost, who finds it for me. *City of God* IV.iv: Take away justice, Augustine wrote, and what are nations but great bands of robbers?

But Shiv also has heard from KCH, which is putting together an offer for next week – perhaps by Monday – a deal that they promise will be much better than ABC's. Shiv is, understandably, euphoric, and though I bite my tongue I also note that, better though KCH's offer is likely to be, it still may be a job getting the Board to accept it. Shiv wants to begin by enlisting Tim, on whom he has by no means given up, and by making the case as air tight as possible. I suggest that Lori Montgomery be given a copy of the offer as well, since, even given the *Post's* checkered history in this affair, we need to make the arrangements as transparent as possible.

Discussion at one point turns to KCH's first offer, the one in which they offered 40 million for the property as a whole, and I say that it was less good than ABC's which at least allows residents the right of return. But Shiv says not really. Citing his perceptive father as his source, he suggests that, once given the choice, very many residents will simply take the $50,000 payment, and be on their way. It's not such a big deal to them if they have to move somewhere else, he says, though KCH's 40 million would have meant that each resident who elected to do so would have received about $215,000 instead, clearly a better deal, though admittedly hard on those who wanted to stay. Thinking about it later, I consider that the ABC offer might just preserve more of the community than KCH's, even though it might do so by defrauding the residents. Still, even a development of 550 units, if that was actually what emerged from negotiations with the City, would change the community here forever. Buddhists are right. All is impermanence. But my sense is that we will probably have a lot more *dukkha* coming at us before we reach Nirvana.

Monday September 19, 2005

A month ago I had naively thought that everything would be settled by now, but now not at all. Yesterday I picked up an email from Lori Montgomery saying that she was going to show the ABC agreement to someone who knows about such things, but that (I gathered she had this from someone to whom she had already shown it) it could be a very good thing indeed. She seemed to say, what is obvious, that the amount ABC has put in is nothing compared to what it stands to reap, but the 15% the Board itself stands to realize from the three lots the City has offered ABC for development on North Capitol Street could more than make up for it. So she is going to show the agreement to someone to get a better reading. From what she says, she also likes Tim's idea of seeing all of this as a new kind of developer-community partnership.

Shiv and I speak again. He agrees that the lots in question are important, but is far from sure that the Board will ever see the monies implied in the putative agreement – my word, but Shiv points out that nothing is in writing, that ABC had not signed off on the document to be given to the residents, and that the City government is likely to have changed at least once before any such an agreement would be signed. How much confidence can we have in those monies then, he not unreasonably asks?

Tuesday September 20, 2005

I found a message from Shiv on my answer-phone giving the vote last night: 120 for the ABC agreement, 10 not voting, 1 against. No question whose vote that was. Shiv says he has heard that a number of the residents had their doors knocked upon last night, and were told either by a Board member or by another that if the vote went the wrong way the residents would be put out of their homes very quickly, with only Section 8 vouchers to fall back upon. Remembering Tim's email I am not surprised. This seems to me nothing but hardball intimidation masquerading as well meant advice. But then he called again about 9am in good spirits, conceding only that the community had no convincing alternative to ABC and had been frightened by the threats of what would happen if the vote failed. He is confident of a better offer within a few days from KCH, and reported that he had taken Wilma to meet officials at KCH yesterday. (I am less so.) The meeting had gone well, and the new offer from KCH will leave 90% of the ownership in the hands of the community. It will also include a loan of $3.5 million (to include interest when cured) to pay off ABC and maintain the property. KCH will also put together a package which will help to identify (and solicit) other developers. We talk briefly about the difficulty of moving the community after such a vote, but Shiv thinks it can be done. I remind him that the tutoring program begins again tonight, and he is happy for it.

The initial session is always a little chaotic and started fifteen minutes late because there is a Board meeting concluding as we arrive. Eventually things settle down, and Christine Nicholson makes a very good speech of welcome to the tutors and the children. The match-ups go well, though in the course of it I had not taken account of anything else, so I was surprised when, afterwards, one of the students tells me that she had seen what she took to be a HUD inspector, clipboard in hand, gaining entry to one of the houses.

Thursday September 22, 2005

Shiv calls last night to say that the Board is moving to oust Wilma, and has sent her a letter, drawn up by Tim, to which she must respond by Friday. Luke had quickly convened a meeting of the Board at which she was not present, saying that two members had brought up objections to her role. A vote of the five present had been taken (the Parson and I, as we are not resident in Sursum Corda, are not voting members), and Shiv's was the only vote against. I have a guest staying, so we cannot talk long, but I am somewhat concerned that Shiv is blaming himself – I should have answered Joe Austen at the meeting, etc. I insist that he has done all that is humanly possible, and he says that KCH (not yet informed about recent developments) is pressing ahead with its offer and is helping him to secure others. I applaud their efforts, but say it is a great pity that they could not have had an offer on the table when the ABC vote came, because without it the community was left a choice between the ABC offer or nothing. But Shiv says that there were people out again the night before the vote, going door-to-door and telling residents that if they did not support the offer they would be issued Section 8 vouchers and turned out of their homes shortly thereafter. He had charged that this had happened at the last Board meeting, but Luke had laughed, and said No, he hadn't done so himself, but was not surprised that others had done so.

Meanwhile Lori Montgomery's article comes out on the front page of the Metro section of today's *Washington Post*, and from what I can tell it does little more than continue the *Post's* tradition of cheering the developers on. It endorses the ABC offer, insisting that the "community" is working with the developers in a mutually beneficial agreement. This is simply not true. Shiv's objections concerning the low amount ABC is paying for the undervalued property, though mentioned, is banished to an inside page – indeed to the very end of the article. Later Shiv says it's not as bad as it seems, and that it will have the effect of having ABC trust Lori, but I suspect she may be having to negotiate her way through a desk editor – like Shiv, I both like and respect her, and in spite of the article, realize that I have rather come to trust her too.

Friday September 23, 2005

I call Shiv before setting out today to hear what the KCH offer has been. Alas, there is not going to be one. As they were finalizing the offer Ted, the KCH senior officer who has been spearheading the offer, came into conflict with another senior KCH partner about the propriety of KCH making one, because of its connection with BAR, which Shiv thinks pressured KCH to pull back. My heart sinks a little when I hear this, but Shiv insists that, having failed to get the offer through, Ted is now willing to offer advice when reaching out to other developers, and that confirms to me at least the sense I had of Ted as a particularly able young man of evident integrity, an interest that I have been pursuing, perhaps too unremittingly, throughout. But if he really is willing to offer advice, I suppose that could indeed be valuable, though I am not convinced that it would compensate for the lack of KCH's offer. After all, if we were working with KCH he would necessarily be on the other side of the desk, whereas now, the theory goes, he will be on ours. Shiv has already been in touch with CIM, a California developer, said already to be working on a project not far from Sursum, who has expressed an interest in the project, and he is going to explore things with them. I know that all this may sound like clutching at straws after yesterday's *Post* article, and in the past I probably would have thought so myself, but given the way I have seen developers work, and given the amount of money involved, I am by no means sure that it is.

Saturday October 1, 2005

It has been a busy week during which I heard from Shiv only off and on, but I gather things have been moving forward. Somewhat surprisingly, Boon is back in the picture, and with general (but also specific) encouragement has come forward with an offer that Shiv says beats the ABC one easily. Chief among its improvements is the amount paid to residents who opt not to return (increasingly, the suspicion is there may be many), $100,000 rather than ABC's $50,000. One or more other offers are expected as well. Meanwhile the Board has been coming down on Shiv, at one point pressing him to sign a confidentially agreement, promising not to disclose anything that goes on at the Board meetings to anyone outside of it, but he had pointed out that since public monies were involved in everything they do, his right to speak plainly was both protected and vital.

Meanwhile I see Luke when I am present for our tutoring session on Thursday, and, him knowing that I ever tilt toward Shiv, we speak to each other with somewhat elaborate courtesy. The second floor, on which we are working while folders are being assembled on the first, is crowded and noisy, and Luke kindly offers to let us expand into his offices on the third floor. I am reluctant to do so, I say because I fear for the safety of the rather large number of personal computers he now has up there, but also because I do not want to been seen as too close to current operations there, which do not seem to me necessarily carried on in the residents' best interests. But later I reflect that the third floor would be perfect for our older kids program, and we may even find PSAT programs on the computers, so I swallow my pride and ask him if we can use it after all.

At one point (in a different conversation) Shiv and I are talking about BAR, which he believes may have found a way to steer KCH away from the table. Afterwards, I reflect upon my own surprise at recent developments, but consider too that even as well-informed a *Washington Post* reporter as Lori Montgomery was, she was taken aback at seeing Jim Moran's well connected wife quite so personally involved in a Washington, D.C. development project. The whole process, to be sure, is hardly above board, a circumstance that emerged again in a rumor suggesting that FBV is involved with BAR, and that it was thus that ABC came to the table. I suppose there must be some way to prove that such connections exist, but once concluded, it is hardly possible to undo them. For these often quite insensitive and often grasping persons, this is business as usual. No doubt it was more convenient for FBV to use ABC's money, rather than risk their own, if that is what happened. But all this dealing was of course carried out above the heads of the residents, whose interests and wishes were hardly in the frame.

Thursday October 6, 2005

When we arrived for tutoring on Tuesday we find a Board meeting in session, so as it is a fine evening, we hold our tutorials in Center Point, the open air rink behind the Community Center, which was intended in the beginning of Sursum Corda for small meetings of the residents, and has seats around an open central area. Some of the tutors break away after some minutes and play catch (with a football: I wink at it) though most carry on with their tutorials, many working on writing since our books are all upstairs, and I decide not to interrupt the meeting to get them, which would take too much time. We end ten minutes early, and my own sense is that things actually went quite well, though in our seminar yesterday some of the tutors complained about the disruption, and one young man took particular exception to the games going on while he was trying to tutor. I hypocritically agree with him, though under the circumstances I still think I was right to hold my peace. But viva industry.

I talk again to Shiv who reveals that there has been an email sent out from ABC's lawyer seeking to keep him away from the partners meetings. Shiv believes he can counter this, perhaps by asking Tim to lend a hand, though I am not entirely clear what he has in mind. Meanwhile the Board is up for reelection, and the ballots are due at 6pm tonight, with the results being announced shortly thereafter (very likely when we are tutoring). Shiv hopes that both he and Wilma will be reelected, and thinks they will, but is concerned that the ballots be counted fairly – I suggest he ask Tim to stop by and oversee the process. In any case though, Shiv believes (I think rightly) that he can be every bit as effective as an informed and active resident as he ever was on the now-hostile Board.

Later that day...

The Board meeting was just concluding when we came into the Community Center just on 7pm for tutoring, and both Wilma and Shiv had been reelected, as had the six other Board members, which was not entirely surprising since there were ten people standing for nine places. But Shiv and Wilma both did well in the vote count, so hope still lives.

I shall be away next week on academic business next week, and even though there are two development offers yet to come in (one of them from KCH which has now reentered the lists), and even though the difficulties of bringing the offers to the attention of the community are as great as they ever were, I have the feeling that with tonight's vote an important milestone has been passed, and that we are approaching a watershed. That will come, no doubt, at the end of the month, when the promised 45 days are completed and the community will have to fish or cut bait. God give us strength to see this business through.

5

Of Conscience and of Good Faith

The whole of anything is never told.
–Henry James

Between the time the last chapter ended and this one begins, things seemed at least to turn around. They didn't, as time will tell, but at last an email arrived from Shiv who had learned that, as a result of the inspection, HUD had agreed to back off, at least for now. The Community effectively 'passed' the inspection, but not by much. It might have received a reprieve of three years if the numbers had been better, but in the event it received only one. So the result was a year's grace, no more, with the clear implication that the buzzards are still circling. The sense was simply that it could now sell itself; no one moved to save it. No doubt HUD understands what time it is, and perhaps the result suited it well since it could more easily wash its hands of an increasingly sticky affair. But there was a sense of anti-climax in the result. What began with a burst of gunfire ended in an email.

Meanwhile the Community's debts continue to mount, and the Board expects to sell the property as soon as ever it can. That won't be soon, but the remaining choice seems to be who will buy us, and what will they pay? The simple answer is not much, at least not when the debts are tabulated, agreed, and paid. Now that the end seems to be approaching other voices are going to be heard, and informal arrangements, some say, may play a role as well. No one is going to save this much conflicted place, where the children still play, parents worry about them, and resentment, whispers, doubt and anger have become the order of the day.

Wednesday October 19, 2005

Much, but also little, has happened since I last wrote, and uncertainty is still everywhere present. During the time I was away the power of the community to address the HUD inspection, thanks to ABC, is now understood, though any sense of gratitude towards ABC is tempered both by a growing distrust of the Board (and particularly of Luke), and by a sense that ABC has become all powerful – and is pursuing its own interests first of all. It is as though the passing of the inspection, upon which so much hope had been fixed, has become a kind of anti-climax, almost a detail, which precipitated almost as many difficulties as it resolved.

The community passed the HUD inspection with a score of 60, so that it has been allowed but a year's grace, though even some things have not exactly fallen into its lap. Thanks to the inspection it has greatly increased its indebtedness, and so institutionalized a relationship with parties whose motives are far from altruistic. No doubt in other cases when there is a single private owner for a dilapidated property such practices as the ones HUD employed here could have something to recommend them, though in the case of a co-op like Sursum Corda, its employment necessitated actions that financially devastated its already markedly disadvantaged resident-owners, and drove them into the arms of some who were by no means their friends. It may well be – it was certainly widely believed – that it was a HUD/City relationship that precipitated the HUD inspection in the first place, and it is possible that the one agency to benefit from it in the long term may prove to be the City, whose interest, from the first, has been to move the community out and to 'develop' the land on which its buildings stand. And although it is not at all unreasonable that HUD and the City (or any city) should communicate with each other, there may, this time at least, have been a line, whether ethical, moral or legal, that was crossed, so that this great federal agency more or less deliberately set out to eliminate a resident-owned community, or so it is believed. If so, this seems to me a great pity, not only because HUD seemed at least to become, at least for a moment, as rapacious as any developer – it certainly viewed as the enemy from within the community, though there were others more worthy of that designation – but also because, historically at least, HUD has not regularly been an adversary of the poor -- who have so many of those already that they hardly need one of their erstwhile allies to join them. But the circumstance at Sursum Corda, though in some ways exceptional, are by no means unique, whether in the ethical, moral, administrative, financial or legal challenges that emerged, or in the answers that, collectively or individually, have been offered, sometimes in evident error, and rarely with the purest of motives. Meanwhile Boon, supported by Ted though not by KCH, has presented an offer, and did so in the same terms that ABC had employed, in order, Shiv tells me, to facilitate comparison by the residents. Like the ABC offer, it calls for razing the property, a fact which I had understood before – that seems to be where we now are – but which still gives me pause, though there is one other contingency ("which no one wants," Shiv warns) that might just cause the present units to remain. In any case, the hopes that have driven those of us who value the community have now, perhaps finally, been set aside. In three (or two or five or ten) years, if either of the present plans prevails, the community of Sursum Corda will be dispersed, its buildings leveled, to be replaced with a new group of residents, certainly a richer one. "They want to bring in white people," one of the children, echoing her parents, told her tutor. Communities of the disadvantaged do not easily resist the rich and powerful, and no doubt that circumstance has abetted the scramble for money that has been going on. But if the possibilities at Sursum Corda have incited greed in some, the community itself, at least in the past, has given evidence of more attractive qualities, and worked in cooperation with those who wish it well, making only such alliances it seemed most useful. But that was then. As for its heralded destruction, such was hardly what the residents wanted, as if that mattered.

Meanwhile the new Boon offer demands to be read. It offers the community 80% rather than ABC's 15%; a free, unencumbered house, said to be worth $235,000, not one with a mortgage attached; and $100,000, rather than ABC's $50,000, should the resident simply decide to move away, and have done with it. But there are difficulties. For one thing the free house will not necessarily be within the present boundaries – both offers envision an unmistakable end to the community that we now call Sursum Corda. The residents will indeed become home owners, but with that will come exactly the sort of responsibilities – taxes, utilities, upkeep – that some or many feel unprepared to accept. It is true that, under the Boon plan at least, there are no resale restrictions, so that it would not be difficult for residents to free themselves of these burdens, but the process of doing so, to some at least, must seem formidable indeed. Better to rent: but where will I find the deal I have had here? Built into the Boon proposal as well is a secondary proposal, the one which no one wants, but which would, in spite of everything, allow for the possibility of converting the existing residences to condominiums and selling them on or about 2010 for $40 million should Boon not be able to exchange the present residences for "a free and clear interest in replacement housing." There is no indication in the Boon proposal that the residents will benefit from any "partner payments" which are expected to be derived from the profits ABC expects to realize from the deal as a whole, and to which some residents have attached such a measure of importance. Finally, in what can only be thought of as a small consolation, the Boon agreement offers 120 days (not the 45 attached to the ABC offer) for the Board to find a better offer, if it can. (But who other than ABC would again come forward?) Battle has been joined, and quite publicly, in the *Washington Post*. In one instance (among many) I noticed again how freely Tim allowed himself to attack the Boon offer at least in part by implying, rightly or wrongly, that Boon is too limited an agency to accept responsibility for the project. "How can they guarantee half of the things they're promising?" Tim is quoted as asking in an October 12 article Lori Montgomery produced in the *Washington Post* ("Another Offer of Millions for Poor D.C. Residents"). "How can they assure there's going to be free housing with no mortgage and no resale restrictions?"

The answer to those questions, if there is one, may turn on the actual value of the 5.8 acres upon which Sursum Corda stands. The ABC agreement assumes a value of about $25 million, while the Boon offer suggests that it is worth at very least $30 million, and probably a good deal more than that. Whatever may happen to housing prices, remember where Sursum Corda stands: it is close not only to the new Convention Center and Union Station, but to

Capitol Hill and downtown Washington as well. But there are other complications, too. The ABC agreement holds out the promise of a profit sharing which it has recently suggested (how firmly and by whom I don't know) may amount to an additional $50,000, thus matching the Boon offer – though there is no promise that it will do so, and I do not know anyone who believes that it will. But it offers a fig leaf to those who want to hold with ABC. There are other matters too, ones in which the Board's ownership will change according to the amount of borrowing it undertakes which, as presently represented in the Boon agreement, hardly comes clear to the residents (or to me). But one other aspect of the Boon offer comes through sharply. In a section entitled "FBV's Involvement" the document pays elaborate courtesy to the group, and insists that "We will be happy to acknowledge FBV's involvement in the project and re-structure the ownership to include FBV after we better understand the contribution that FBV has made to date and intends to make going forward on the community's behalf." This is not an unreasonable objection, though the second part of the sentence is problematic, since if the residents settle elsewhere there will be no effective contribution for FBV to make.

Still, it is not clear that the Boon offer is gaining much ground. From the beginning Shiv has been in favor of real change, if only so as to break the bonds of dependency, as he saw them, which have held the community back. From the reactions of residents reported in another Lori Montgomery article on October 16 ("Sursum Corda's Troubling Choices"), these bonds have by no means been severed. One resident believed that the ABC payments will indeed amount to $50,000, so matching the Boon offer; another doesn't want what the article calls "the burden of home ownership." "Maybe your mortgage is free," this resident notes, "but you still have to pay taxes and electricity. And at the end of the year those taxes are going to eat your checks up." A third reasonably thinks that "with housing prices like they are" $100,000 won't go very far in securing new accommodation.

Increasingly, it is clear to everyone that the world in which they have lived for the past 35 years, will almost certainly, at some point, come to an end. For those paying $100 or less in rent each month, many of them elderly, unemployed, or partially employed, and often without regular income, the transition, however managed, is going to be very difficult, and it seems inevitable that there will be feelings of betrayal. But by whom? The management companies who may have led the community into fiscal ruin? The City, which put its own plan first? Those members of the present Board who have all but married ABC and BAR? Or ABC (or BAR) itself? There is no good ending here, though in yesterday's *Post* yet a third article ("Affordable Housing at Sursum Emphasized") quotes City Administrator Robert C. Bobb as saying "We're committed to staying with the residents for the long term and to ensure that we have very low-income housing." Mr. Bobb also called the Boon offer "presumptuous" because it was undertaken without consultation with the City. The City remains fixed on developing not only Sursum Corda, after all, but also the land around it as a part of its New Communities program, and "ABC's offer comes closer to meeting the goals of the New Communities program," Mr. Bobb said.

But in writing thus I have obscured the amount of confusion, ill-will, general doubt, well-meaning ignorance, and outright anger that eddies around all of these proposals. After the last election, which added three new members, the Board effectively broke down into a 5-4 grouping, with Wilma and Shiv's side represented by 4. The result was that Wilma was removed, and Luke's ally Mimi Norman put in her place. Mimi took a very strong stand against both Wilma and Shiv, and charges of duplicity have become common at Board meetings, so much so that after one of them, Shiv guesses, Luke sought out Mimi's husband and induced him to threaten Shiv with physical violence (Mimi had evidently called Shiv corrupt at the meeting and he had responded in kind) – and she apparently did so while Lori Montgomery was standing nearby. Shiv talked the man down, but when Lori included a reference to the event in her story, together with a further description of Luke, her desk editor cut both out – or so Shiv was able to deduce from their conversation. At another meeting another Board member said that as she was driving into Sursum Corda she had seen Shiv and Wilma standing together talking – and for a brief instant had been tempted to run them both down. Under these circumstances it is clear that the Boon offer is going to get short shrift from this Board, and if it is going to be attended to at all it will have to be by the residents.

Meanwhile, since I got back late Sunday night I have been twice to Sursum Corda, once yesterday and uneventfully with the undergraduates, then with eight Law School Students who are tutoring there this semester. There had been some difficulties both with identifying children with whom the Law School students could usefully work, and also with deciding where they should tutor, but when a meeting was obviously about to begin on the second floor, Luke appeared and provided us with space on the third, thus leaving the second free for such meetings and projects connected with the competing offers, as are now underway. His new, smart secretary, Mary, offered three of her own excellent children for instruction, and we expect to gain three more next week, from a family who fled Hurricane Katrina from the Dominican Republic. I spoke to him only briefly, but Luke seemed to me a little more distracted, perhaps even a little more anxious than I remembered him, and then he asked one of the Law students to review the two offers to see which she thought the better of them, and to look at the details. But the fact that Boon, which had earlier been driven from the table, is now back again may be more than a detail, particularly since it had been Luke who had earlier pushed them off. But even so, this new attitude, if that is what it is, is a little hard to explain. He has a new Board to work with, and a President who will almost certainly follow his direction, or so he evidently thinks. New offer or not, from his point of view, what can go wrong?

Friday October 21, 2005

I talk to Shiv about the way things are going, and we take up an issue we have rarely engaged before, the involvement of FBV and BAR in all of this. Neither of us really understands their present roles, though in the beginning FBV, with its three well-known former Redskins, had the very good effect of neutralizing some at least of the bad publicity to which the community was subjected as a result of Princess Hansen's murder, among other things. In those now distant times (last May) they were also going to invest in the community; teach its young; and bring HUD around. But the connection was thought to be long term, not short, and to serve to preserve the community, not bring it to an end. What it did, of course, was to bring BAR and through them ABC to the table, with a result that has been all too evident. It now appears that the connection between FBV and BAR may be even closer than first appeared, and both are now involved financially in what has been going on. Apart from the extraordinary 3.75% which FBV will reap from the 15% ABC has promised the Board, we have the sense that it may have extracted a further commitment from BAR as the price for bringing it on board. Did it also, I wonder aloud, put up some or all of the $2 million ABC represents as the cost for defending against the HUD inspection? It struck me that, in all of our summer meetings, ABC never once raised a real objection to their costs, and if they had done so that would account for the evident respect they had been accorded – far more than FBV had enjoyed.

Shiv has doubts, but (politely perhaps) says Maybe. More to the point is a meeting the community had last night with Ted and an element in the community that Luke had specially invited. I suppose that the results were predictable, though they surprised me. Ted had been brilliant, Shiv insists, answering all the questions posed to him, and all the objections lodged, with an easy eloquence, which left nothing for the opposition to say but, Don't believe him; he's a liar. And indeed, apart from those residents who don't want to own a home, the chief objection to Boon's plan is that it's too good to be true. A free house? But nothing's ever free. What strings are attached? Who's really benefitting?

Joe Austen of ABC had been present too, and after it Shiv thought he had had a good conversation with the man. What do you really want, Joe had asked him? And Shiv had said for ABC to improve its offer, or for it to withdraw and for Boon to win. He pointed out that if Boon did so, one effect of that outcome would be to free ABC from the clutches of BAR and FBV both (unless BAR had simply made ABC a loan to defend against the HUD inspection against the expectation of future profits – which seems unlikely), or that Boon and ABC could then enter into negotiations. He means to arrange a follow-up meeting with Ted and Joe, to see if anything can be agreed. But now I too have begun to entertain doubts. As we were coming in for tutoring last night Joe Austen had just come out of the Community Center. He looked neither right nor left as he was getting into his car, and threw his briefcase into it, his face a study in suppressed anger and evident frustration. Shiv is surprised when I tell him so, and this time seems to share my sense that any such accommodation is a pretense. ABC and BAR and FBV have smelled blood (and money). Whatever they represent, Shiv says, they're still in play.

And this: Shiv reports that Phil, an active resident and for so long the vocal backbone of the opposition, seems at least to have gone over to the other side. He and Luke chat together, and from what Shiv observed of their interchange, their confidence is mutual and complete. It is possible, Shiv speculated, that someone played up to him and brought him round, treating him with sufficient courtesy that any embarrassment about his change of direction would have been mitigated. But nothing is certain and the sliding surfaces that we stand upon now seem to have acquired a thin veneer of ice. As far as the game's end goes, things are falling into place, and it seems to me less and less likely that the community as such will prevail. One final point. Looking back, the reason this all began, apart from Princess' murder which, Marc Fisher notwithstanding, simply is a red herring here, the real issue still turns upon the failure of an earlier management company to do what was necessary to prevent HUD from beginning the actions that would have resulted in a foreclosure. We have all been accepting this from the first as an outrageous, possibly even illegal action (depending, to be sure, on how the contract was written), which the company undertook more in its own interests as in Sursum Corda's -- but was it acting alone? Speaking the other day Mr. Robert Bobb, the now famous City Administrator, remarked that the ABC offer fit with the City's own initiative best of all, and it strikes me that the City's plans may figure more deeply in all of this than we have understood. Certainly the City has kept its hand in from the first: it was the City that first approached Jane Walters and brought her around; the City that when the ABC deal seemed all but in the bag, approached Luke, and asked if it could make a counter-offer; the City which offered a deal with ABC, offering free land for a substantial development, if only if could have its way at Sursum Corda.

Wednesday October 26, 2005

I talk to Shiv about recent events, those that are still developing. At the last minute ABC brought forth another proposal: $80,000 instead of $50,000 for residents who simply want to leave, and 49% rather than 15% as the Board's share on the project as a whole. At the Tuesday Board meeting, ABC initially sought to withdraw its offer, but ended by reaffirming it (unsurprisingly: they're in too deep to quit), which Luke thought a great victory. The Board (except Shiv) is still firmly attached to the ABC offer, and will no doubt accept it, probably at the next meeting, and almost certainly without giving the residents a chance to vote before they do so.

In the meantime, Shiv says that he has been to visit Jane Walters, together with Wilma and six others, who at once offered to help. She asked any resident who wanted to take part in a law suit against the Board to come back when she had had a chance to talk to Northwest 1's lawyers, but in the event only Shiv and two others had returned. The lawyers are now said to be getting ready to file an injunction on Friday to prevent the ABC agreement coming into force. Shiv was taken aback by Wilma's absence, which may suggest that, not for the first time, things are not quite as they seem. Of the two residents, both women, who returned, one is well enough placed to look after herself if (when) the community is forced out, but the other, a very poor young mother with two children, exactly the sort of person whom, over the past years, Sursum Corda has best served, is not so well placed, and she trusts neither offer, sees both of them poised to destroy her home and what asylum she has found at Sursum Corda. But Shiv is glad of her support whatever the circumstances, since the participation of these residents is what will give the Northwest 1 lawyers standing.

In conversation with Shiv I say what I really feel about the Boon offer: that yes, it is clearly better than ABC's, and if I were a resident it is of course the offer I would support; that Ted (like Shiv himself) has performed yeoman's service in advancing it, and that ABC's recently revised offer (unthinkable without Boon's) shows yet again that ABC had left itself a generous margin of profit. But even so, I say that I cannot fall at its feet. Its bottom line seems to be to obtain the community's land free and clear, and without encumbrance, but also without residents. Apart from the backout position – that the property would be reserved and enhanced, and, as we had hoped from the first, only in a small way developed – it too writes a final *finis* to the community of Sursum Corda, this place where, for all its faults, the poor ruled, sometimes badly, sometimes well, but in any case without apology. It has also been the place where the poorest mother could keep a roof over her children's heads, even on those nights when they all went to bed hungry. Such was, when all is said and done, the reason for its founding, and its sustaining grace. ABC's offer, for all its faults, has within it at least a nod in the direction of the residents. Perhaps in time a better will take its place, and that the happy and unhappy mix of 550 poor, moderate incomes, and market rate residents will rise as one. But it seems unlikely. Whether they do or not, the really poor mother, whether on welfare or not and with children to raise, will no longer be welcome here, since current plans are to accommodate those among the present residents that can afford it, not to encourage the poor to find a place here. So that, for good or for ill, in time to come, such a fellowship as has met here shall never again be in company together.

Thursday October 27, 2005

Shiv called in last night, but only briefly, and we discussed possibilities. Among them is that of an injunction, which Shiv thinks may be necessary since it seems unlikely that Luke is going to arrange another vote in the community to allow residents the choice between the ABC and the Boon offer. A lawyer could bring it to a judge, if one can be found to do so. A vote of the Residents would (or should?) be necessary in order to sell what is after all the co-op's major asset, the land on which it stands, and that requirement would certainly not expire on October 30.

Monday October 31, 2005

More developments, how important is hard to say. Luke cancelled the Thursday night meeting at which the Board was to vote, but during the day on Friday the Board visited HUD for the first time since the inspection, for what proved to be an interesting – I am

increasingly reluctant to say an important – meeting. In it, HUD rejected virtually all of the charges which some members of the Board
had made against it, and reported instead that it did not at all require the community to accept the ABC offer; it would not foreclose
on the property if its demands were not met; it could indeed work
with Boon, as it often had in the past, etc. Although none of this
should have been news to the Board, because of the representations
of some of its members it indeed was, and had the effect of so shak-
ing the ABC offer that the meeting was at once reported to ABC,
by Luke and others, the delegation including Pastor Gray, so that
ABC would not be encouraged to repeat its bait-and-switch tactics,
and could be held accountable for whatever it proposed. What it
proposed, and this time in writing, was a new agreement, which
seemed to some of the Board to approach, or better, the one from
Boon. It would match Boon's 49% for the community, and raise
the amount each resident could either attach to his or her new residence, of take away with them, from $50,000 to $80,000, still under
Boon's $100,000, but not by as much.

This proposal became particularly attractive because it turns
out there is a provision in the Boon agreement that seems to rob it
of some at least of its moral high ground, and its status as a offer
intended only to provide for the community. At some point one
of the parties – Shiv thinks almost certainly officers in Boon itself,
not Ted – introduced a requirement that if, at the end of the 120
day period of delay, the Board does decide to accept another offer
(which would be possible, particularly if one came forward that
offered to preserve much or all of the present community), then
Boon would be paid back *twice* its investment in the project. This
contrasts sharply with ABC's requirement that it be paid back only
the $2 million (or whatever it is said to be) it had invested to defend
against the HUD inspection, and would have the effect of leaving
Boon with a good profit for only a very limited period of investment. It would also, of course, eliminate all risk, a concept about
which I have already written, but here is another aspect of it. No
doubt it was the thought of winning the contest with ABC and then
being robbed of its victory in the end by an unknown that made
Boon insert the clause, and given the early history of Boon's association with the project, I suppose this development should not

be surprising, but to tell the truth it was, if only because it seemed to underline, yet again, the itch for quick profit that seems to infect anyone who comes near.

On Friday night the 28th the Board met and voted, 7-1, to accept the revised ABC offer. Later Luke sent an email which recorded the vote, but also added that the so-called "Advisory Group," composed of those persons, personally attentive to him, whom he had appointed, had voted 5 to 1 to do likewise. The Board's lawyers had acknowledged the strength of the Boon offer, but unsurprisingly, had supported ABC's. The clause I have just referred to figured in the discussions, Shiv, who was embarrassed by it, acknowledged to me.

The next day I went with the Georgetown students to collect the children in our program for a Halloween party and stopped up to the Board's office on the third floor to see what was up. In the office with him, sitting around a large table and evidently discussing things, were Phil and Wilma, Shiv's former allies, who now seemed to have made their peace with him. Wilma and I greeted each other, and Luke was as cheerful as ever, saying only that he had been able "to leverage the Boon offer" to get a better agreement out of ABC, but there were details still to be worked out, so that they had made no public announcement yet.

Talking with Shiv on Sunday I found out that things are not quite over after all. After the Friday meeting ABC had sent an email to the City saying that it had been chosen as the developers, but the City had responded in part by sending a squad car to protect Shiv and his family, which seems unnecessary. Shiv agreed that Wilma has now allied herself with Luke, an event possibly precipitated by Jane Walters's re-emergence (she is pressing ahead with getting signatures to remove Luke from office). For now at least, Shiv is disinclined to pursue an injunction since he says that he has now no real support in the community, and could be seen to be acting out of pique. But he is as strongly opposed to letting Luke prosper at the expense of the community as ever, and regards the whole business as far from concluded.

Two days ago (I think it was) I saw on a local TV station a recording of last week's outdoor meeting at Sursum Corda, which Jane Walters was chairing while a number of City officials, including

City Administrator Bobb, sat, somewhat uncomfortably I thought, in a row of chairs behind her. She was trying to encourage residents to join her in examining the offers (at least I think she referred to more than one), and her strategy was to agree with whatever a resident said, and then asking him or her to join with her, and give advice. This offer of consultation, however, rode somewhat uneasily on her powerful administrative style, and so much so that when Luke came forward to try to clarify a point she effectively batted him down when he asked to speak – "No, Mr. Gratian, you may not" – and I had the sense that at least Mr. Bobb looked a little uneasy at the rejection. Although as the meeting went on I was surprised how few details of the present plans she knew, the meeting itself showed to perfection that she was indeed allied to, and trusted by, the City, and seemed to confirm Shiv's judgment that it is with her that we should seek an alliance if there is to be any effective progress, and if some at least of the malfeasance which has emerged is to be brought to book. But sadly, that seems to me a very big "If."

Wednesday November 2, 2005

As a result of a community meeting last night, which announced the revised ABC offer and the Board's subsequent vote to the community, the *Post* ran a story today about both events, written by Lori Montgomery who has emerged in recent months as the most sympathetic and knowledgeable *Washington Post* reporter ever to write about Sursum Corda. Today's article presented the deal as all but concluded, and as a victory for the community and the Board. Curiously, there is no mention of the fact that it was the meeting with HUD, for once acting very much in the community's interests, that precipitated the new ABC offer, and it cites primarily Wilma and Shiv as the architects, Shiv in particular for having brought both developers to the table, the second when he became "disappointed" with the first. In what seems to me an evident sign of authorial and perhaps editorial disapproval, Luke is not mentioned, a circumstance that will certainly annoy him. Wilma, whom I saw briefly as we were going in for tutoring last night when she declared herself happy with the deal, is quoted as urging residents to remain, not to take the $80,000 and leave: "We've been through it all. So why leave now when the rain has finally stopped and the sun is now shining." All the residents quoted are those that approve the agreement. "All the board members, they did a heck of a job," one said.

It is difficult to escape the impression at this point that the curtain is indeed poised to come down. And with all of the *Post's* evident approval thereof, it continues to sound like Pangloss, as though what has emerged is "the best of all possible worlds." "Possible," perhaps, but some, not "all." The community, all but hidden by the initial attacks on the community after Princess Hansen's murder, flourished briefly, but is now to be like the living flame it once was, quite put out. Though $80,000 richer (if everyone delivers on their promises – but does anyone think they will?), the residents will either leave for other places, or return to a new and more mixed apartment complex, one designed both for low and moderate, but also for market rate apartments. Or so it seems. It is of course a pleasing, if not altogether reasonable proposition that this new apartment complex may develop its own sense of community, in the way of such places, but perhaps here crossing class boundaries, so that the affluent and the disadvantaged may speak to one another – and their children too. May it be so.

Later I meet Shiv and a friend for lunch at the Tombs. After today's article I reckon that he has become something of a celebrity, and amuse him by suggesting that he sit on the outside seat, so that he can sign autographs more easily. Alas, that service not required. He does not believe that justice has been done for the residents, and considers that the City's Office of Economic Development will think so too. And since it is that office who will have to issue the permits ABC needs to begin work, he thinks that things are far from over. Maybe. But at some point everyone in authority is simply going to want the whole business out of their hair. He adds that Luke has hired a Public Relations firm, perhaps to address just such an issue. Meanwhile, Deputy Mayor Stan Jackson has expressed an interest in what exactly happened, a difficult question to answer given what has passed for procedure with this particular Board. Mr. Bobb did not attend the community meeting last night at which things were announced, and to which he had been invited, so perhaps Shiv is right, and there are some indications that the City is far from satisfied. Meanwhile Shiv thinks that Jane Walters has continued working with such residents as best she can, and thinks that she may be drawing up a petition. But whatever happens, there probably will have to be a community vote to approve the revised ABC offer, a vote at which the Boon offer may well put in another appearance.

For myself I certainly hope so, and suspect that the City's interest, never entirely absent though not always operating to the community's advantage, may prove paramount. The "New Communities Initiative" may be running into difficulties however, because the bill for the baseball stadium which the City is supporting has proved larger than expected, and there may be less money available for other things. That could make the City less willing to hand over grants of land to developers from whom the City will realize little profit, at least until the property taxes roll in. Or it may simply make the City less willing to put any money at all into the project. I suppose that time will tell, but more and more I am reminded of the green light Fitzgerald refers to at the end of *The Great Gatsby*, as we press on, boats against the current, born back ceaselessly into the past.

Saturday November 5, 2005

I had lunch at the Dubliner's yesterday, a fine but not too fine Irish restaurant, with an old and close friend who knows Sursum well, and the day being fine we sat outside, so that we could speak quite freely, and we did so. She has kept up with what has been going on at the place, and though she does not live there, understood what it once stood for, and what brought it into being. It's a mess, she says at once when we begin to talk. The people don't know what they're doing, or what's being done to them. Eighty thousand is nothing, and anyway, people she knows are already talking about buying cars with it. They think they can live anywhere they want, and it won't cost them anything. They'll get a voucher and it will be just like it was. But they're going to be cut off federal assistance once they've got all that money. The ones who are going to be hurt worst are those who are least able to understand it. Many residents have never paid utilities – very rare, she says, the only other place she knows where this is true are some federal apartments in Southwest. Most of them are older, she adds, but even the young ones have no idea what they're getting into. They just see a check for more money than they've ever had before. That's the way it is. Wave a little money in front of them, and they'll do whatever you say. Some of the ones who are worried are even blaming Shiv, she says.

I object, and say that anyone who blames Shiv simply has no idea what's been going on. I ask who is relaying the false information on which these opinions are based, but my friend doesn't know. It's just around. As for the rest, I say, other things are driving the way people are reacting: a sense of inevitability, present from the beginning, that has now been reinvigorated and added to by talk of large amounts of money being owed or paid for this and that, confident white people all over the place, being nice, but acting as if they owned it and obviously used to having their way, and the behavior of the Board, all now following Luke, asking no questions and doing what they're told. And there is also, I say, even after all these years, a sense that the government – City, Federal, who cares – is driving all this, which in a way it may be, and that the people must comply. The Board could have made a stand, but hired Luke, and seems to have put out its collective hand instead.

In the end we agree that, in recent years, the management teams seem to have worked to their own advantage first of all, and my friend recalls when the utility bills had gone unpaid, and management had simply divorced itself from the community, which it treated simply as not a very bright client. We disagree about Jane Walters, whom my friend thinks has been proven right, but I recall the way she had attacked the community in the *Washington Post* after Princess Hansen's murder – "there's no hope there, no hope at all" – and consider that it may have been to her own past power that, then at least, she was still attached. Perhaps she had a grander plan as well, and believed that in time she might come forward again, alone this time, or with the City's help, and save the day. But her connections downtown, Marion Barry no longer being mayor, proved less powerful than she anticipated, and she found herself drawn into the City's plans instead.

But my friend is incensed at the way many of the residents are already making plans, and not only those who have moved in during the last few years, and for whom Sursum Corda is but one stop among many, but also, more surprisingly, some who have lived there since the beginning, since they were children. A year or so ago a real estate agent had canvasses the residents in her (Perry School) neighborhood, just across First Street NW from Sursum Corda, and had been offering residents $325,000 for their homes. Most apparently refused. But as our conversation continues she grows increasingly warm to the subject, and now cannot restrain herself, but tells me about an exchange she had with one of the residents. It's such a shame, she had told him. And it's wrong. Father McKenna worked so hard to make a good place for you to live in, and you've sold it for a dollar. That's so stupid. But her interlocutor, perhaps remembering the eighties when the community had become a co-op for a payment of ten dollars, answered, A dollar? No, we really didn't sell it for a dollar. Yes you did, she replied. You sold it for a dollar. You wait. You just wait.

Sunday November 6, 2005

The academic year is by no means old, but the semester is, and it is high time for the Seniors to be thinking about next year. I have brunch at Martin's with one such, the only Senior who has been with the program four years, who was (and indeed is) much involved with a family associated with Princess Hansen, and has generally been among the very best tutors in the program. She hopes to work with learning disabled children and wants to go on in Special Ed, an aspiration I both encourage and admire, though I suggest that, if the opportunity in graduate school presents itself, she might consider course work in Public Policy too, since this is a field now little known to her, but one that in the future may engage her.

Because she knows Sursum as well as she does we discuss the current situation, and though she has read all of the *Washington Post* articles on the subject this year, she has been convinced by none of them, and thinks, as my friend did yesterday, that what is happening is simply a disaster both for the community and for the residents, many of whom, and particularly those with children, will have great difficulty finding like accommodation, not to speak of the loss of their community. She is particularly concerned with what will become of two of the young boys with whom she has been working, who are beginning to make very effective progress, but whose family circumstances she knows to be very difficult.

Occupied as I have been with other contingencies at Sursum Corda, I have not written much about the tutoring program recently, which has been going, under the circumstances, surprisingly well, in spite of being crammed onto one floor, a circumstance which contrasts with past years. During the semester I have been seeking, not for the first time but with somewhat greater purpose, to encourage tutors to teach their learners simple words in other languages, usually in Spanish or French – the words for hello, good-bye, thank you – both to engage their sense of language, and also to try to open their schemata to other linguistic influences. The idea is not to teach a second language – though it is not difficult to imagine circumstances in which literacy might be accompanied by second language study – so much as to awaken and encourage interest in language acquisition and comprehension by holding up easily intelligible commonplace phrases in a second language, and my sense is that, although it certainly is not effective on all our young learners, on those who embrace it, it could indeed prove a most helpful supplementary strategy. But, influenced by a language student who some time ago tried to interest her learner in Italian, I thought it best to begin by encouraging some at least of the tutors to take a first step.

This year the tutors have been sitting with their learners around what is in effect one large table – actually four or even five long tables left conjoined by a previous meeting of the Board, which could easily have been separated but which, for whatever reason, we left as they were. I had initially been concerned that the proximity of the tutorial groups would make distractions easy, but in the event exactly the opposite happened, and, in some cases at least, the children concentrated better, taking their cue from those about them. I was not sure how this arrangement would affect the strategy I had proposed, and candidly, I am not sure that I encouraged it. Because I had said that tutors need not press the language issue if their learners proved unwilling, two tutors (both at the tables) had asked their learners if he or she would like to begin a new language, and in each case received an unequivocal refusal. But now two other tutors, neither at the tables, have simply gone ahead and done so, and been rewarded for their pains, including a burst of interest from one child who does not much embrace new challenges. But in doing so they have taken their own direction as to which words they teach, and one has taught his learner to count up to thirty in Spanish, an accomplishment to be sure, but I am not sure of its actual effect. Still, at least with this relatively successful beginning I can return to the subject in our next seminar.

Saturday November 12, 2005

I was not mistaken about Shiv's new celebrity, and on Thursday he was interviewed with Lori Montgomery on Kojo Nnamdi's radio show, which I had to miss, but which, from all reports (Shiv's anyway) went very well. Luke had been invited as well, and intended to send the now-trusted Wilma, but in the event, pleading an interview with the City, no one from the other side appeared. From all reports Shiv had been most diplomatic, holding his fire and praising Jane Walters, in whose agency he now has placed much trust. Lori is said to have been in good form too, speaking to some issues closed to Shiv, but deferring to him on details. On the other hand she also referred to the community's "wonderful lawyers," a quite extraordinary description, even given the sympathy which we all feel for Tim.

The next day Shiv and I have lunch with Ted from KCH, more or less just to see where we are. The City's new plan for North Capitol is going to be revealed shortly, but Shiv has had advance notice. The City has set aside $585 million to acquire properties in and around Northwest 1, he says, and (following the charette, which the City had effectively managed) hopes to keep low density in Sursum Corda (current plans will call – can this be right, I remember thinking? – for only 138 units there!), but with a total of 1,700 units overall in approximately 15 acres (the plans now include Bible Way's Golden Rule apartments and its nearby nursing home, together with the other apartment blocks, Tyler House, Turn Key, Temple Courts and some or all of Sibley Plaza), to which will be added 3 acres on the other side of North Capitol Street. There will be commercial and office development involved as well, together with new schools (Walker-Jones Elementary School and Terrell Middle School will be torn down), and the mayor wants to advance the project before he leaves office in about sixteen months' time, Shiv says.

But Ted points out that the numbers sound all wrong, and wouldn't work for any developer he knows. The bill for acquiring all those properties would be huge, he points out, and without higher density on Sursum Corda the project simply could not pay for itself. Equally, the idea of one-for-one replacement can't be right. He's interested in the details, but thinks that the people who drew it up may not have taken all contingencies into account. But of course this is the larger plan into which ABC has wanted to go, even though now it may have to limit itself to Sursum Corda instead, in which case they will indeed need both a higher density and City permits for allow the construction to begin. Still, and more to the point, none of this will be complete until long after the mayor has left office, and his successor, whomever he or she may be, is unlikely to embrace so ambitious, uninflected, and costly a plan. Indeed the present plan seems to be so costly that it will probably not go very far now, Ted points out. Only look at the attacks on the Nationals' baseball stadium, and the way members of the City Council went after the costs there. Would they do less with this ballooning project? But if so, even with a putative new plan, nothing really is decided. Ted also talks about owners (one in particular) of Northwest 1 properties who of course would benefit greatly with the gentrification of Sursum Corda and the surrounding areas that KCH has been intending to develop.

In the beginning Ted seems a little removed, and I wonder if he may think it necessary to put some distance between himself and the whole business. If so, I cannot fault him for it. Motivated not only by the game but also by a sense of evident injustice, he put his considerable knowledge and experience to work for the residents of Sursum Corda (who collectively at least, did not understand the extent to which he had done so), produced a plan much better than the one that prevailed, and did so at his own cost, and without any reward. From any point of view it must now be time to cut bait, and not to pursue indefinitely something which, to mix my metaphors, probably will not pan out. Warmest and best thanks for what he did, and every Sursum Corda resident owes him (and Shiv) at very least, $30,000 (the amount ABC was forced to raise its individual family offer), in the unlikely circumstance of the offer coming to fruition. He now suggests that Shiv approach ABC himself and say what it would take to get him on board (not *the* Board).

We had been talking about how much the units were actually worth, and Ted estimated their actual value between $300,000 and $400,000, and then asks how many residents would simply take that sort of money and run. Many of them, we believe. Yes, says Ted, but what if they could both have a new residence in the rebuilt apartment complex and bank, say, $200,000? We agree that would change things. It was then he suggested that Shiv approach ABC, a reasonable suggestion, but not one Shiv's history with ABC would encourage, even if ABC would agree to the suggestion, which they won't. He asks why we think the ABC offer had been successful when the Boon offer was so much better (intimidation, disbelief and ignorance, we suggest), and he adds that of course even $100,00, still less $80,000, is but a fraction of what, in other circumstances, is probably their true value.

We also talk about how we might convince the courts to mandate an audit, which seems quite essential if we are going to see where things really stand. Trust is at a premium just now. When Shiv returned a new suit Luke had left for him at his parents' home he had told Luke that he was returning it because he was concerned that Luke was beginning to develop a reputation within the community for educing Board members to support his position by means other than reason, and he did not want to be seen as included in that particular remit. Luke had affected surprise. We decide that a petition of residents might help get an audit, together with as the City's new found interest in the details of the proceedings. Shiv thinks Jane Walters can make it happen by calling upon old contacts; I am less sure.

So where are we then? In one way, nowhere at all. The original HUD and City plan has been foiled by ABC, with whom the Board, induced to do so by Luke, partnered without seeking other bids, indeed (from what we can tell) without any real negotiation at all, and certainly without effectively guarding community interests. But the ABC plan, though slightly improved by a now withdrawing KCH, will of course destroy the community (hooray!, cries the *Washington Post*) in spite of the several legal issues posed, for HUD and the City, by the fact that Sursum Corda is a coop, and by the bourgeoning costs always implicit, but not now easily explained away as the true value of the property becomes apparent, even as it is fluctuating, to everyone.

All this should be comforting, especially as I doubt that the next mayor will attend to this morally ambiguous and administratively contentious project with quite the same pertinacity that the present one has, but it hardly is. There's too much money flying around. There are too many flat screen TVs that need to be accounted for, too much talk of money under the table, and the Sursum Corda Board has run up bills that will one day come due. If there is to be a general, Northwest 1 plan for everybody, the new unacknowledged heroes are likely to be Shiv, some other members of the Board, the City, and some developer, possibly, I suppose, even ABC – if the City trusts them, which seems to me unlikely. But time and money may not permit them the latitude they need, and in that case the parts will probably come apart and the plan, such as it is, will operate piecemeal, and higher, even much higher density, could then become the order of the day.

After our lunch Shiv gives me a ride to Georgetown in his new second-hand car, a 1992 Acura Legend in very good shape (or so it seems to me, who am no expert) and with only 70-something thousand miles on it, which he got for $2,500, which he assures me is a good deal. During a lull in the conversation I quote him my friend's remark about Father McKenna having worked so hard to produce a good place in which the poor might live, which, not at all as I had intended, troubles him somewhat. He agrees that, in a way at least, such indeed was so, and agrees that the changes which will come about will certainly spell the end of the community as it once existed, for good and less good. But he says too, what seems certainly right, that now at least the community is simply being defrauded, and that he must do what he can to limit that depredation.

That night...

That night I am invited to dinner by five tutors, several of whom share an R Street townhouse a short distance from the Georgetown campus. In the course of conversation it turns out that all are active and practicing Catholics (three have been to Jesuit high schools), and that most of them understand their work at Sursum Corda in that context, as I do. I tell them something about what is going on, and assure them that the reference they have seen in the *Post* to ground being broken "in the spring" does not mean that the community itself is under imminent threat. It is very likely, I say, that it will still be there, with children for us to teach, until well beyond the end of the year. In the course of our discussion we talk about the way in which one group among the partners had represented its motivation as born of religious commitment and so supportive of the community as a whole, even though it now seems as somewhat profit-driven too. But that in turn leads to a consideration of how far our work as tutors responds to a Catholic dimension yet present in our university, a question I have entertained elsewhere. Given the setting, the question embraces as well what it means to be a Catholic Christian these days, when the phrase has had attached to it, in the media and elsewhere, associations of a kind of conservative traditionalism which certain Vatican pronouncements only apparently support, and when the Church's traditional role as a supporter of the immigrant, the poor, the outsiders and their communities, seems less now than it once was, as rapacious Republicans jostle smug and stagnant Democrats for votes.

But this is the world in which these young ones must live and thrive, and if they are to retain their faith beyond graduation – or in some cases even while they are here – they must learn to negotiate between the Scylla of a newly friendly if finally false fundamentalism, and the Charybdis of an all-encompassing American secularism, itself attached to a social compassion which is rooted only in the individual, and inclined to instrumentalize human suffering (which David Hollenbach thought a matter of ultimate concern in any Catholic university worthy of the name), in the interest, not of a common, but of a putatively greater good. No doubt we did not entertain these matters long enough for them really to register, and it would be mistaken to think that we achieved anything like a consensus, but that the questions themselves were lively, cheered me somewhat. I should probably confess too, lest it all sound a little too uplifting, that the evening concluded with a game apparently called "Beer Pong," involving a ping pong ball, twenty plastic cups, and varying, if (last night at least) small, amounts of beer in each – I suppose there is room for negotiation there too – a game previously unknown to me, but one round of which I observed (but did not participate in) before leaving. I think we all knew our conversation had not ended, but these are issues we do not engage as often as we should.

One other conversation which is still continuing – and no doubt will do so long after I have finished this journal – concerns our little experiment with using languages other than English at our tutorials, which some tutors at least have been trying out. When I first urged the practice I had hoped that it might help make the children (well, and some of their tutors) more sensitive to English nuance, and so improve their writing – something of a stretch, I now consider. It seems instead to have had the unintended effect of getting a very few children briefly interested in Spanish, when, encouraged by their tutors, they try their hand at counting, or at the most simple of sentences. But what are the long term effects, if any, like to be, and certainly, we have not made it last.

And this: I spent the morning writing this entry and then went down to the National Gallery to meet a well-known art historian, a medievalist friend who is in town for a lecture he is giving tomorrow, and we see a woodcut exhibition – "Origins of European Printmaking" -- now on exhibition there. Earlier, he had helpfully assisted me with an article I was writing, and when he very reasonably asked me how it was coming, I had to confess that it was not yet done, and that writing these poor pages was the reason why. But my real excuse came a few minutes later, when we came upon number 104 in the exhibition, a late fifteenth-century German woodcut of the fourteenth-century Dominican Henry Suso (d. 1366), kneeling, the catalogue avers, before a representation of "Eternal Wisdom in her female incarnation," as the Christ child himself looks on from a nearby tree, and, in an almost Kafkaesque parody of academic industry, painfully inscribing the monogram of

Christ onto his own chest with a metal stylus. But at his feet there is a somewhat angry-looking small dog, waving a bit of cloth in its mouth, whose purpose is said to be to recall the holy man from his asceticism, and compel him to involve himself in the lives of others.

Wednesday November 16, 2005

I talk to Shiv who has been increasingly drawn into the proceedings, so much so that the Board now courts him, and tried to get him to come to its meeting with Mr. Bobb. But his attachments to the City are better than their own, and he made excuses. Tomorrow however he will have to go to a meeting which will involve everyone, ABC included, and he is getting ready to speak as the voice of moderation (a new role for him), so as not to take sides, and to oppose neither the Northwest 1 plan (which really seems to be the City's), nor the Board's attempt to improve its position. He is still taken by Ted's suggestion that if the individual units are worth, as they may be, between $300,000 and $400,000 each, then it should be possible for some residents at least (especially the old, Shiv says) to secure a unit in the new development for $150,000 and have an additional $200,000 to live on.

He has been keeping in touch with Lori Montgomery for some time now, and reports that the *Post* is working on a story about the increasingly evident corruption which has so clearly influenced events at Sursum Corda. It may be out soon, though exactly when he doesn't know. Not surprising. The *Post's* sub-editors had ruled out any allusion to such goings-on earlier on when they might have helped challenge the first ABC agreement (indeed if what Shiv had been told was true, they had not only discouraged, they had actually stricken from Lori Montgomery's earlier accounts, her references to them). Now of course the publication of such doings would strengthen the City's hand against the Board, which, from the City's point of view, has now filled its purpose. The more Sursum Corda's Board can be discredited, the more likely the City's plan, now put forward by Northwest 1, is to succeed. To be sure this Board has brought such a fate upon itself, but Ted's suggestion is hardly in the City's interest, and anyway this particular administration has only fifteen months to run. And who knows what will follow then.

On the way down to tutoring tonight Stewart Morris, one of the more perceptive and thoughtful of the tutors who has been very much keeping up with things and has a keen interest in urban education and in the forces that guide it, asked me what I wanted to happen now. So caught, I said that this is not a community that needs leveling, but that if I had to choose suppose that I would have to opt, however reluctantly, for Ted's most recent idea (the bare outlines of which I then briefly explained). Yet as I think about it later, I realize that it's not an easy question, and that I had hardly answered it for this excellent young man. There has been so much greed, prevarication, and outright duplicity involved in everything that has been going on that it seems to me invidious to invoke reason – but what else? – and say in effect: This is what I think should happen now. To do so gives a certain stamp of legitimacy to what has gone before, one that it by no means deserves. I understand that the answer to this is to say in effect, Well, that's very nice for you, but you don't live there. You can stand apart and judge because, in the end, you're finally not involved. And it is true that I don't live there, and if I did I might well continue to approve simply and with fewer questions whatever seems to me in the "best interest" of the residents – worth remembering when Wilma's change of heart occurred or Phil's involvement come into the conversation, I suppose. But I am reminded too of a story, I think in Boswell, in which Sam Johnson, approvingly told of a Spanish university whose professors were approached by the national government and asked if the practices then enforced in the Americas could be condoned. Indeed they could not, the professors replied. Their judgment changed the national policies not at all, but at least they did not accede to the depredations of the hour.

Later in the day...

After writing these paragraphs I go off to the Russell Senate Office Building for the ceremony awarding of the Robert F. Kennedy Human Rights Award, ably moderated by my former student Douglas Brinkley, and this year also celebrating what would have been RFK's eightieth birthday. The honoree is Stephen Bradberry who has been working with low income communities in New Orleans, and with particular heroism following Hurricane Katrina, which devastated the city, and particularly the disadvantaged areas. My needful if expensive taxi having gone walkabout, I arrived in the middle of Senator Kennedy's rambling and (to tell the truth) somewhat sententious remarks, but the ceremony comes together when Kerry Kennedy takes over and speaks very much to the point – I don't think that there were very many members of the Bush family whom she left out – and especially when Illinois Senator Barack Obama give a short but powerful keynote address, hitting especially effectively at the "Can't do and O well" attitudes which lead us to stop working for the possible, and settle for what seem to be probable, particularly where the poor are concerned.

But I was especially struck with Mr. Bradberry himself, a modest and unassuming young man, but also one deeply committed to his work. One of the more attractive aspects of the RFK award is that it rarely brings coals to Newcastle, so that its recipients are usually quite unfamiliar, and they themselves often admit, as Mr. Bradberry did, to having been surprised by the award. It did not escape me, of course, that compared to the victims of Hurricane Katrina, indeed compared to the great majority of Mr. Bradberry's clients, the residents of Sursum Corda, whether they have access to $300,000, $80,000 or even $50,000 are in a position somewhat to be envied. (That is why, of course, I am permitting myself this digression.) Prior to Princess' murder and to the subsequent, really unrelated, assault on the community, many of the Sursum Corda residents lived in very difficult personal and social circumstances, but thanks to Father McKenna and the other founders of the community, they had at least a decent place to live. Now, however, if in a way unknown to the law, they have been all but defrauded, though unlike the disadvantaged of New Orleans they are not penniless, nor have they been stripped of their possessions. But their foe is Man, not Nature. There is nothing impersonal about their adversary, and a different construction, whether born of law or of ethics or of simple morality, would not have taken their homes and sent them on their way. No doubt the catastrophe which the residents of New Orleans endured is worse in every way, and as Kerry Kennedy would have it, it too was enabled, if not produced, by humankind, but there is still something horrific at having a group of rich white people, aided by some who are not white, legally, but assisted by half-truths and guile, strip from the poor their greatest asset, and pay them but a fraction of its worth. If Hurricane Katrina showed government incompetence or worse, the selling of Sursum Corda shows other forms of depredation, ones in which we all participate. I understand that there will be those who will insist that the two events bear no comparison, but with greatest respect to the victims in New Orleans and to Mr. Bradberry, in the intellectual and moral life of this our often good, but certainly improvable, Republic, who can say which may be worse?

Thursday November 17, 2005

Lori Montgomery reports on the meeting Shiv told me about (though he is not himself mentioned, and now tells me that he had to leave the meeting early on) in today's *Post*, which was before Council member Ambrose of the sixth ward, into which Sursum Corda was moved, out of the more prosperous ward two, a few years ago. Ms. Ambrose is the Chair of the City Council's Economic Development Committee, and also, the representative for the 6th ward, where Sursum Corda stands. She is holding the meeting to inquire, not for the first time, into the City's plans for low and moderate income housing in and around Northwest 1.

Later I see yesterday's committee meeting on TV: a very interesting production. It opens with Mrs. Ambrose on her own (other council members joined her as the meeting progressed), and its business commences with the redoubtable Mr. Bobb, followed by some of his colleagues, offering an overview of what has transpired so far, and what is intended for the future. He stresses three "Guiding Principles," which he insists will direct the development of the mayor's "New Communities Initiative": One-For-One Rebuilding; Building First (that is, before homes are demolished, other residences will be constructed to house displaced residents); and the right to stay, the right to return. A colleague adds information concerning the "human capitol" in the area, and offers these statistics which Mrs. Ambrose asks her to repeat: that the Northwest 1 redevelopment area comprises 28 acres and 980 units all in all, and that within that area 60% of the residents live in poverty, according to the government definition of the term; 40% are single mothers; 38% have no high school diploma; 21% are unemployed (the D.C. average is said to be 8%); and 33% are retired or disabled. From Mrs. Ambrose's reaction to these figures it was clear that, for her, there was no more to be said. And as the conversation developed she responded with equal enthusiasm to the suggestion that the "grid pattern" be reintroduced, so that the police can operate more effectively. Though no one says so, it seems that Sursum Corda is implicated in this plan, which Mrs. Ambrose thinks particularly useful to combat prostitution.

Overall, what is being proposed is about 1700 new units to replace the 920 now there: of these, 520 will be dedicated to subsidized housing, 600 for work force (moderate income) housing; and 600 for market rate housing (later someone refers rather to 500 such units). Construction will begin along K Street and North Capitol Street, where the City already owns the land, and there is a further expectation that the development will realize about 95,000 square feet of commercial development along K Street. These constructions will be high-rise buildings, comprised primarily of 1 and 2 bedroom units; low rise constructions will be reserved for the inner areas, including places like Sursum Corda, which will have 3 and 4 bedroom units. Mr. Bobb is certain (from other developments he has observed) that he can realize a mixed-income development, so that people making six (or did he say seven?) figure salaries can live right beside families making $12,000 a year, and until you step in the door, he avers, you can't tell the difference. There is much talk of site assemblage, and of the places to be assembled, Golden Rule, Temple Courts and Sursum Corda, are the three that must be acquired: the City now owns 60% of the 28 acres that make up, Northwest 1, and these three developments make up the lion's share – 90% – of what's left. Bibleway Baptist Church, which owns Golden Rule, has indicated a willingness to talk turkey, so has Temple Courts, no doubt assisted in its resolve by having failed the HUD inspection, and by the HUD support that, if rumors are to be believed, its owner is seeking in Baltimore. Though nobody says so, Sursum Corda will prove the challenge. There is $6 million in the 2006 budget, which Assistant Mayor Stanley Jackson confidently asserts can be leveraged to $70 million so as to pay for the land that the City needs to acquire.

I have put the City's plan thus baldly because for the moment at least, it looks like the one most likely to survive. But there's many a slip twixt the cup and the lip, as my mother would say, and though the change of City administration – the mayor has announced that he will not seek another term – may alter things, the fact that the City Council is invested in the project may lend a certain weight to it, which may encourage a new mayor to let sleeping dogs lie (assuming that they are still sleeping in fifteen months' time), though if the City's investment becomes too large, he or she may have to kick them awake. But that is why this meeting of the City – the mayor's office – and a sympathetic Council sub-committee has a certain importance, and one that attaches to the persons involved, as well as the now well-honed plan itself.

I have already mentioned Mrs. Ambrose, the Chair of the sub-committee, a careful, evidently hard working and autumnal woman who reminded me at once of a now deceased but much loved aunt, who had worked for years at a Hartford bank, rising, through industry, attention to detail, and mature consideration into the ranks of the bank's officers, so esteemed by her colleagues that when, in the early 1950's she was denied a promotion to vice president, the president of the bank himself called her into his office to assure her that the denial had nothing whatsoever to do with her work, and that had she been a man she certainly would have been promoted. In my childhood the president's explanation was sometimes recounted as if in praise of my aunt, but by the time I had reached adolescence, the man was execrated.

I digress again, but not by much. Council woman Ambrose seems indeed to have my aunt's evident dedication to her work, matched by an equally evident moral compass which no doubt adds to her effectiveness. At several points it became clear that she had studied attentively the documents which the City had already produced relevant to the Northwest 1 development, and early in the proceedings, as I have indicated, she made one of the witnesses repeat some of the statistics she had brought forward – that 40% of the Sursum Corda residents are single mothers, 38% are without high school diplomas and the like – but I had the sense that these cold numbers were being twice cited to offer a kind of moral justification for the project. Such people cannot be trusted to look after themselves, the logic seemed to run, of course we should strip them of their homes, insert them in new ones, and never mind, or only deal summarily with whatever their wishes might be. She had certainly done her homework (not a claim, candidly, that all of her colleagues could have made), but even she seemed to know the community hardly at all, indeed it was not clear that she understood that there was a community there to be violated. Like it or not, these people are going to be helped, and the razing of their homes is a small price to pay for this evidently needed assistance.

Her evidently knowledgeable colleague from Ward 7, however, Vincent C. Gray, mentioned that he had played football for two years in association with the Northwest 1 boys' club, and that he knew the neighborhood around it, including Sursum Corda, very well. Indeed he did. Perhaps because of that youthful experience he seemed most familiar with the area and the people both, though not particular ones, even though he paused, if memory serves, to greet Jane Walters, present in the audience. I believe (but am not certain) that Mrs. Ambrose may have done so as well, and the acknowledgment of her presence served to show both her evident profile on the City Council, and also that the Council does not always understand the nuances present in the circumstances that call for its attention. Mr. Gray did not much challenge the City's plan, or even dig into it, but his experience seemed at least to presage further contributions.

Finally, Mr. Kwame Brown, the third (at large) Council member present, seemed to bring a kind of youthful energy to the proceedings, and I looked to him with particular interest, as a putatively bright and engaged young African American who might serve as a model for some at least of the children whom we teach. But as an icon he would have burned a good deal brighter, to tell the truth, had he studied the relevant documents in advance of the meeting, and with the attention Mrs. Ambrose had brought to them, so as to have familiarized himself with the larger issues – and perhaps too concentrated a little more attentively to what was said to him at the meeting itself. It would certainly have been better for him to repeat: "Keep it simple for the people," less often than he did, since attention to detail is one thing that "the people" most need from their elected representatives. Sadly, his questioning was uninformed and quite imperceptive, and, worse of all, he seemed to have no understanding that this was so.

The City was best represented by Mr. Robert Bobb, who has not infrequently appeared in these pages, but who now manifested a more complex, even brooding presence, fully informed, in some ways more knowing than anyone in the room, but like a fallen angel apparently unmotivated by things that used to drive him ever on. I am not being entirely serious, of course. He was in fact very much on top of his game, and on top of the project too. It was impressive, rather than the reverse, that he resisted using the phrase "eminent domain," even when young Mr. Brown was waving it about, resisting I thought not only the action but the theory, and more than any of them, certainly more than Deputy Mayor Stanley Jackson who spoke after him, superficially as it seemed to me, and mainly about finances. Robert Bobb seemed to exude a kind of consciousness that embraced all aspects, human and institutional, not only of the City's plan, though of that too, but also of the city itself, and all of us who seek to make it up.

The council Chair did her very best in questioning the Sursum Corda/ABC agreement and almost by accident, as it seemed to me, winkled out of ABC the now evident truth that very few, if any, residents will be able to sustain the mortgage payments the ABC plan would impose on them, even if they should manage to secure a mortgage, which in many cases may prove unlikely. Joe Austen revealed that the actual cost of the new units is likely to be $400,000, not the $235,000 that earlier had been mooted, so that even with federal vouchers many residents would encounter a shortfall of some $500 a month, which HUD, or more likely the City, would have to pay. But none of this had been at all clear to the community, which, except that it was acting under duress, would certainly not have approved an agreement which would have effectively bankrupted or driven out virtually all of its members. In the end it was only council member Ambrose's good and persistent questioning which finally brought this extraordinary feature of the agreement into general view.

What came clear in all of this was how important ABC's withdrawal of what I and others believe to be its initial offer of a free unit for all residents has proved to be. Simply put, that action had poisoned the well. Had it stood, and had ABC held to it, some, perhaps many, of the residents would have been able to remain, and most of the rest to obtain something like the true value of their present houses, even though they would have had to sell their new residences in order to do so. The present "agreement" however strips them of their property for a fraction of its worth, and effectively sends them on their way. And none of this needed to have happened.

As I said, Mr. Stanley Jackson, Deputy Mayor for Planning and Economic Development, who has been much involved in the City's plan, also spoke at some length, and in the course of doing so seemed to make it quite clear that the City's plan for Northwest 1 in general was funded and settled, though the one ABC had proposed for Sursum Corda was not. I wonder if it is. Subsequently I gather he sent a letter to Chairwoman Ambrose rightly and forcefully challenging certain of Joe Austen's statements concerning ABC, and pointing out, *inter alia* that, contrary to ABC's assertion, zoning restrictions in particular prevented its accomplishment, at least as things stood now.

Later in the evening

Later in the evening, after I have come back from tutoring, I catch the end of the meeting I had earlier written about, which had taken place the day before. Though only a part of a session of day-long hearings, I was present at the point when Paula Knox, now suspected to be Luke Gratian's sister, whom both council members had been treating very gently, and who has been a great supporter of the ABC agreement, urged the council members not to treat the residents (whom she referred to as "us") as victims, which in one sense at least, they certainly are. But even though earlier the City had been willing to fall in with the HUD foreclosure, now at least they seem to be solicitous for the residents, if not for the community, and in any event to have ABC's number – council member Ambrose summarily forbade Joe Austen to make a concluding statement when he asked to do so, partly no doubt to save time, but her tone communicated as well a weariness, if not a wariness, of ABC's behavior. In the event Mr. Austen shrugged her ruling off, indeed he seemed almost amused by it, but I thought that he might be better advised to reflect that the city council, and all of its well-founded suspicions, will be around long after Mayor Williams has left office.

And not only the City Council. At tutoring tonight I walked back towards the Community Center with one of the tutors who has remained attentive to such developments at Sursum Corda as appear in the *Post*. (His tutee had forgotten that there was tutoring tonight and was washing her hair; it was cold enough that she asked to defer until Tuesday.) Without any prompting from me, he looked down First Place and suddenly remarked, Look at these houses. There's no way they're only worth $80,000. What a gyp. Really, what a gyp.

Friday November 18, 2005

I talk to Shiv who says that one result of yesterday's meeting with the City Council is that Liz-Ann Hall, President of BAR, has hired a lobbyist with connections on the Council to press the ABC case, since it may well be there that things will be decided, and that she realizes that yesterday's meeting did not auger well for its fortunes, or hers. He agrees with me that this is the first time we have heard about the individual units costing $400,000 each, though we agree that the number must have been known to Joe Austen and ABC for some time, and the "everybody knows that" strategy he and it are now using will fool nobody (or so we hope). Can ABC actually be expecting those funds and the North Capitol Streets lots as well? It seems unlikely, but there are precedents. He notes too, however, that recently he has heard recently from Ted from KCH, who now wants to involve Luke Gilmore of Northwest 1, whom he believes understands what is actually going on. The good news seems to be that Ted himself has by no means lost interest in the case.

We talk about the suddenly attractive actions of the City, though we know well that the City's first plan was to lay hold of the property cheaply, through HUD's attempted foreclosure, and he confesses that the last thing he wants to do in opposing ABC is to recreate that particular scenario again. At the same time he hardly has confidence in ABC itself, and even if the City would hand over all the money Joe Austen now wants, something that would be helpful to the residents, it seems most unlikely that it would do so. So the quandary again is Ted's disarmingly simple question of last week, What do you want to happen now?

Friday December 2, 2005

Although many battles no doubt lie ahead, it seems to me increasingly that they are of less problematic, less ethical a character than those that have already been waged. The November 16th meeting was, in its way, a watershed, and it hardly matters now, as Shiv reports, that other Board members are now trying to fire Luke, the more so since, in yet another turnabout, Wilma has now been defending him, and has so postponed any action. But one member is now believed to have allied herself with Jane Walters, who still seems at least to be very much supporting the City's plan, a plan that would be easier to implement if Luke were not pushing the ABC agreement. Even Luke may have begun to sense that his moment has passed, and that his uncritical advancement of the ABC agreement to the exclusion of any other has left him either unnecessary (once the Agreement passed) or vulnerable (as its limitations become apparent). The Board member in question is less likely to be concerned with the details of the grand plan as Jane might, but evidently she has now taken exception to Luke's many dealings, and wants him out. We'll see. Wilma notwithstanding, Jane may indeed find a way to do so. That would certainly open the way to the City's plan, and my sense is that ABC would hasten to make its peace therewith.

But as things now stand, the time when the Board enjoyed an important role in what is to happen is all but over. Circumstances alter cases, but effectively the Board's fortunes, like those of the residents, lie in the hands of ABC, and ABC's prospects are increasingly at the disposal of the City. It is of course now unlikely that the residents will realize the value of their homes, though it remains to be seen how many will opt for the current offer, and how many will try to return. The letter Deputy Mayor Jackson sent to Councilwoman Sharon Ambrose forcefully contesting some of Joe Austen's assertions at the November 16th meeting certainly shows that that struggle is far from over, but since the City holds, in two or three vacant lots, what ABC most wants, it is hardly the sort of issue that will engage philosophers, and their present aegon makes them sound less like two *hommes d' affaires* than like two boys pushing each other on the curbstone of the pavement (Emerson's image; different context). But there are flashes of daylight, too. Tim, now freed from the burden of defending a plan, has become a good deal less responsive to ABC, and has been working vigorously in the interests of the residents and the Board both. Among other things, a recent memo reminds everyone of a base payment of more than $15 million, that the Cooperative will retain 49% ownership of the Sursum Corda property, and points out that there must be no misunderstanding about the $80,000 payment. "The Agreement contains numerous protections for the residents," he has written recently. "These are the early stages of a long process."

An addition in April...

Now the pace picks up... There is, of course, no end to history, and events continue on at Sursum Corda, though without the sense of possibility that once attended upon them. There is talk that ABC now wants to avoid paying the agreed upon $80,000 to the residents (a figure few had believed), and is seeking legal ways of doing so. More clearly, the Board has engaged the services of several outside agencies, the expensive ones – mainly from Baltimore says Shiv, who has seen the relevant documents – to perform a variety of services. In one case I met members from such a group, which had been engaged to advise residents about home ownership, not simply back at Sursum, but in the very likely circumstance that they could not afford to return to Sursum, then elsewhere in the city. The people I met seemed decent and, in the case of one young man, motivated and even principled, but just as during the past year, the forces that play upon the equation here are both personal and impersonal, and money leads the parade. The young man may be as well-meaning as he pleases, but it is far from clear what effect his efforts will have, or precisely why money was spent to engage his services. The community's increased indebtedness to such groups will of course be cured when the community is itself liquidated, so, probably at least, all the bills will be paid. Let's hope that includes the $80,000 minimally owed to all of the residents who live there, but who deserve at least twice or thrice that sum.

But time and tide wait for no man. On March 15, 2006, the City Council held another public hearing under Chairwoman Ambrose, this one to listen to community and other responses to "The Northwest 1 / Sursum Corda Affordable Housing Protection, Preservation and Production Act of 2006," which would allow the City, as part of its "New Communities" redevelopment plan, to invoke its power of eminent domain, and so obtain the property upon which Sursum Corda stands. The balancing of Northwest 1 and Sursum Corda in the bill's title was notable, and reflected those for and against, though it was difficult to believe that the Sursum Corda spokespersons, many still attached to the discredited deal with ABC, represented the whole community. Those hastening to embrace the City's plan, now represented as Northwest 1's as well, included those who in other times and circumstances might have stood by the community, but found themselves alienated by the events I have been describing here. The City's plan was again represented as the rebuilding of an enlarged community, and as so often the word was used according to its dictionary definition, without the sense of shared values, attitudes and assumptions that in the past at least, have often made it real. A community is certainly being leveled; but what is being built is a connected group of low, moderate and market rate houses and apartments, the market rate houses being intended, as speaker after speaker intoned, to finance the cheaper ones.

A few days before the March 15th hearing a flyer issued by "We Are Family," one of the many new groups now semi-involved in the project, went around Sursum Corda, further supporting the City's "New Communities" initiative. "We are often suspicious of plans to 'redevelop' low income communities," it ran, "as this is often code for removing low-income residents. In this case, however, we have worked side-by-side with the city and other members of the NW One Council over the past two years to get help craft this plan [*sic*]. If adopted, it will ensure that the new housing on North Capitol and M Streets NE will be built first; that ALL of the existing units of affordable housing will be preserved in the end; that all residents will have the right to stay in the community at their current rent; and that new resources will be brought into the community to help lift folks out of poverty. Given the reality of 'big money' encircling our Northwest One area, "We Are Family" believes that this is the ONLY way to preserve your homes, while also using the power of a largely united community and city government to keep outside developers at bay." At their current rent? All of them? The community may at some point be devoured, but at least it appears that ABC will not be the only one to eat it.

Three Months Later...

Nor will they. On July 25 now outgoing Mayor Anthony A. Williams signed into law legislation approved by the D.C. City Council which will give the City eminent domain over Sursum Corda, effectively ending further discussion, except over money and details. Megan Greenwell's story in next day's *Washington Post*, now banished to an inner page of the Metro section, lists what the City has promised to supply: a new neighborhood elementary school (already projected), a new recreation center, a library, a health center. The last two are already present nearby, and if they are rebuilt, surely they should and will serve the whole neighborhood. Of the 1,600 units the City now projects (evidently for the whole project, though the article is unclear on this point), 520 are to be designated for low-income families, the rest to be divided between moderate income and market-rate units. If things go as they should, this number could indeed accommodate all who now live in Sursum Corda (hardly what was proposed under the ABC plan the Board had embraced), and it may not be too much to hope that any who choose to leave will now be offered payment for their seized property. The City expects to attract private developers to the project, and the article quotes Jane Walters, whom it describes as "a former resident who was a major force behind the redevelopment plan," as saying: "It'll have a wonderful effect on the neighborhood."

Later I talk to Shiv about the article and the circumstances it describes. We are both surprised that Lori Montgomery had not written it (and agree that it would have been better informed if she had, but Shiv thinks she may have moved on), and also that the

City had resorted to the threat of eminent domain, which was only possible thanks to the recent Supreme Court decision. But ABC's maneuvering, not to speak of that of the Board, also forced the issue, and it may be that people wanted the whole business resolved before the September election. Shiv expects that both the Board and the City will now each get an appraisal, one high and one low, for the land on which Sursum Corda stands, and that the lawyers will find a number in between. He thinks that individual payments could total as much as $100,000 for those who choose to leave, and that it will be difficult for officials, whether on the Board or elsewhere, to exclude current residents for whatever reason, nor will it particularly be in their interest to do so. We agree again, as we had before, that the present community will probably remain until well after 2010, so as to give the City time to construct the apartments on North Capitol Street and K, into which the remaining residents will be moved, after which Sursum Corda will itself be leveled, and new projects built there.

Now it is December again, and both the semester and this whole business draw toward a close. Tutoring has gone well, and although the real triumphs of a program like ours are connected with learning to read and write well, and so are inevitably private, the social high point may have been when, at the very end of September, a group of the tutors and I took some of our young learners to the National Book Festival on the Mall. Not everyone went, but even so our numbers were large enough so that we broke up into smaller groups of tutors and learners. Two new second-year students, both of whom had developed into excellent tutors over the course of the semester, later described their experiences in their journals. One learner loved the excitement and the Polaroids, but then delighted her tutor by picking up a book and reading on her own, without prompting. "She even said she wished that we never had to leave," her tutor noted. The other tutor's learner was a little more quiet and shy, but later reported that her favorite part was the interactive computer games. The group I was with enjoyed it too, and being photographed with Elmo went down very well, as did the Magic School Bus, when we finally got inside it, the extraordinarily patient scientist-entertainer who worked magic-like experiments to distract us while we were waiting in line, and the general sense of celebration for authors and writing and books. I had been rather hoping to meet John Hope Franklin while we were there, and had even brought one of his books for him to write in, but the logistical requirements of our expedition prevented, and we had, as always, to put first things first.

Meanwhile back at Sursum Corda difficulties continued. A month or so later the City demanded financial information which the Board was unwilling or unable to supply, and then indicated that it was prepared to break off further negotiations with the Board until it did so. In mid-September the Board retaliated in kind by threatening to return to the earlier ABC plan (the threat seemed something of a paper tiger however, since in order to proceed ABC would probably need permits that only the City could supply), but then barred City officials from entering the property on grounds that they had not checked in at the office as was now required, and anyway may have been among those spreading disinformation regarding rental and other charges to community members which the Board was seeking to impose, but which, without HUD approval, were prohibited by law.

Meanwhile Northwest 1, championing the City's plan for the break up not only of Sursum Corda but less contentiously for the area around it, began to attract some residents, one of whom called HUD to complain about some of the new charges. The pushing match thus continued, and November 14 saw another particularly adversarial column in the *Washington Post* by Marc Fisher, which began: "In the concrete cul-de-sac where, for too many years, parents disappeared into a stupor, children sold themselves for a quick high and dealers proved how cheap life could be, there is an eerie peace on the streets. The war has moved into the conference rooms." Earlier in the semester we had been discussing in seminar the way the media's representation of communities like Sursum Corda, and of the poor in America in general, had conditioned the reaction of many members of the class before they set foot in Sursum Corda, and served the interests of the developers as well. Now that lesson appeared again, brought home by the students' new-found familiarity with some aspects of a community they had begun at least to understand, and which Fisher's melodramatic and stereotypical description in no way fairly represented.

At this point, Fisher's notion that what has emerged is a war of conference rooms was both wrong and right. Any moral battle is apparently over, for now at least; what remains is, in Emerson's words, a scramble for money. Thus when the City discovered that, through an accountant's error attributable to management, the community had not filed certain required tax forms for five years it insisted that they do so immediately, and stood ready to impose a fine of $2,000 a day, even though as a non-profit organization the community owed no tax. The speculation that followed turned in the idea that what the City really wanted was gain control of the land on which community stood without having to resort to as politically unpalatable a method as eminent domain, and so to bring the whole matter to a close before Mayor Anthony Williams left office. In the general election of November 7th City Administrator Robert Bobb had been elected the new President of the DC Board of Education, and Council Member Adrien Fenty, mayor of the city. On January 2, 2007 they will both take office, and Fisher's article also reports that Fenty has indicated that in the matter of Sursum Corda he will be advised by a new Deputy Mayor, Neil Albert, replacing Mr. Jackson. Behind all this smoke a consensus may be emerging, and not for the first time, the two sides have begun to look alike.

But as I am writing these words, at least, the community still stands, though for how long remains to be seen. Whether the projected new development, by whomever constructed, will become in time the sort of community that the present Sursum Corda, for all its faults, has so long been, only time will tell. There is of course no requirement in the City's plan for civility, never mind community, and though the projected disparities in income may militate against it, only time will tell. It is at least to the City's credit that it means to resist any tax-driven temptation to opt for unrestricted, high-income development, and to insist that among the market-rate apartments there be space reserved for the less affluent, and the poor.

Toward the end of the year I call a friend about another matter, and we also talk about "the development," as he and many others now call it. He is very happy with the City's plan, which he thinks will be continued under the new City Administrator Dan Tangherlini, and will work out, in that now-familiar phrase, in the best interests of all concerned. In Northwest 1 there said to be are plans afoot to replace 520 units with 1600, more or less equally divided between market rate, moderate and low income families. From the outside the units are to be almost identical, to avoid invidious distinctions, and to obviate any social issues that might otherwise present themselves. The School Board has determined not only to rebuild Walker-Jones School, but also (it now promises) to give the matter priority. Other facilities may be developed as well, and a new, and very welcome, supermarket is already under construction not many blocks away. Shiv is well informed about these and other developments, and knows far more than I now do about the false rumors that, deliberately or not, are now in circulation. Though the City may begin by constructing new apartments for Temple Court residents before it is Sursum Corda's turn, Shiv still thinks that eventually, and sooner rather than later, Sursum Corda will certainly be torn down. He does not seem as resentful as he has been in the past, though he continues to hope that Sursum Corda residents will reject the highly problematic $80,000 that they have been semi-promised for their present homes when they see the newly built apartments rising around them, and opt for one of them instead. I don't really know if he is right, and continue to have my doubts. And of course there is more to come.

6

Mousetrap

Neither a borrower nor a lender be,
For loan oft loses both itself and friend,
And borrowing dulls the edge of husbandry.
–Shakespeare

If the last chapter ended in a kind of victory, it was a pyrrhic one, and everyone associated with it knew that the end was still to be. That realization became general (it was already widely believed), and the Board was now well and truly discredited, so that everyone in the community, it seemed, now wanted a change.

For a short period it seemed as though things might muddle on, but it soon became apparent that the residents would not be satisfied by those who, at least in theory, led them, and only a new election might change the game. In a world of recrimination, anger and contention, a new election was announced, and everything seemed to be finally on the table.

Friday September 26, 2008

Soon after we arrived at tutoring last night, indeed just as I was approaching the steps leading into the community center, one of our young learners rushed up to warn me that there was a meeting of the Board and the residents taking place, and that we should work up on the third floor instead of the second. I went with two of the tutors to collect some books from the closet in the second floor where meeting had just begun, and we set to work in the closer space above, for a focused and what turned out to be a very good session. An hour later the meeting was still going on, and when I went in to return the books, it was obvious that things had become heated. I deposited our books and withdrew, and the next day (today) I called Shiv to find out what happened.

Quite a lot, it seems. Luke had called the meeting at the insistence of one or more members of the Board, who were reluctant to vote for the new agreement with the new developers, both of whom had become involved about a year ago, the result of the City's public offering. The new developers are said to have the reputation of being sensitive to what is sometimes called minority aspiration, and the change went ahead without consultation with the residents, most of whom had no idea what had happened, or what was being planned. In brief, the Board was going to accept an offer of $27 million for the land on which the community now stands, which of course would be leveled as the larger plan was put into effect. The Transfer of Deed would take place in 2010, with the understanding (written and explicit) that the property would be emptied within six months, sometime early in 2011.

From that 27 million would be deducted numerous fees, debts and other obligations, to ABC (now renamed), for a yet unspecified sum, unlikely to be less than 2 million dollars, to FBV (about a million, Shiv thought), and to a number of other persons and bodies to whom money had been promised – about half, Shiv reckoned, perhaps a little more when all was counted. That would leave about $62,500 for each of the remaining families, a good deal more that the $50,000 they had first been promised by ABC, though a lot less than the $80,000 to which the offer had been increased. As it progressed, the meeting had grown heated, though one surprise was that Phil, who had changed sides more than once, did so again, and now, having taken a measure of how things were going, had resolved to cast his lot with the residents.

In the course of all this it emerged that Phil is no innocent, rather he had in the past been a Housing Inspector, knew much about rules and regulations, and had a good sense as to how to proceed. At his suggestion, in the middle of the Thursday meeting, he and Shiv retired to the third floor (the tutors and I had left by that time) and there drew up a Limited Liability Company to protect the in-

terests of the residents. Naturally Luke had objected to this, revealing that there are now 184 residents (a certain number of families
having been recently introduced), and suggesting to the suspicious
that what may have concerned him was that an LLC would make
it more difficult to exclude a certain number of families from the
final settlement. Phil is also said to have a petition signed by 93
residents insisting that the Board not misdirect or misappropriate
any funds received for the sale of the property, and that, once the
legal debts are paid, the rest go to the residents.

We talked too about Shiv's present exclusion from the Board,
an exclusion he had discovered when Tim told him that he would
now need the Board's permission to reveal any information to him
at all. Shiv had decided that the path the Board seemed to be following was not one he wished to trudge, so at the time he was not
much concerned, but at one point last night Phil remarked that,
thanks to ABC, he was no longer welcome to the Board, and when
Shiv replied that the same was true with him, Luke had agreed that
that was so.

Shiv also had remarked, and admiringly, that our friend and
adviser (as he calls her) Christine Nicholson had for the first time
spoken at the meeting, against what it had seemed to her and to
some others that a man who works for Luke was trying to push
through, and had spoken with feeling. But Shiv also remarked
that Luke has a small group of residents who are very much in his
pocket and who do his bidding, and that they had been much in
evidence as well. I suggest that Shiv do what we had talked about
before, and have a talk with Wilma to see where things now stood.
I say not for the first time that he and Phil may need the services of
a lawyer, and wonder if the Harrington Institute might be willing
to become involved, though I have my own doubts that they will.
So does Shiv.

In the end Luke had actually thanked Shiv for his contributions
to the meeting, probably because at one point when things had become difficult Shiv had tried to cool things down by suggesting
that we now had to play the ball from where it was, not where it
might have been. The meeting had broken up shortly before 10pm,
having run for almost three hours. Tim's wife had recently given
birth, so although he was on call, he was not present. As a result

there were no white people involved in the meeting at all, a circumstance that may have contributed to the candor that developed.

Monday September 29, 2008

On Saturday some of the tutors and I took nine of the children to the Book Festival on the Mall, sponsored by the Library of Congress and First Lady Laura Bush, arriving about eleven in the morning to collect our young learners. For the first time I saw that Temple Courts, a K Street high-rise that looks down on Sursum Corda from the next lot over, has now been stripped of its windows and, eyeless, looks gutted and dying. Remembering Michael, born on Christmas day, a bright and lively ten-year-old whom I formerly had tutored, and whom I had more than once visited there, I felt a tug at my heart, even while recalling his and his mother's hard life together. Later, when I mention my reaction to Shiv, he says that seeing the neighborhood buildings being gutted has had a like effect on a number of the residents, particularly those who hadn't really believed that the community was ever going to be razed. He was taken aback the day before, he said, when he saw how far things had gone at Terrell Junior High School on First Street. He hadn't been by for some weeks, apparently, and rather a lot had happened in the interim. But, son of Sursum Corda that he is, he seems not to share my response to what's been happening at Temple Courts.

Traditionally, it was said that there was no love lost between Sursum Corda ("that's where the drugs are") and Temple Courts ("that's where the violence is"), but such contention almost never flourished among the children – or into our program. Boys like Michael roamed freely in Sursum Corda at all times of the day or night – I had first heard of him from a perceptive Carmelite priest who lived for several years in Sursum and even founded a "Carmelite House" there, and who reported the boy as a surprisingly late nighttime visitor. Nor did we turn away from our tutoring program children from Temple Courts who found their way to our door, though in deference to the Sursum officials from whom we took direction, we somewhat preferred it if they had some member of their family – a grandmother, an aunt – who lived in the community. But we rarely stuck at such details. Howbeit, there certainly were drug dealers who operated out of Temple Courts, and openly enough so that the DEA mounted an operation and closed them down – a whole floor had been dedicated to their occupation, it was said, and the whole business had quickly grown far beyond the power of the private management company to address. But during my visits to Temple Courts I noticed a certain guarded sense of community there too. Not among all the residents perhaps, but among those living on a given floor, so that doors were left open and very young children, sometimes at least, circulated from one apartment to the next.

No such permissiveness seemed to obtain at the nearby project known as Turnkey, poised on the land between Temple Courts and Sursum Corda, and built on the model of the Sursum Corda townhouses. Doors were locked, and only opened with a knock; neighbors watched each other, but carefully; and in the twenty odd years that I have sojourned among them, only a very few children from Turnkey ever presented themselves for tutoring. But now the destruction of Turnkey has now begun in earnest, after only a brief pause made necessary, Christine tells me, because the forms indicating the approval of the former residents had not been secured.

The visit to the Book Festival was again excellent – we have been before, missing last year, however, because it conflicted (ahem) with Georgetown's homecoming football game. Our tutors and children cheerfully endured the long line into the Magic School Bus, or marched all the way up to the Pavilion of the States where they obtained stamps on some diminutive US maps there supplied them, which could have been redeemed for a prize, had any accumulated all 50. Another group simply remained at (or near) the Children's Tent, though all groups found time for ice cream and more. But the event had too the effect of confirming to the children our little program's focus on reading and on books, and showing them that adults both old and young (the undergraduates) thought they really mattered. And modest though it may have been, the venture also provided a very good opportunity for the children to get to know, and to interact with, their tutors, who may have been a little hesitant to address matters other than academic in the protected environment of the tutoring room, but quickly understood that here at least they had to be a little more engaged, if only so that we would return with the same number of children with which we set out. In the end we did, with hearts more or less content, and with thanks both to the Library of Congress and to Laura Bush.

Monday October 6, 2008

Last week Shiv came to the first hour of our Wednesday seminar, and again talked to a new group of students about growing up in Sursum Corda, and about his subsequent work in the tutoring program – he spoke with great effect, at least in part because he enjoys the unique distinction of having been both a learner and a tutor. Referring to Sursum Corda, he said he had been "a kid in it" since he was ten, but initially he had not been entirely welcomed there by the other children, and he described the tutoring program as "a life changing experience," a phrase to which I noticed his audience at once responded. It had been to some of them as well. The program he described as having "a colorful history: it was founded by the Jesuits" (quite true), and he himself had "felt comfortable" there, thought he reckoned too that it had been especially helpful to the community in the late 1980's, "when crack came," and by the sense of continuity it provided to the children after Princess Hansen's murder. He spoke a little about Mayor Williams's "New Communities" project, and the effect that was having and was likely to have on Sursum, but did not emphasize the approaching apocalypse, so as to focus on the still-vibrant community which the students now serve. Shiv thought the children unaware about the present state of play; I'm not so sure.

There was a question period afterwards, and in the course of it the question came up about what effect the program had on the tutors (Shiv perhaps is not a typical example), and I said that it seemed to me to change not so much what the tutors think, as what they assume, and in particular what they assume about people who live in such communities. But it often it does more than that. I remember a passage in one of Robert Coles' books where he describes himself as a young psychiatrist being enjoined by an older and more experience colleague to stop fitting his patients into the medical and psychiatric categories he had learned, and rather to regard them as distinct human beings. No doubt I have put the incident too crudely, and it is difficult for me to consider, even on his own testimony, that this greatly admired man (by me among others) would have done any such thing, but I certainly have seen tutors do so. But sometimes a tutor, instructed by the media, will enter our program with self-confidence amounting almost to a fault, only to discover, in the young person committed to his or her charge, a wider and a richer world than the one he or she had hitherto imagined.

Sunday October 12, 2008

I see that I have not written about our new student director, Megan Bush, who began the program last spring, but who quickly distinguished herself by a perceptive and quick eye for the children, and not hers alone, and an evident ability to talk to other tutors, and to carry things through. I had it in mind to ask her if she would like to manage things even before I met her parents, inner-city principals in New York, who visited our little program last spring. Megan has as good a sense of herself as anyone could wish, and as a Junior will be able – if she wants to – to continue next year, when we may, who knows, be drawing to the end, and experience will be particularly helpful. But she is among the most alert and perceptive of students, warm with the children and unobtrusively helpful to some at least of the other tutors. She also drives well, and when I say so she replies that having driven in New York, Washington has no terrors for her. So I am reminded of an incident now many years ago when I and a very able graduate student tutor, Tom, now an English professor elsewhere, were taking two of the children on a little trip. Tom was driving, and, knowing his origins, every time he passed a car the boys would shake their fists in triumph, and shout in unison, "New York driv-ing! New York driv-ing!"

Tuesday October 14, 2008

I forgot to bring the keys to the Community Center to tutoring, only remembering as we were approaching Dupont Circle. We were late starting, the result of a missing van and a consequent rush to find a student car, so there was no turning back (we were late enough already), and I could only hope to find someone with keys once we arrived. But luck was with me, and Christine was not going to bible study this Tuesday, so kindly lent me hers which I promised to return directly. Once we got in it was obvious that recently there had been another meeting of the community: the chairs were in rows, the tables positioned, and it was almost as if another one was about to begin. The tutors found their young learners quickly (in the end we were only about ten minutes late), so once things were coming together I hastened up McKenna Walk to return Christine her keys and have a word about next week, when I will be absent.

However it happened (I am writing about 90 minutes after our conversation and even so cannot remember how we launched upon it), we quickly moved on to the recent meeting, which had brought to a head frustrations, lies and deceptions of recent years. I had noticed when I first came in that she seemed a little distracted – not surprising given both my interruption and the bustle of children about her – but her customary reserve and calm seemed to me a little shaken, and her account of what had recently happened supplied reason for it. The meeting was one of many in which Luke had sought again to secure the written agreement of the residents for one of his many schemes, and increasing these have been distrusted. Christine had spoken at the meeting, forcefully and to the point. She had brushed the representations Luke had posed aside, naming them for what they were, and when his nephew had intervened on his behalf, she had squashed him, too. Then she had announced her departure, and followed by others, had left the room.

She and I had never before spoken as directly about Luke and his exploitation of the community, but now we abandon our customary reserve and spoke candidly to each other, and to the point. She and some others – Phil among then, I suspected, from what she said of him earlier – had been in contact with the FBI, and she also knew a sympathetic reporter on the *Washington Post*, to whom they had promised quite a big story – within two or three months she thought, maybe sooner. "We don't want just to get rid of him," she had insisted. "We want him to leave in handcuffs." She asked if I knew about Tim's connections to Georgetown's Law School, but apart from the fact of his graduation from it I had no idea, though expected he may well know people in the Harrington Institute. I opined that he was responsible to the Board, not to Luke, and though she agreed with that, it was evident that she thought he had not always been an honest broker to the community itself. Luke's mistake was apparently to have played with, possibly, if the report be true, to have embezzled, federal funds – that had enabled the FBI to take an interest in the case, and the result of that, she thought, would soon appear. For whatever it was worth, I offered my support of her, and then, as some of her family appeared, returned to my students.

On the way back to Georgetown one tutor recounted this experience: she had managed a breakthrough with her very young learner, who, after much hesitation, had suddenly begun really to read, and to understand that she could do so. After tutoring, she brought the girl home, who then, as she watched, excitedly showed her new power off, both to her mother (herself a tutee of some years ago) and her grandmother. It seemed not really to register with her mother, who said that it was good and left the room, but her grandmother, knowing better what had come about, broke into tears.

Wednesday October 15, 2008

Times being as they are, I call Shiv to see if he could be on deck – that is, available to the program – on Tuesday next week, when I am away. He can, and I sound him out about community developments. Phil has been after him to talk about Luke, and he has had a word – not more – with Christine, but agrees when I say that my impression is that she has always seen things as we have, but had been necessarily constrained by her position. He thinks Luke tried to fire her after the representations she made in the meeting, to which she had replied, with the directness I have always associated with her, that she does not take kindly to threats. Luke has also been trying to see Shiv, but he has been fighting shy of meeting him. Like Christine, Shiv is also frustrated by Tim, who will communicate only with the Board of which, for unknown reasons, Shiv is no longer a member, though how that happened, or when, he has not been told. But Shiv has also been in touch with KCH again. Ted has promised another offer, and Shiv thinks that it might possibly succeed.

But writing this, I am struck by the fact that this is the first time that Shiv and I have spoken about events at Sursum Corda in anything less than complete candor. True to my promise, I did not report my conversation with Christine, though the tenor of my questions could have suggested that I knew more than I seemed to. But neither, I thought, were Shiv's cards entirely apparent. Honest man that he is, he replied to my questions and suggestions with his usual directness, but I came away thinking without such hints as I had had from Christine much would have gone unsaid. Of this I make less than nothing, but it may be another indication that we are all waiting for some version, or possibly some vision, of the end.

Wednesday November 5, 2008

Today we all have much happiness in now President-Elect Obama's great victory, albeit over a very decent man. It brought joy to my heart and a lump to my throat. I can hardly believe that it is so, and that I have lived to see a Black man elected President, but it is and I have. Of course we will do what we can to get the children to write about it at tutoring tomorrow.

Last night as the tutors were settling in I left the Center and knocked on Shiv's door, partly to thank him for having looked after things when I was away, partly to see what was developing in the community. Much news, none of it very good. Phil has a petition written by Shiv which he, Phil, is to circulate which seeks to dismiss the present Board, but since it needs one hundred signatures to take effect, its success is uncertain. But even if it does succeed it is hard to know what will follow. There is now an offer pending of $25 million for the community, which is the arrangement that might yield $60 thousand (about) per family unit: Luke is trying to get families to move out, Shiv thinks, so as to preserve as much of it as possible for other uses. Meanwhile the offer itself stands to be accepted in about 90 days, hence, I suppose, the petition.

But the difficulty is that Sursum Corda now has begun to appear to developers no longer as a fair damsel to be diligently courted for the advantages she can bring, but as a kind of tar baby, and one to which, once attached, there is no escape at all. Friendly developers have told Shiv that they don't want to get involved, and even the offer that is in hand was made reluctantly, and only because, having acquired many of the parcels of land around Sursum Corda, the developer had to have that one as well. The advice Shiv has been getting has been simply to sell the property outright, and divide whatever profits there may be (at this point he has no idea how much would be left after all parties have been paid). From the beginning there has been the sense that some properties should be reserved for low and middle income tenants, but apparently the definition of such units – to be priced at a stipulated percentage of the median income of the residents – is such that Shiv thinks only a handful would qualify, and he doubts that many or any would take the offer up. No doubt that is now the reality, and indeed the stipulation does seem to have become nothing but a fig leaf, calculated more for reasons of publicity and apparent sympathy, than for any practical effect it might preserve.

Without it, the affair does simplify: to realize what the property will yield, and to divide that amount among the current residents, after an audit has revealed what the outstanding debts are: 6 million for this one, 2 million for that? Meanwhile the only parties engaged in at least putatively strict accounting seem to be the creditors. Perhaps the City (or the HUD of yesteryear?) will insist that some such arrangement be preserved if only to maintain the present policy, but the vision upon which Sursum Corda was founded, inexpensive and well-kept housing for the poor, and particularly for those with children to look after, is no part of that dispensation, if only because, unless changes are made, the income of the present residents would fall below that which would be required to return to the rebuilt apartments.

I have been thinking again, and perhaps more critically, about the newish HUD policy of moving away from Section 8 vouchers, which of course restrict their holders to properties where landlords will accept them, effectively forcing them to live together, embracing instead a kind of twenty-percent solution, in which HUD invests in projects at their inception, so that, say, twenty percent of the units are reserved for low and moderate income residents. The idea has evident and real advantages, since children could be reared in situations where, for example, drugs were neither approved nor (usually) winked at; they could, at least in theory, mix easily with a diversity of families, and not less good than any of these, they could attend schools not reserved for them alone. Certainly I know families where such circumstances would have been most welcome, and where there was everything to gain. As well, such a purchase, such a renting, answers well to the mantra of many a real estate agent, that it is better to buy or rent the least expensive property in a development, than the one most dear.

But why must it be all or nothing? Attractive as this project surely seems, for some it is no such thing at all. For them, the circumstances of ownership are not such as can be easily managed. Others balk at even the hint of condescension that indeed may be, in some such cases, present in the mix. It is not only the rich who do not wish to be encroached upon. Some families want to live not far apart; to find their own way; to choose, as far as possible, their own neighbors; and not to be directed how to live. In an age where, alas, pilotless aircraft can drop bombs thousands of miles away, it should not be beyond human ingenuity to devise a way to monitor and advise, as well as sanction. But these are not propitious times for such an effort. In Washington, all is party now, and preaching. Opposition is the order of the day. When the economy falters, who cares what the causes of poverty may be, or who can make a better future for poor children? Quite overlooked for some much greater cause, without the means or practice to prevail, the poor are easy pickings for the rich, who quite despise them as they pick their bones.

The land in Sursum Corda is its asset: the rich must have it, and pay for it as little as they can. What's needed is help not *in extremis*, but to assist the texture of the place, the very thing the papers most deride. What business does not manage its investment? Well, this is business too. So what's to lose? Don't look right or left, but at the thing. Not that the government should rule the poor, only that it should engage and, as need be, quite prevent such predatory practices as are now too widely present in this industry. These, since usually not illegal, too frequently are unconstrained by law. It really needn't be a party issue. Developers may not care much for the poor, but Christians, Jews and Muslims favor them. Let them say so when it matters. It matters now.

Writing these pages I have observed an evident difference between two great developers, here called ABC and KCH. Throughout, it has been evident that the actions of one, but not the other,
were sometimes, even frequently, informed by considered ethical
judgments, ones based on experience, and by the circumstances
of a case. In their operations (at least from what I saw) they took
a certain care not to deceive the poor, with whom, inevitably, developers in an urban setting work. Their practice (as it seemed to
me) was to be truthful, at least in part because they understood the
advantages that education, wealth had given them over those with
whom they had to deal. They seemed at least to be trying to act eth-
ically – though from what I could tell they did not call it that. But
what they showed most of all was how useful a Code of Conduct
would be. When apartment residents are turned out of their homes
much money is made: and some of it should surely go to them, and
whatever replaces the Section 8 vouchers, too. This was, to be sure,
the plan at Sursum Corda, and the one announced in the *Post* — but
no one quite believed that it would happen. Almost as soon as the
payments, first 50, then 80 thousand dollars were mooted, a question rose: Who, exactly, are the residents? Whatever answer was
proposed, the intent seemed to be to limit the number so as not
immoderately to inconvenience the developer or the Board. Then
reasonably came then the question: Does length of tenure matter,
or is an owner an owner? Do ethics ever matter more than law? In
the real world, I mean.

From what emerged here, the law responds to property and
money -- it's only practice that maintains the common good. But
these practices need a Code of Conduct now, if only to give direction to the willing, and one inscribed by the experienced. I know
this sounds unlikely, but this occupation has a reputation that,
while not in every case undeserved, is largely the result of considering profit first of all, and leaving ethical concerns, should they
arise, to others. Do developers enjoy destroying the homes of the
poor, or simply see it as their occupation? Some shrug their shoul-
ders, and say, That's life. The dog barks, but the caravan moves
on. Some see the wrong, but don't know how to stop it. But in the
end, it's really up to them. When both law and public opinion are
constrained, misled and contaminated, as happened here, the poor

have no defenders. And though much of what I saw was the result of unconsidered practice, greed, arrogance and vanity have played their part as well. A Code made by the willing is needed now, one that will be acknowledged, if not always followed, by those who are involved in these affairs. In the end, that might be better than a law.

Or put it this way: single and married persons, if young enough, can wander as they will, but age and children need a sense of place, and if Section 8 vouchers, popular neither with HUD nor with landlords, have really had their day, the need they answered has hardly disappeared. And speaking realistically, many who hold them are versed neither in real estate law nor in management, though their interests, and certainly those of their children, are also those of the State. Against all this, what can these pages do? Most parents, rich or poor, much love their children, and very often do as best they can; though sometimes not. But in Sursum Corda the poor have made a place to live in. We brought them here as a convenience to the rich, to preserve property values elsewhere, so must admit their independence now. And though we no longer forbid the poor to read, or publish, or enter the professions, the centuries we did so left their mark, and changing that needs a metaphysical snow plow, but one shaped like a scalpel.

I return to the Center to look for Kathy, the seven-year-old for whom we had no tutor but who kept coming until our informal tutorials became regular, but she is not there and I talk instead to a somewhat older boy, once in the program, about changing schools. The tutors have been encouraging their children to write about Halloween, but there is of course a greater event on everybody's mind, the expectation of the one with which I began this entry, and I leave the van more hopeful than apprehensive. Would that I felt the same for Sursum Corda, too.

Friday November 14, 2008

Last night before tutoring I call by to invite Shiv to our end-of-semester Christmas party, but he is at a work-related meeting and I chat instead with his wonderful mother who is concerned about the next step for one of her daughters, now finishing high school. Later Shiv calls me at home.

His mother had mentioned that he had been talking with the Board's lawyer, so getting involved again with the whole business, and was a little worried that it would somehow be used against him. But Shiv says the conversation had been perfunctory: the man had no doubt rightly declined to discuss anything with Shiv that he would not at once reveal to the Board whom he serves, and could hold no opinion on the petition demanding Luke's ouster. That document, with ninety-nine signatures Phil obtained, had that very day been turned over to the Board, which at once acquainted Luke with its contents. The Board now has ten days to reply, or to call a public meeting, but the wagons seem to be drawing into a circle: Wilma, again the President, agreed to meet with Shiv to discuss where things stood, but in the event did not do so.

Not long before we spoke, Shiv had encountered Luke on his way home, and asked if his signature was indeed on the document. It was. He seemed a little perplexed, but generally unfazed. He holds still, Shiv thinks, to his plan to obtain $150 million from a hedge fund (evidently one he knows about? Does anybody else? It stinks) to become in effect his own developer, though when Shiv told Tim about the plan Tim let slip that the Board had heard about it already, and had discouraged him from pursuing it. I ask if he had thought of contacting our old friendly enemy the *Washington Post* about the petition and he had, emailing Lori Montgomery only to be told by return that she now works on other things, but offering the name of one of her colleagues, who later contacted Shiv directly. But by then (all this must have happened very quickly and recently) Shiv had talked to Ted at KCH who had counseled patience, and suggested that the City, HUD and the new developers all had an interest in the proceedings, and that less noise might be better than more. It is the end game, after all, that matters now. I have my doubts, and am all for being open, but recollect that Shiv and I have somewhat different hopes and expectations for the outcome: he very honestly and with no small amount of courage wants the best deal the residents can obtain, so that, though driven from the homes they fairly own, they at least can realize the best return on them, the better to defend what is to come. I on the other hand am captured still by the vision that Fr. McKenna and the other founders shared, for a community of the poor and disadvantaged responsible to no one but themselves: it is too weak to speak of right and crime. But then Shiv sees on his caller ID that Phil is trying to reach him, and we agree to talk again over the weekend.

After visiting with Shiv's mother I had returned to tutoring, but dear Kathy, who does not live in Sursum Corda though her grandmother does, has not appeared, and I defer the little lesson I had prepared. But it proves to be an excellent session, quiet, focused and on task. Really the best sessions are the ones when I have nothing much to write about.

Afterwards I try to consider what Luke has in his mind. The idea that he can – through a hedge fund! – become the developer seems so outré that I wonder if he really understands everything that has transpired – with the City, with HUD, with the developers – or if I do. The perception that he has been trying to use Sursum Corda as a giant ATM machine is now so general that it is easy to see why a petition calling for his removal was as successful as it proved, and yet difficult to see who he expects to stand with him, except perhaps for the present Board, and a handful of residents whom he has recruited for the purpose. Emerson again. It's become a scramble for money.

Tuesday November 18, 2008

The front door to the community center was locked when we arrive at tutoring, and I retrieve the key from Christine and then return it, afterwards putting my head in to have word with Shiv, whose difficulties have not grown less. After Luke had accosted him about the petition, Luke's relative, Paula Knox, had done so too, asking why he had signed it. When he cited the lack of any meaningful communication from the Board she had agreed, but said, in effect, Well, yes, but even so. But this is no answer, and Shiv points out how, at the very beginning, when it was still possible to do so, he had championed an independent plan, but Luke had scotched it, in favor of the very dubious deal, as it now transpires, with ABC. Too much water now has gone under the bridge, he thinks, to change things now. Shiv has also talked to Wilma's son, and understands that she is now convinced by Luke's new plan. Shiv had remonstrated with the young man, reminding him how Luke had effectively turned his mother out of office when it suited him to do so, and wondered why she trusts him now, but she does. Finally Phil has been pursuing him, seeking an assurance of his support, and not minding how in the past his own had somewhat wandered.

Meanwhile the Board's ten days to respond to the petition are up on Sunday, and between now and then a community meeting must be called – or so Shiv thinks. Tim, whom Shiv still much respects, knows as much and, though he keeps Shiv at arm's length, may yet effect one. Under the present circumstances HUD's rules trump those of the Board, and Tim knows it. We talk about the possibility of the residents obtaining a lawyer, if only to present the petition to HUD effectively, and Shiv seems to have some good leads. I wonder again about the possibility of more openness. Shiv has also been talking to Ted, who has been helpful, but who had advised him to talk to Tim, another dead end. As we talk Kavir, Shiv's very dear little son, not yet two, has been sleeping on some pillows at his feet, but now wakes up and without a word climbs into his father's lap. Shiv kisses him, and he silently watches us with wide, gentle eyes.

Afterwards I return to the community center, where Kathy has at last appeared. We work together with Lou, a friend of hers, and write a letter to President-Elect Obama, which turns into a somewhat complicated task. I have discussed with the tutors the importance of retaining their learner's "ownership" of the texts they write, and particularly those we print in our little "literary magazine." This can be a little complex, because I also urge them to be sure nothing appears that, from meaning or expression, would embarrass its author, and so to be attentive to such matters as grammar, sentence structure, and spelling, as well as to content. There is nothing wrong with suggesting topics – but not ideas – though this, experience has shown, many tutors are reluctant to do.

Kathy in particular needs little assistance: she jumps on the project, beginning with schools and President-elect Obama's daughters, but in due course turns to Senator McCain, asking the President-elect to help find him "some work," evidently believing that, having lost the election, he will now need to find gainful employment. She asks me if he was nice to the president-elect, and remembering the moment toward the end of the campaign when he had replied "No, Ma'm, he isn't," to the woman who had asked if then-Senator Obama was not in fact an Arab, taking the microphone from her hands as he did so, I say that he has been. But they are even more interested in helping the homeless, now in evidence around Sursum Corda, for whom they ask his help. After some discussion and revision then, this is what emerges:

Dear President Elect Obama,

Hi! Isn't it wonderful to be President at last? We were wondering how you are going to make the schools better? In D.C. and in the U.S.A. too. We think our uniforms could be lots better, and we could have less homework too.

We love your daughters, and invite them and their mom to come to Sursum Corda so we can meet each other and be friends. You can come too, but if you're too busy, it's ok.

Also, can you please, please, help the homeless because they are homeless and hungry. And it won't be fair if we have a home and they don't. And we really mean this. Please help them. Thank you.

And can you help Senator McCain with some work? Even though we were very, very glad you won, we thought at the end he was nice about you.

Also (this is Kathy now) when the TV said you won, my mom jumped right off the couch and said "Obama won! Obama won the election! Yeaaah!"

Your friends,

Kathy and Lou

Tuesday November 25, 2008

Shiv called last night to say that he had received a registered letter requiring him to present to the Board proof of the putative allegations present in the petition at a meeting of the residents called for December second. (Other residents had been informed of it by a circular.) Shiv now reads me the petition, and I offer the praise it deserves, though I also think it might have said somewhat less than it did. There is also to be a meeting of certain of the residents who support the petition next Tuesday night, Shiv says. This is the Tuesday before Thanksgiving, when we won't be tutoring because experience has proved that too many of the tutors (ahem) will already have left for home, and their absence causes difficulties with their children. Shiv believes that the letter he has received might amount to intimidation, and though I am not sure that this is so, I am at least very glad to hear that he has at last contacted a lawyer. If the registered letter achieved nothing it achieved this, that Shiv now seems to understand that the whole business cannot be resolved without tears. He wonders if he should call the Board's lawyer again to see if he will discuss things, and I express doubts, saying that my sense is that he really can't, that it probably would not be ethical for him to do so. Shiv's regard for the man is again apparent, and not surprising: he is certainly what the British would call a very decent young man (I show my age), like Shiv a young new father (a bit older), and, again like Shiv, with a clear-eyed understanding both of what has been going on, and of the character of those involved. I try to say, probably not forcefully enough, that though he certainly need not think of the man as an enemy, he probably should conceive of him as a possible adversary, at least for the present.

We also wonder if Chris Martin, a senior partner in the same law firm, is entirely out of the picture, even though he is not much in evidence. It was he who had drawn up the first $50K per resident offer, and has certainly left the impression of believing, alas like many others that the residents – really the owners – should shut up, sign where they're told, and get out of the way of progress. Then, as he is about to hang up, he remarks that Luke is again trying to get Christine fired, urging ABC simply to eliminate her position. He's not yet got an answer back, however. We agree to talk again after the Tuesday meeting.

Wednesday November 26, 2008

The meeting was a small affair, consisting of Shiv, Phil, Christine and two long-term residents whom I don't know, but who feel strongly that the community is being defrauded. They discussed things, deferring to Shiv (whom they came regard as the leader, he somewhat nervously reports). But what's Phil's role to be, I ask? To keep the residents' support, Shiv gently says. They discussed strategy: Shiv had wanted to contact Wilma again, and see if she would be willing to at least talk to him, but the group first advised and then voted against it, and Shiv agreed to defer to their collective judgment. Among the narratives they took up was one of Christine's: some time since (but apparently not so very long ago) she had spoken to an associate of Luke's who had been with him when he had cashed a check said to have been donated to Sursum Corda by some unnamed charity (or person?), and who claimed that he had been paid $1,000 for allowing the check to pass through his account. Since then the man says that he has not felt at one with himself, knowing that whatever he had done was far from right, but reluctant to report it for fear that the whole business would somehow redound on him. Christine had thought his regret was real, and that he might in due course speak about it. I sympathize, but have doubts.

Like anyone who has followed these affairs, Shiv's account echoed things I knew already, though I had never heard of them before. I also understood what Christine had meant when she said that she wanted to see Luke leave Sursum Corda "in handcuffs," as though here at least was a simple and obvious crime, and one not subject to mitigating explanation. As with Augustine's apple, the issue was the will, though the chump change involved bespeaks not only greed, but also the easy contempt of a confident thief for his victim. I have known Luke now for years, and have in the past responded myself to his ready reply, his evident, if never quite believable, openness of manner, his reasoned propositions. But recently I have been reading Claire Tomalin's life of Samuel Pepys, and have been struck by the sense that there is something of Pepys in Luke – or perhaps the other way – though Pepys, for all his engaging self-love, had not exactly what seems to be Luke's sense of entitlement.

In all of this, however, I am concerned that Shiv has no higher authority to whom he and his new group may yet appeal (they seem, after all, to be urging an entrenched Board simply to dissolve), and suggest again that HUD or the City somehow be involved. We both have some doubts about HUD, Shiv because of past experience of them, me because I fear that they will not want to reopen old wounds, so that even in the unlikely circumstance of certain of its members regretting their past behavior, they may choose instead to look the other way. The City's administration having now turned over, I gather Shiv has lost some of his contacts there, though he says that he has others, but Luke does too, with some of whom, Shiv thinks, he still plays golf, a story I somewhat doubt. But the City has its own plan for the shaping Sursum, and doesn't fear its formerly noble past. We don't speak of such things, however, and I only remind Shiv that there must be a lawyer at the December second meeting, if not Tim than another, and he agrees. December second may prove a lively time: the resident's meeting will begin at 6pm, and an hour later the tutors will appear. This has happened before, and when it has we have been banished, willingly enough, to the third floor, where the cramped quarters have induced the simple expedient of sitting on the floor, a practice that detracted from our lessons not at all. Only an immediate lack of books did, locked in the second-floor closet as they were, so we interrupted long enough to grab a few. And Tuesday next all that may come again, and – who knows – more besides.

All this matters because it now appears that things are not quite as final as they appeared to be. Shiv has learned that the developer's offer of 27 million dollar appeared only in a letter of interest, and that the putative agreement is in principle only. It will take another vote of the community before the promised destruction can begin. That is what has been keeping Luke active, and as ABC has begun, apparently at least, to put some distance between themselves and him.

Later, recollecting what has come about, I am pleased that there is some agreement concerning Shiv's evident virtue, and also, when one might believe the dye is cast, a larger sense that there is more to do. It was not always so. A hint of inevitability is probably always present when the rich confront the poor, and be the poor ever so well ensconced – in their own homes, for example – rapaciousness will often find a way. But Shiv's honesty and perseverance, Christine's decision not to be lied to yet again, Phil's, I don't know, resolve to see the whole thing through, commend themselves. One of Emerson's great questions was whether, faced with someone like Napoleon, moral categories could yet apply. There's no such here. Long live this little village. Power can license outrage, not contain it. We live our lives on sliding surfaces.

Tuesday December 2, 2008

In the event the meeting went very well indeed, though Shiv thinks, rightly as it seems to me, that the Board has by no means folded its tents. No lawyers were present in spite of my best efforts, and probably a good thing too, though Tim's absence is a little curious. But Wilma, as President, began the meeting by saying, in effect, now let's hear about those allegations, but Shiv intervened to say, in effect, No, let's just agree to new elections instead, and, evidently speaking for the Board, Wilma agreed. The date was set for December 18th, and it was only then that Shiv pointed out to the Board members that, having now served three terms, they could not stand again. Surprise and alarm, but no consternation, which points to the conclusion that noting was really written in stone – in Leo Deroucher's immortal phrase, it ain't over 'til it's over.

Such expedition did not prevent the meeting from lasting two hours, though Shiv reports that no one got out of hand, and in spite of some little acrimony evident when we were leaving tutoring, the victory, for now at least, seems to have been more or less complete. When we arrived they had been in discussion for about an hour, and though we taught on the third floor, we had to gather up some of our books in order to do so, and these were locked in a second floor closet. Passing through the meeting it was impossible not to take the temperature, particularly when an older man in the audience, pointing towards the lectern, said pointedly, "No one's disrespecting anyone, but we all think that..."

And this: after the meeting Luke tells Shiv that he has spoken to a man from KCH. "Well, what did he say," Shiv asked. "Exactly what you told him to," Luke returned. "As if," Shiv says later, "I could tell KCH what to say." But he allowed too that, by the end, both sides were deferring to him, and it seems to me quite possible that Shiv has become the *de facto* leader of the community, at least unless the present Board finds a way to claw back what they certainly seem to have surrendered.

Thursday December 4, 2008

I call Shiv to invite him to our end-of-semester Christmas party (tonight) at the Community Center, which will begin traditionally, with the presentation by one of the children of a gift to Christine, followed by the children reading from their contributions to the little *Sursum Corda / Georgetown University Literary Magazine* that we produce, and then by a party of cake, cookies, etc. This year the magazine, produced in a press run of 200 copies, will be dedicated to President Elect Obama, whose name will also feature on the Christmas cake, bought from Safeway. Shiv says that he can and will come, but then reveals that already the Tuesday meeting already has begun to unravel: Tim has told the Board that, in spite of the by-laws, they can indeed run again, because there is no law in the District of Columbia forbidding them to do so. No one knows if this is true, and Shiv has been seeking another lawyer out.

Shiv also solved the apparent mystery of Ted having called Luke: he did no such thing. Rather Ted had called Tim, offering an opinion about the way recent events are being perceived among some developers, and Tim had reported the call to Luke, who then fabricated the story of Ted having called him. No wonder he couldn't tell Shiv what Ted had "said" to him, and simply said "what you told him too," when asked. So perhaps Shiv's position isn't quite as secure as I had begun to believe, though I think it may be moving in that direction. And at least the election still stands, and still for December 18th.

Friday December 5, 2008

The party went as well as ever it could, and both the Safeway cake and the literary magazine arrived when they should have. As custom has it, we began by presenting Christine with Christmas gifts in imperfect acknowledgment of her help and support over the past year, a study bible, and exactly the edition she'd been looking for, she told me this morning, and some Godiva chocolate for the coming winter. She had responded with a short talk directed to the tutors, a model of felt brevity, which set the tone for our reading, which then began.

Doug Whence, an American Studies major who writes for the student newspaper and is on a club baseball team, proved to be an excellent MC, urging the children to come forward with their tutors and read aloud their contributions to the just-published literary journal. With varying degrees of enthusiasm they did so, some almost in a whisper, some so very quietly that their tutor took over the duty for them. But this year as in the past, the readings went splendidly: the children were attentive to their colleagues, went (for the most part) dutifully to their own, and basked in the applause. For many, the experience of writing something of their own, albeit something based on another written text, and then seeing it attended to by others, was a real one, and gave as good and clear a closure to the semester as anything we could devise. This time again it seemed to me to invest with significance and power the written word, to draw our little authors into a fellowship of the literate, and to show than, better than any words of ours could do, the meaning and the purpose of our work together.

Thanks to Doug, the reading went expeditiously and well, and 45 minutes saw us done. The party followed, and decorum rushed out the door. Gifts and laughter and noise were general, no bad thing to be sure, except that it was only when the reading was over, the party begun, that some of the parents and other care-givers appeared, and I wondered if they thought it was always thus. When I offered a tentative apology, however, it was brushed aside, and I was thanked in no uncertain terms for the difference the tutors had brought.

Shiv however stood us up (yet again, I almost want to write), but then so did all the former tutors I had invited. No great surprise. The point of what we do is not that they should ever visit us, but that both tutors and children should indeed move on, perhaps taking with them, if with an effort, a memory of what we sought to do. Later Shiv says that he had a meeting in Maryland he had forgotten about; that the lawyer's point about D.C. Law allowing the present Board to run again may not have been mistaken, and that, though still lawyer-less, he is trying to arrange a slate for the election.

I hope I have not represented us as fiddling while Rome was yet aflame, and have not forgotten the larger storms that rage around this place. But my purpose in all of this has been to show, or at least to testify, that things connect, that the greedy and the innocent, newspapers and football heroes, undergraduates and developers, murderers and children, the poor and the State, are all involved together. In the events I have been documenting here they depend upon each other, so much so that such personal forces have a voice at the mercy of impersonal ones, but these in turn depend upon those voices, written and spoken, that are finally the reason for our little program.

Sunday December 14, 2008

Last week Shiv had emailed me a copy of a *Washington Post* article "Building on Broken Promises," that detailed the real estate dealings of former D.C. City Council member H. C. Crawford, who had used public money (more than $8 million in one instance alone) to renovate housing projects, employing means, and securing ends, that were by no means above reproach. Among other things, he made deals for friends, offered inducements that sounded very like bribes, and, through an intermediary, convinced renters that if they relinquished their tenancies they would one day return as owners, but the properties he constructed were beyond their reach.

As Shiv had pointed in an accompanying email, the parallels with Sursum Corda were obvious. A contract to install 10 Dell computers at Sursum had come to $20K; a Home Buying Counselors firm, which nobody had objected to at the time because it had been represented that their presence was a HUD requirement, had been budgeted at $1million, but ABC had balked at the price; and the security firm "Fruits of Islam of Baltimore" has been paid $64,000 a month, an extraordinary fee, in spite, to tell the truth, of the evident courtesy and good cheer they bring with them.

Earlier today Shiv and I have brunch at the Daily Grill in Georgetown, which, as it has before, proved a good time to discuss things before Thursday's now crucial vote. The importance of the election had become apparent to Shiv in another meeting with the Board last week, evidently called to clarify things, wherein each side finally appreciated how entrenched the other was. Indeed my sense was that Tim's willingness to have a new election in the first place may have rested on a belief that the general plan was now finally in place, though that of course is exactly what Shiv and his colleagues now mean to contest. Shiv now considers that the first order of business after the election may have to be to fire Tim's firm as well as Luke, and to have an audit – always provided that the result of the election is what is hoped for. We talk, not for the first time, about what can be secured for the individual families from the community, and Shiv thinks that individual payments could exceed $150,000, if things are done right, since he doubts the $16 million debt figure (to ABC , FBV, etc.) that Tim keeps advancing. This would of course be a very great help for the current residents – 171 families, Shiv now thinks – and far, far more than they are likely to receive otherwise. Fifty thousand, I guess, not more. But Shiv thinks the figure could be as low as fifteen, with Luke offering to cut such a check for an individual family only if it will leave in, say, three days. Many, most, all, would very probably accept, if only to be done with it, and for fear of the Board's lawyers, who they will never beat. Shiv has been talking to Ted at KCH, and some of this thinking comes from him, who has always felt that the "new apartments for residents" argument was a sham, and indeed as we came to understand this thing the sense that fewer and fewer residents will actually be able to remain is increasingly obvious. Thus Shiv has come to believe that a very large one-time payment is a much more realistic prospect for the great majority of residents than the plan, which no one now believes, to rehouse a certain number of them in apartments few of them will finally be able to maintain.

Such an arrangement is only possible because Sursum Corda is a cooperative – the residents are actually owner-residents, and so, until the present Board sprang into action, had certain clear legal rights, which they were effectively persuaded to surrender. In other circumstances, in other places, it might be difficult to make the same arrangement, if only because the residents would not enjoy the property rights present, or semi-present, here. But of course, speaking morally for a moment, that is exactly what should happen. The poor are being driven from their homes to suit the rich – but if there is enough money to level and rebuild their homes, there is also enough money actually to support them elsewhere. It is the love of profit, and not financial necessity that prevents them from being treated fairly. It is just possible that their legal rights are, strictly speaking, being observed, but their human rights are not. As a general rule, ejected residents will not have access to a meaningful legal defense, and, as we have learned too often, HUD's support cannot be relied upon. The ground is thus laid for intimidation: take your children and go. This is our property now. Are you still here? Still upset? Hard cheese. It's the law, don't talk to me of justice, of equity. Even if we have been guilty of wrongdoing, you'll never prove it. Not in our legal system.

The amount Shiv and I have talked about in the past – $100,000 more or less – seems about right now, perhaps a little high, but given the saturated condo market that obtains in Washington just now, probably ok. There is of course nothing magic about the number, and in five years' time, depending upon circumstances, it could be more – or less. It is not just inflation that matters, but also what actually is available.

In the midst of all of this, I ask Shiv if the more direct sale will mean that the community would be razed any sooner (I ask with our little program in mind), but he doesn't think so, though he admits that since the land is to be sold and the money distributed to the residents without any middle state, it might. But the present semi-proposal, even as now projected, seems to be a sham and a delusion. Few if any – I think none -- of the present residents would be in a position to take it up, and the effect would be to buy them off cheap, and to argue that really, it's their fault. We talk about the failed morality everywhere apparent, and agree that no one will ever admit that they were guilty of wrongdoing, even to themselves. I at least am prepared to believe that Luke may have begun with good intentions, and we both agree Tim did, though neither of us thinks he has them now. Shiv now agrees with me that there may be those in Tim's law firm who are influencing things, but we both know it doesn't matter if they are.

Shiv tells me that at the recent meeting, the designer of the new community was present too – Shiv thinks he may be paid both by ABC and the Board – and his jaw dropped, Shiv thought, when it suddenly became apparent to him that all the ducks are not in a row, and that the monies only apparently dedicated to the development of his grand design may yet find their way into the hands of the owner-residents instead. That brings us to the new HUD plan that involves placing the poor in apartment complexes really operated by and for the rich, what effectively had been the plan for Sursum residents, and having observed one such arrangement already in place in Washington, Shiv confirms my doubts. Not only is it well known who the poor are, but their voting rights at resident meetings are affected; the appointments within their apartment units are intentionally made inferior; their names are known. The argument is sometimes advanced that such things may be true, but it will be better for their children anyway. Could anything be more foolish – the question answers itself.

As I am writing this Shiv calls to say that a friend of his from Georgetown, now himself a lawyer, has received approval from his firm for 400 hours of *pro bono*, to be directed by the senior attorney in the office who deals with real estate law, while he himself does the day-to-day. If Tim decides to leave after the election, he points out, at least we will have someone to put in his place, and I am struck again at how Shiv has grown over these past five years, so that he now understands what is going on better than I do, and has by no means relinquished his moral compass, so that his actions are at one with his beliefs, and both work to the advantage of the residents.

Throughout our brunch we had talked, and not briefly, about the trajectory the whole business has followed, really since 2005, if not before. By the end of 2006 the community was effectively sold and delivered, and the darker purposes of the Board all but accomplished. Some of those who once worked with one or other of the older boards, or for the management firms, have begun to sense what now is going on, and some of these rejected ones are beginning to pick up their weapons once again. I tell Shiv, not for the first time, about this little addition to my journal, and again make sure he understands what I mean. But together we realize too that now, after a year and a half of silence, things are again in play, and that has been the work of this good year. It seems just possible that HUD, the City, the developers, the Board and Luke may not, in the end, effectively divide the profits from the sale of the community among themselves. Alas, this refuge for the poor and for their children will surely die, but at least it may not drag down its current residents with it, who may instead, we'll see now, take both good heart, and what amounts to damages, away with them. *Laus Deo.*

Following the meeting with the Board and residents, Shiv meets again with his small group. At the larger meeting he had agreed with Tim not to pursue the matter of the petition since it would all be decided by the Thursday elections. Phil, who circulated the petition with considerable effort, is irritated thereat, and thinks he might well have not done so. Shiv understands that there could be a problem here, but hopes to placate him, at least in part by taking him to a meeting with the City that he has set up for Wednesday, a good idea in any case. We agree that he must explain the new arrangement to the City, so that it will be seen as a pro-residents proposal, and not simply as one to let the Board and the City off. Shiv also hopes, what seems to me an excellent idea, to convince the City to run the elections on Thursday, since he no longer trusts anyone to do so. We talk again about arrangements for the election. Phil is against the idea of running a slate since he knows that there are some residents – those whom Luke has brought down from Baltimore, for example – who are against him in any case, and will equally vote against any associated with him. Shiv has heard that someone opposed to the present Board is going to circulate a flyer, and I approve the effort. Still, an opposition is forming. Apparently – not certainly – Wilma may be the only one from the Board to run again, though I am far from sure that this will prove so. But others will take their place, this one's nephew, that one's daughter, so that the Board can thus perpetuate itself   It's only to be expected.

Wednesday December 17, 2008

Shiv calls about 9:30pm with news about the meeting he, Phil and one other colleague had with the City, which seems to have gone very well ("amazing," is his word). Shiv had arranged it through the office of the Deputy Mayor, and met with two representatives. They seem to have spoken with great candor, and Shiv had explained the new arrangements to these representatives of the City, which embraced them, and then had been particularly hopeful that the new, higher amount (that is, in excess of $100,000 per household) might be realized. They seem too to have understood that only a handful of the residents could have been accommodated in the newly projected buildings, and even those few, in many cases, briefly. They cleared up one point nicely, however: the City never began to implement eminent domain, and has no plans to do so. Shiv was greatly pleased, and though any such action had always seemed to me a non-starter politically, I hastened to agree. I try to be hopeful, I later consider that the amount of money they are expecting for the individual residents may be unrealistic.

We discussed tomorrow's elections, and not without a little trepidation. Shiv asks me to come and count the ballots, and I agree, even though it is far from clear that we will succeed. I sing again my lawyer-song, and insist that we must have one, someone who knows the City code this way and that. I insist, I plead, Shiv somewhat agrees. But I realize that he has been talking again with to the Board's lawyer, partly to understand what needs to happen tomorrow, but they seem to have connected in other ways as well. He is concerned that, for the first time, the man seemed to him afraid of something, and, though sure of the law – or at least the D.C. Code – less happy at what his own part may prove to be. I sympathize with the young man, whom we both like, and reformulate my objections to say that, very sadly, under the present circumstances, the Board's lawyer perhaps cannot have the best interests of the community at heart, but only those of the Board. Shiv agrees, but rightly insists that he knows things we don't, for example that the quorum of 57 must be present tomorrow for the election to be valid, that absentee ballots must be separately and formally applied for (which means effectively that there will be none), and that the Board's Secretary can decide who is in good standing, who not, and as a result who actually can vote. Paula, Luke's relative, holds that office, and for that reason, among others, I urge as many City officials, able lawyers and others as possible be invited to attend, and that in any case, our side must prepare, prepare, prepare. Shiv agrees that we shall talk again tomorrow (about 10am), and I suggest that he postpone a dentist appointment he has for tomorrow so as to concentrate on the business at hand, and he is very willing to do so.

Thursday December 18, 2008
12:30pm.

As we agreed last night, Shiv and I talk twice on the phone, at 10 am, and then, when that proves inconclusive, again at noon, but in a city awash in lawyers, it seems there are none to be had. The one Shiv and I had been hoping for has declared himself engaged, though Shiv considers that he may know Tim, and not want to oppose him. Another lawyer-friend has a reception he must attend, though he promised to see if he could secure a colleague to come to the meeting, without success, as it transpires.

Friday December 19, 2008

The meeting, which took place last night on the same second floor of the community center where we tutor the children, could not have gone better, though it hardly seemed so in the beginning, as tempers flared about who could and could not vote, and whether the newly enacted regulations had actually been promulgated. In fact, they had. It was hard not to sympathize with Tim, however, who bore the brunt of some simply uninformed accusations, and in the end accepted such arrangements as the residents there present came to agree upon. I do not think the depredations of protocol were many, since the residents had a way of looking over each others' shoulder, and, as a general rule, seeing who should have voted, so that no one did so more than once, and usually it was the head of the household who cast the ballot. No doubt there were some irregularities – though fewer than in many an election – but the result, when it came, was so clear that there could be no doubt that it was indeed the voice of the people.

The ballot had eleven names on it, and there were nine places on the Board. The meeting, scheduled for 6pm, finally got underway about 6:30, by which time most of the residents had filled their ballots in, and after an opening prayer (largely for peace) and some discussion, a Reverend West, pastor of a nearby Church, and I were appointed to count the votes. He is a tall, formal man, with a fine ringing voice, which was perfect for the occasion. The residents remained attentively in their seats as we counted, he opening each ballot and reading it out, as he and I marked it down independently. The process took an hour and more, but in the end the transparency was such that no one contested the result.

And the result was devastating: most of the candidates received between 50 and 60+ votes. Phil had the most, Shiv came an equal 5th but two of our chief adversaries were in the mid-twenties, by far the lowest of the low, and so utterly repudiated by the residents. What they had in common, of course, was unwavering support for Luke, whom a great majority of the residents thoroughly distrust. But about Wilma, if not exactly for her defeat, I had nothing but regret. It was for her, in her youth, that Sursum Corda had been built, and for her it had, over thirty years, done rather a lot. The single young mother who is constrained to send her young children to bed hungry, but had at least a bed to send them to, was what gave this place its reason and its virtue, as I have said before, perhaps too often. But the vote and the voice was the community's, as decisive, clear and as final as it could be.

After the election Shiv kindly gave Tim and me a ride to our respective homes – it was cold and damp, we were both grateful. Tim knows that he has been identified with the old Board, and wants to make amends, or perhaps to have his actions and obligations understood – he not unreasonably thinks that his actions may not have been entirely understood, though he certainly seems to me to have acted as he was obliged to. My sense is that he will indeed continue, if only because his skill set is precisely what the new Board will need most of all.

And now it is evening, and I have talked to Shiv about the day's events. The new Board has met and elected its officers: Phil is in charge, Shiv Treasurer, but Jessica, a carryover from the old Board, is number two, and personally, for some reason, is opposed to Shiv, based on a family rivalry, Shiv says, though he does not know what caused it. Shiv wants to inform residents about the options they have, whether for sale or placement, but Jessica will have none of it. The only agreement was to dismiss Luke, and Tim will draw up a notice of dismissal, which may be served as early as tomorrow. But at least the City is pleased with the new leadership, and hopes to meet with them in January. And so it begins again.

Sunday January 4, 2009

Sometimes things actually do improve. I was away from Washington over Christmas, and returning, again called Shiv to see what was happening. All is motionless until the holidays have past, but there was one development. After the Board's first somewhat fraught meeting, Shiv had spoken to Phil about his difficulties with Jessica, and Phil seems to have understood that such tensions were no help at all. He talked to her as Shiv did afterwards, and the difficulty seems to have been that Jessica had come to believe that Shiv was on Luke's "side" in all that has gone before. Whether this is the result of Luke's representations or Jessica's blinkered incomprehension is hard to say, but whatever else it may be, it is certainly another example, if any was needed, of the way mistrust and rumor, a lack of information and outright lying, have all but steered events here, really for the last three years, if not more. There is simply no one who has done more to represent the best interests of the present residents and to confront the previous Board, of which Jessica, of course, was a member. Perhaps she had reservations about Luke's performance in office – the vote to remove him as COO was unanimous, after all, and in thirty days, it is hoped, he will either leave or be evicted from his rent-free house – but if a Board member understood so little of what actually was going on, how many of the residents have been adequately informed? A handful, starting with Phil, seem to have become so, but what has really ruled here was insecurity and doubt (perhaps not entirely vanished), a lack of any hard information, which, when mixed with threats and blandishments, lent power to the unscrupulous.

But Shiv believes that he and Jessica have reached an accommodation, enough at least to permit them to work together. Time will tell. Meanwhile Phil has been in conversation with Luke, Wilma and Paula, whom he described as "upset" by the outcome of the election – but wanting most of all to be allowed to retain the community-owned laptops they have, as Board members, been using. Of course this seems a very bad idea, and Luke's in particular could have important information on it. It may be, of course, that he will delete it, but such things can sometimes be recovered, especially if there is ever to be an investigation.

Later...

Shiv and I have brunch at the Daily Grill again and talk about Sursum, mostly rehearsing what I have just written, but Shiv has been in touch with the City, and there will be a meeting next week. Luke had let his connections with the City lapse, and there has been little if any communication for some time. He also says that Luke had been working up in the Office during the small hours after the election. Whatever else he accomplished, he had sent Tim an email saying, in effect, Let's meet and discuss how we can deal with this election, but Tim had written back saying that the result was final, and urging him to make the transition a smooth one – but that was before he was fired. I say again that the new Board must develop a relationship with HUD, because, however difficult it may have been in the past, there must be the possibility of making representations to counter some accusations Luke is reported to be making. But the danger may not be so very great: surely in HUD as in the City, there must be few if any who will credit what he says. Or am I, not for the first time, being a little too hopeful?

We also talk about the older residents, those who will have difficulties with any transition. Shiv has talked with the new developer and with Ted, both of whom say that the best way to get a larger offer from a developer is to offer the land unencumbered. But if that is the path, it is even more important that all the residents, the old in particular, be given help in finding a new home, one that (given the saturated market in Washington) they can buy outright, and have money left over. But they also need to understand about utilities (Sursum was built at a time when it was still possible to fund these through the main office), and condo fees, which will appear to be a kind of rent, but which will need to be budgeted for in any case. Shiv agrees, and is going to try to see if the new Board wants to hire an agency to address the issue. He also in trying to get the Board to agree to new security measures – cameras and lighting, as well as hiring off-duty police officers to replace the present guards. He has encountered some opposition from the Board because of the expense, which would, he says, amount only to a month of the current charge.

Saturday January 17, 2009

It is the beginning of the semester and things have been busy, so I have not much talked to Shiv since our last conversation. Our first session was to have been last Thursday, but then I got a message saying that the Board needed the room for a community meeting, and could we put off our first session until the Thursday after President-Elect Obama's inauguration. We can indeed. In any event, I am most interested to know what, if anything, has been developing, and call Shiv to see if he would like to have brunch again, increasingly the only time during which we can talk more or less uninterrupted. While doing so we talk too about how things have been going, and I gather that the powers that be are not so very keen on selling the community outright, and dividing the profits among the residents. A proposition I have not embraced either, to tell the truth. Even if each family was given $100,000 or more (which Shiv still believes quite possible), some think that, in some cases at least, the money would be gone in three months, and that older residents might have difficulty in simply keeping hold of their windfall (they'll discover relatives they never knew they had, etc.). Better the new Board should work with the City again, the thought now is, and together see what can be done to ensure apartments for some at least of the older residents. Shiv understands, as they say, where all this is coming from (it's a prospective we have often enough talked about ourselves), but he is a little impatient with effectively beginning again, at least in part because he is not at all sure of what the City's attitudes toward Sursum may be. But he understands too that that's what needs to happen. Selling the place will be a last resort, for reasons both humane and practical. If the more vulnerable residents can be thus protected, they must be. But as it stands, present arrangements for getting Sursum residents into one of the new units clearly advantage the relatively affluent, those who have their act together, for whom details like utilities, condo fees and even mortgages hold no terrors. Those, in a word, who need no special favors, but are accustomed, in some cases at least, to receiving them. But our brief should provide for the others. It's complicated too because, even with all that has been agreed, I recall that it was with such discussions that our project began, but for reasons that I trust are obvious, I hold my peace.

And now it is Sunday, and I have just come from brunch with Shiv (this has been a continuing leit-motif, I realize). He notes that the meeting with the City went well, though Jessica's hostility appeared again, but what was most apparent was the fact that the City wants to keep to the unworkable arrangements Luke had negotiated, though they are now willing to pay more than the 27 million agreed for the community. But the situation is complicated by the present recession, which has meant, among other things, that the City, like most of us, is in debt, and though it has already contracted with developers for other projects, thanks to the Recession it has not the funds to honor its contracts. Not less important is the apparent collapse of the luxury condo market in the District. The only things selling now are townhouses, which is one reason that the City balked when the Board asked about increasing the density. More surprisingly, the City did not want an independent audit made, which might indicate that, even in these hard times, the land is worth a good deal more than is thought. Shiv suggests that a better reason for *having* an audit would be difficult even to imagine. Yet not only the City, but also the current developer is effectively out of money. This means that the present contract, approved by the City, could probably be honored by neither of them, and it may be that other possibilities can again be considered.

The Residents meeting for which we cancelled tutoring last Thursday also went well, and Phil indicated the two choices – sell everything or more or less (some changes) follow the deal with the City. But Board says it wants more feedback from the Residents: who wants to move, who doesn't, and will send out questionnaires. A resident asked a question which Phil tried to defer to Shiv, but Jessica interrupted and said in effect to Phil, No, she asked you, you answer it. Phil pressed on, but Jessica insisted. At the end Jessica stood up and made a speech denouncing the old Board, of which, however, she had been a very prominent member. But probably many of the residents have already forgotten.

I am going to work in my office after our brunch, and Shiv drops me off, but we talk in his car before I get out. There is one other possibility, he says. It goes back to our earlier conversation, and would be the one way to effectively save the community, though he doubts the Board will go for it. But he thinks that we might possibly turn it into condos. A bank loan, perhaps 30 million, might be needed to pay off debts and recondition the units. Residents could then secure individual ownership of their units, no doubt paying their own utilities, etc., but able to sell their units when (after an initial period) they want to. The "Sursum Corda Cooperative Association" would retain the right of first refusal, at market rate. Such an arrangement might work now, with a recession on and the condo market saturated, and the association could begin (once the loan was secured) by reconditioning the now vacant units, and selling them. This is not unlike a plan he and I had discussed long ago, in a very different economy. But, as Shiv says, the real difficulty is getting 200 people to act together – some will want to move, and simply want money, others to stay. But it is only one of many plans possible, and any resolution is perhaps years away.

Wednesday February 11, 2009

Shiv came and again talked to our Wednesday seminar for the tutors, again engaging the students with his tales of having been raised at Sursum, and of the present difficulties there. Afterwards, as his usual fee, I take him to dinner at the Tombs and we talk about the course of events, over the years, that we have seen. He is concerned by the inability of the Board to deal effectively with matters at hand, but he says too that under present circumstances it may be no bad thing. We are still in a recession, after all, and one effect may be that the high-end condo market in Washington is more or less saturated, at least for the next few years. It's not that Sursum Corda wouldn't sell, but it wouldn't sell for enough. That being so, there may be no reason now to proceed with the sale of anything, and perhaps what the Board could best do is to address the extraordinary financial legacy it has inherited, begin again to rebuild a relationship with the community, maintain the property as best it can, and seek to practice openness and visibility in all things.

May it be so. But this has been a long and winding tale, and I hardly think it is at an end. Still, this may be as good a place as any to break off. After a ten month period, in 2005, of shock, frustration, duplicity and the kind of fog that flows from half-truths, deception, and simple ignorance of what the rules are, the last five months have taken a very different turn. Nirvana has by no means arrived, but some at least of the most egregious difficulties have been driven from the field, and those who remain have a fair chance of success, if they do not grow fatigued by fighting among themselves. It may also be more honest to stop here, between acts, as it were. If my sense of inevitability has not entirely been dissolved, its presence has. One of the hallmarks of Sursum Corda is that the residents, not the rest of Washington, still set the tone. Their writ runs here, at least for now. Legal powers may lodge elsewhere, but even these had better proceed with caution. Good advice for the new Board too.

But in the end, these pages have been less about the interactions of an opaque and perhaps too-powerful Board, the residents and the developers, than the continuing presence community itself, in and around which we all moved, of which we all imperfectly spoke, against which wave after wave of half-truth spent its force. Emerson's anguished but confident, "There must be a relation between power and probity"– as American a proposition as there is – was all too rarely proved. Law, an easily climbed fence when the rich confront the poor, was not a particularly formidable barrier, and threats and intimidation danced around. But was that all that finally happened then? No: not at all. Power didn't exactly go limping home, but neither, in the end, did probity. A stand-off then, at least for now. As often happens here. It could be worse. It could be better, too. The world goes on.

September 2012

Two years and more have brought a kind of balance to the place, and it registers upon our little program too. Thanks to Christine Nicholson the children continue to come to be taught, and, without claiming anything like perfection, our work has flourished. Our student director, from Chicago and a Republican, has been excellent, and I am reduced to my traditional worries, that this learner has missed too often, that that particular linking of tutor and learner is not working out, that the student who fronted for (say) the Halloween party has not yet been reimbursed for her outlays. Meanwhile around us the community has gathered itself again, this time led by motives less devious than before. The new President of the residents Association is not only a Georgetown graduate, but was a member of the Georgetown basketball squad during the heady days of Coach John Thompson, and keeps a weather eye on the fortunes of the present team. My sense is that Christine is happier with the present arrangements than with what went before, and that her contributions to the community are now better understood, and I hope appreciated, than previously. But the recession has slaked, and although a developer may now have partnered with the Board, conditions and stipulations follow, not unnaturally in a city as saturated with unoccupied high end condos as Washington now is. But these are complicated by the requirement that, rather to its credit, the City has by no means abandoned insisting that there should be provision for low and moderate income residents in whatever finally emerges, and that the density be appropriate to the setting. Once gone, as soon we will be, we will never have again this fellowship, but perhaps its legacy will allow something for the disadvantaged. It's nice to think so.

Thoreau began and ended *Walden* in the spring – for in some parts of New England, during some years at least, early July can just be called spring. I am going to end a little later, in an approaching autumn, which seems appropriate. Like Thoreau, I stop writing this little urban *Walden* for as good a reason as I began it. Like the residents, I too have other lives to lead, and as I am writing these words I have the sense that what I have been writing about will never end, whatever Sursum Corda's fate may finally be.

Yet for a few years, much of the old Sursum Corda will probably remain. I do not want to fall into the trap, against which, as I may have said, I warn my students, of romanticizing the community because it has become familiar, or because they have come to know and cherish one of its younger residents. But recently a student put my admonition to flight when she named her course paper "Literacy and Love," and argued that both, not one, are central to our work. And indeed, even the narrative I have recounted here provides no immunity to such love as hope, perseverance, and commitment can supply.

But again, there is no end to History, and for the new Board, as for the old, the die seemed all but cast, if not quite yet. The Recession of

252 *Power and Probity in a DC Cooperative*

2008 had left its mark, and so the expenses and charges that the old Board had run up continued still, so that for five years the project stalled, and no one (not the City, nor any willing Developer) had the funding to advance it, at least not yet. The debt was in the millions, after all, and and more would be needed to construct whatever was to follow on. So for a while at least, life continued as it had, our program flourished, and Shiv changed jobs, moving with his young family to Florida.

But then the Recession slackened; new ways appeared; and with them a new developer appeared, one with a good reputation and enough money to move the project forward once again. Phil took the bull by the horns, though there were those who wished he hadn't, and signed where he needed to, and it was done. When the end finally came, it took no time at all.

Not without a struggle led by Christine, vouchers were supplied to the Residents, who were thus induced to leave first by the end of August, then by a final dispensation by the end of October, 2017. In the end, a moving company was hired to speed them out. Whether or not they went happily didn't now compute, since the debts were large and growing. Was there no other way to address them, some wondered? But by 2016 the Board was of one mind and the end seemed well and truly inevitable, though how it finally came about was a wonder still

Envoy

Ending Up: Last Days at Sursum Corda

We are left alone with our day, and the time is short, and
History to the defeated
May say alas but cannot help or pardon.
--W. H. Auden

And now, suddenly, it is January 9th, 2017, and I am getting ready for what looks to be the beginning of the end of our tutoring program, the last semester in which the children at Sursum Corda and Georgetown students will work together. In case you may have forgotten, our program began forty-seven years ago by Fr. Horace McKenna, S.J. and certain of his brother Jesuits, and it is the one I have been effectively directing for the past twenty-seven years. It still brings Georgetown undergraduates twice a week to work with those Sursum Corda children whose parents, grandparents, or care givers desire it. In the very beginning it may have been attached to the university's Catholic Solidarity which has ended long since (and its records have vanished), but it still responds in its way to Catholic Social Teaching, though of course it is by no means is limited to Catholic students, nor ever has been. It now operates through an English department elective that I teach, one open to all undergraduates, in which we travel to the Community of Sursum Corda for an hour's work on Tuesday and Thursday, and meet for a Wednesday seminar on campus.

My participation in the program is only one factor in its operation, and initially it owed as much to our contacts there, to Sister Diane Roche, rscj, who was for many years the Resident Director and with whom we remain in contact, and to Ms. Allene Harper, who was employed by the university for many years to assist us with the program. After Allene's death, we continued with the help of the then Resident Manager, Mrs. Christine Nicholson, who, now in retirement, continues to assist us, and without whom we could not have continued as we have. The current Chairman of the Residents Association is Mr. Lonnie Duren, works with Winn, the development company that now enjoys effective ownership of the place. He is engaged with them in curing past debts, selling the property once its residents have left, and thus bringing everything to an end. It is hoped that the sale will make it possible for those who were here at the end to receive a "windfall," as it is being called, a percentage of the money left over from the sale once the debts have been discharged. I consider that I will keep a kind of record of events, but only off and on, recording what happened and when, and sometimes reflecting on what is happening now, and what has gone before.

I had a good indication that things were soon coming to an end from Mrs. Nicholson in December, but there was also the possibility that one section of the property might be built on first, and the rest reserved until that was accomplished. But now, speaking with her on the phone, she tells me that 143 vouchers are to be requested, and will be distributed to the residents on January 18 and 19, or so it is hoped. They are good for six months, I am told, but the residents will be encouraged to start looking at once, and if they haven't found a place in two months are to come to the office for help. We agree that some of the residents and the children may find the distribution upsetting, and that it would probably be best to wait until Tuesday the 24th to begin the program. For some reason Christine herself, who has done so much to obtain vouchers for the community, has not been assigned one yet, but she expects a reason, and probably a voucher, will be revealed shortly.

Thursday January 12, 2017

Everyone whom I had been expecting came to our first class meeting yesterday, the one without the children that takes place in Walsh 492 at 6:30pm. A few of last semester's tutors have opted out, one has had to miss today but will rejoin the class next week, and I admit three then six, new members. I sense a seriousness of purpose (along with beginning of semester good humor), which pleases me and seems at to promise reasonably well for the future. After discussing things at some length, I say that we must take care to run a tight ship this semester, and not let anything slide just because we are ending. I ask the students what FIAT stands for, and they are amused, some groan a little, but, among them, come up with the answer: Factual, Interpretive, Applicative, and Transactive, the kinds of questions we pose to our young learners to ascertain whether they have actually understood the texts they have been reading. We do not discuss them, however. I remark that choral answers are always easier (some smiles), and say that we'll meet again before the 24th, when I mean to return to the topic.

Saturday January 14, 2017

I hear from a resident of Sursum Corda who has been to the meet-ings in the Community Center where things are discussed, and who has already had one of the two interviews required in order to obtain a voucher. But neither she nor anyone else has asked any questions, as everyone is afraid they will be seen as "troublemak-ers" if they do so and prevented from getting a voucher or anything else. She thinks she knows what she should ask, but doesn't intend to push it. Still, it looks as though everyone knows what's been go-ing on, and what's to come.

* * *

Tuesday March 14, 2017

I had intended to write in this journal only intermittently this se-mester, but have not added to it for two months, dissuaded by the sometimes painful nature of the topic, and a general sense of things now drawing in, though also by having to spend time finishing my excellent little book *Vygotsky's Children*, soon to be out. Sursum cer-tainly has a role in it, but the book is largely about the fate of three like programs I helped to bring about and advise at Oxford and

Cambridge. Still, there have been reminders all the while of where we are. Just before spring break we had what I realized would be our last session at Sursum during a rainy night. On January 25 water was pouring down, and as a result the night was particularly dark, making the drive down treacherous, and imparting to Sursum Corda an aspect all its own, somehow separating it from its surroundings, so that it became more than ever a place unto itself. I spend perhaps a quarter of our hour looking into the rain and the gloom, as if seeking to penetrate a mystery, remembering how under such circumstances Sursum can reveal a certain presence, and understanding that, since daylight savings time will arrive before we return again, this will be the last time I will ever see it so. Some of the students look a little puzzled at my rapt attention to a rainy night, but I could not of course explain what I was feeling.

Tuesday March 21, 2017

One of my concerns has been whether we would have enough young learners to occupy all of the students in a rather full class, ones who would remain until the end of the semester. HUD vouchers, apparently enabling the families to move where and when they like, were to be distributed in late February and early March, and if many or all immediately availed themselves of the opportunity to move at once that could effectively empty our program of its younger participants. I had formally mooted this possibility to Ricardo Ortiz, our Chair, and to Chet Gillis, our Dean, both of whom had agreed to let me finish the class with readings and discussions if necessary. But it is becoming apparent that no such dispensation will be required. Within two weeks nine of the 133 families had moved out, followed by a few others soon after, so that the number soon fell to about 120, where, for a while at least, it seems that it will remain. Another nine may leave by early May (by which time our class will have concluded), but others have been prevented by the circumstances in which they live.

Apparently in Washington, but also in Maryland where some of the residents hoped to move, landlords are disinclined to embrace -- or even to allow -- people holding vouchers to rent their properties, the result, I am told, of bad experiences in the past with persons who abused their apartments, and left with unpaid rent. Additionally, people holding vouchers are liable to have their credit histories examined closely, with attention paid not only to evictions and to times in which they had not paid their rent until a court order had been obtained, but also to the times in which an order against them had been sought but not obtained, because payment had been made before the court could proceed. The result has been that, for these and other reasons, very many residents have had their vouchers refused by landlords, particularly in Maryland I am told, and returned home angry or dispirited, or both.

But now the residents are being advised by those who know the game. They must not think of vouchers as money, they are told, only as a possibility. When they seek an apartment they should consider dressing as if they are seeking a job, so as to make the best possible impression on the landlord. They should not ask too hard questions, so as to leave a good impression. And I am told that there are ways, over time, of at least moderating credit reports, though I have no idea what they are. The result has been to slow the evacuation of the place, and leave the community intact for a few more weeks. Good for our little program, I suppose, and for the longevity of our class, but it is of course a further indignity for people who are in effect being ejected from their homes.

The other issue has been the children themselves. At first I thought the dislocation might have escaped them, though it seemed unlikely, and reckoned, what was not entirely mistaken, that since everyone was involved, the shock might well be less. But if that was the case in the beginning, it has begun to wear off. Jojo, one of our liveliest and most loving learners has just turned seven, and increasingly has been unable to contain himself, and his energy, when not constrained, enters too easily into general circulation. Last semester he was obedient (mostly) and enjoyed working with his tutor, and seemed to all of us one of the happiest and most engaging children in the program. But this semester the passage has been harder. He runs about when we are getting organized longer than any of the other children, and sadly has begun to fight, quite physically, with other boys who are his friends. His loyal and attentive tutor is taken aback by this development, but is if anything even more attentive to him, and does everything he can to bring him home. Another boy, a year or two older, can hardly concentrate at all, and a third will now read only when he has his best friends close about him, and hardly then. I continue to press the tutors to employ FIAT questions, but increasingly what they report is the number of books read, not the questions asked, before they resort to the playground. I find myself acceding too easily to requests to go there earlier and earlier, not ten minutes before we end but fifteen, even twenty, all the while encouraging other tutors to remain and work, not to join the gallop to the door.

It would be too much to say that there is desperation in their energy, but there is certainly something unfamiliar about it, as if reacting to something known or known about, but hardly understood. To be sure, we've seen it all before, but in a different tone. Tonight Jojo tosses the little red book he has been reading over his shoulder when he is done with it, and turns to a friend. It's not that he's never done so before, but all at once, and now more frequently, he's tired of focusing, and doesn't really want to read at all. His smart, quick, tutor, a year younger than the norm this semester, has other ideas however, and shortly thereafter they carry on reading. A girl who has behaved very badly in the past, is suddenly so attentive that the tutors talk about it on the way home. Another boy has started acting out as he never has before, and not only his tutor, but all of us are a little concerned. His tutor, who has connected with him in the past, now finds doing so difficult, until late in one lesson he puts his head down and says, almost to himself but also to her, "Stupid moving." Yet another boy now reads off and on, but his tutor can't get him to respond even to the simplest FIAT question, only to plunge ahead with his reading. Of course children everywhere respond to an unwelcome move in roughly similar terms, but the situation is different here, where the community is not so much moving as being moved, in an action that their parents, their caregivers, never elected, so that there hardly seems to be a saving grace. The behavior of the children is by no means unknown, indeed it's all happened before, but not quite so often and all at once, as if some gentle sense of panic is gaining ground.

Sunday April 2, 2017

One difficulty I have always had with this course is in encouraging the students to look beyond their young learner, to the community in which he or she lives, and then beyond that, to whatever else concerns them. This encouragement is complicated by the fact that I also insist that their first duty is to their young learner, engaging him or her as best they can, and learning the strategies with which we work. Normally, and encouraged to do so, the tutors will look beyond our upstairs classroom to the community that surrounds it, but less often, unless they are already minded to do so, to the larger implications that reveals.

I have never really insisted on the practice, partly because we come to help, not judge, partly because I do not want to suggest that we seek to instill or approve political attitudes of any sort. When we began work, now many years ago, we attracted a certain amount of criticism from the Left respecting the attitudes our tutors brought to their work, but the Left was where many of our tutors came from too, so we fought shy of any confrontation. Although I tend to lean left personally, though not precipitously so, I remain embarrassed and angry at the increasing nonchalance with which both parties have, effectively at least, observed with detached interest the disadvantaged of any class, as President Trump's election may have demonstrated. But I am anxious not to repel Republicans, conservatives, and those of no fixed political view, from participating in our program.

In point of fact, our study and practice can have a powerful effect on those who have never encountered them before, though their first effect is usually on what is assumed, or simply taken for granted. This year I have insisted that the students incorporate Peter Edelman's *So Rich, So Poor* (2012) into their course paper, insisting that they, not I, decide where it is relevant therein, and why. In the best of all possible worlds I would like his to be the question that, in the future at least, most concerns them -- Why is it so hard to end poverty in America? Byrne's own and highly principled resignation when President Clinton effectively abandoned welfare reform is one thing I would like them to reflect upon (but few of them do), the more so since such gestures are hardly encouraged these days, still less practiced, in either party. But addressing the growing divide between the very wealthy, the wealthy, and the rest of us is one thing I would like them to include in their list of things to do, if not now then perhaps in time to come. Who knows what their futures may bring?

Thursday April 6, 2017

One other question I have never resolved concerns the extent to which our tutorial sessions carry with them an element of mentoring as well, and if so of what kind. Certainly a good deal more so than I first imagined, when my focus was almost exclusively on helping tutors know what they were doing (few at Georgetown then did), and teaching our young learners how to read. The one-mindedness of my early focus may have been partly due to our critics, one group of which insisted that, after some initial instruction, the students should be left alone to get on with it, making mistakes no doubt, but finding their own way forward, and a second group who believed that our students brought so much cultural baggage with them that there was little chance of real communication and change unless we privileged what seemed to me a somewhat radical left-of-center agenda in our work, which we never did.

In those days I was more concerned with the first group, which very much seemed to me the Georgetown norm, than with the second, largely because, I naively believed, it could be easily fixed. It was, I thought, in nobody's interest not to prepare the tutors as best we could, since otherwise we were effectively instrumentalizing the children we intended to serve for the education of Georgetown undergraduates, not the other way. A considered letter by me explaining all this to the then-president was effectively brushed aside by a lengthy, polished and highly superior denial from the then-Dean of Students who refused to take any of my objections seriously – besides, they had all been attended to, he insisted. With the second group I did nothing, believing that, in spite of their rather ideological utterances, they were not an entirely unfriendly lot, with very little understanding of our practices whatsoever, and disinclined to attack a literacy program operating in the interest of disadvantaged children for very long, even if it did not conform to the prevailing ideology.

But now I am in our teaching room on the second floor of the community center at Sursum Corda, and looking around it I remember some at least of my earlier mistakes and misperceptions. For one thing, it is certainly right that any tutoring program involves an element of mentoring as well as teaching, to a greater or lesser degree, I suppose, depending on the case. But in a program like ours such instruction is mutual as much as it is anything, individual certainly, but even then based mostly on exchange. In recent years we have been working not only one-on-one, but also two-on-two, or even one-on-three or -four, so that our young learners learn in consort, or sometimes in competition, but in which the act of learning is also one of mutual agreement, in which the presence of a friendly mentor, one who is also present at other times as well, is often is the reason that learning happens. Recess is as important as reading even when time is short, as it is for us, and a quarter-of-an hour in the playground has unlocked many a mind.

But the distinctness of the culture and circumstance between tutor and learner that our critics used to decry has had its advantages. Some years ago a woman from the community, with whom we worked for years, asked one of our younger learners what he wanted to be when he grew up. I don't know," the boy replied, "I live in Sursum Corda." She replied at once that his answer had nothing to do with her question, and that he could be whatever he wanted to be. A good reply, I think, but he was of course answering her question, only reminding her that he might not have a future, both literally and figuratively. This happened during a period in which I was trying to understand what effect an evidently increased level of violence was having on our learners, and was beginning to believe that for some at least it yielded, if only for a time, a sense of futurelessness, less in a philosophical than in a very practical way.

I agree that it is easy to overestimate what we saw, or thought we saw, to make too much of little, but often the violence came very close to home, and many families had a member with a connection to the drug trade, sometimes a close one. And if that connection could be proved, as it sometimes was, then under HUD regulations the whole family could be, and sometimes was, evicted. So that, as happened, a young man's engagement with the drug trade, however small, could lead to his mother's losing the house in which she had lived for many years. And when there were children, they went too. In the closed world of Sursum Corda these things were widely understood, including by the children, for whom it was something else to be concerned about.

With these larger legal and bureaucratic matters we had, of course, no traction. Our transaction was with the children, but whatever our students' putative philosophical limitations may have been, they did not lack an apprehension of the future, and it was that, among other things, that they brought, twice-weekly, to their work. No doubt it sometimes distracted them, but in the context of the time it may have proved one of their more effective, if unintended, lessons. In any case, when sitting in the room in which we work, what I saw was our excellent young learners, concerned indeed for what might lie ahead.

Wednesday April 19, 2017

We were away over Easter, and now suddenly have less than two weeks left for a program that has lasted for forty-seven years. But our return last night was almost an anticlimax. This year the Spring Holiday came the week after Holy Week, a time when many parents take their children off to visit grandparents, and our numbers were way down. As bad, the floor in the upstairs room in the community center had just been waxed, in anticipation of yet another meeting there tomorrow night, and all the chairs had been removed. In a moment of what proved to be hubris, I suggested that, since the evening was fine, we read outside in Center Point, a small area designed for community meetings that had been included in the original plans, as we often had in the past. A handful of students retrieved chairs and pursued their agendas in our usual upstairs room, but the majority gave it a try, and for some minutes it succeeded. Children and tutors read and talked together in a Washington spring, and all was well.

But there were distractions too, and this time they were not to be overcome. By 7:40 some of the children present had begun to pull away, some almost literally, and in the end we decided to end early -- but to allow some time for games and happiness before we left. Such latitude will not endear us to a small collection of tough, square-jawed residents who sometimes stand around, and believe that children were made for discipline and little else, but such has never been the way we teach. Looking back on the evening, I wonder if we may not have come upon a way our final meeting might proceed, a week tomorrow. That we should then read our little magazine together for a last time, eat pizza, and end our forty-seven years with games and laughter.

Monday April 24, 2017

I had been thinking, too much as it developed, as to how we should tell the children that we will end on Thursday, and considering -- worrying would not be too strong a word -- in what way we should break it to them. Cupcakes and conversation tomorrow, on our last tutorial of the semester, indeed the last after 47 years, I had richly imagined, but then had the good sense to ask Christine's advice, who laughed and said not to worry, they know already, having been told by their parents, or if not by them then by other children. In any case, she said, it was already general knowledge, as such things often are at Sursum Corda, where there really are no secrets, and where the spoken word has an authority all its own.

In the meantime we had, on Wednesday, our last general meeting as a class, intended finally to get our ducks in a row, at which DC Police Officer Darrin Bates, himself a former resident, in childhood and youth, of Sursum Corda, addressed the students. He spoke very well indeed, and the students rose to the occasion and posed good questions afterwards, asking about Sursum Corda's past, about his upbringing and choice of career, and they asked as well what he had learned from our program. He told the students, among other things, that he had grown up in two Sursum Cordas, one by day, where there was warmth, friendship, games and a family-like comradeship, and one by night, where there was fear and the ever-present threat of violence, and that he still remembers both. He suggested that our program was one of the things that had helped him to negotiate the differences. Then on Friday, as a last excursion, and thanks to Rob Sgarlata, Georgetown's generous football coach, we took the older children to the football team's "spring game," so they could see some of their tutors in action on the field. We have had a number of football players in the program over the years, starting really with two excellent young men, Darius Baxter and Troye Bullock, who pointed the way to some of them, and have since founded an excellent organization, *Good Partners*, to work with disadvantaged youth in Washington. But athletes in general, and football players in particular, seem to me to make excellent tutors, properly instructed. Not only are they less concerned than other mortals may be with the rough-and-tumble of the Sursum Corda playground, but they often have, as other students do not, a sense of teamwork, of doing things together, so that tutor and learner are not only on the same page but also on the same side, and certainly they can make their way together.

But after the game was over, it proved to be Student Director Charlie Nester's campus apartment that became the hit of the afternoon, partly because of his lively roommates, partly because, for some of the children at least, the game went on a rather long time. But it was the last time we were to bring Sursum Corda children to the university, and as usual, they loved it.

The excursion had been effectively organized by Charlie, one of our two drivers as well as being this year's Student Director, and one of the best we have had. He made a practice of always being there, and also has a habit of thinking ahead, anticipating not only what will happen but what's needed, and he has so made this semester easier for everyone, even those who don't know that he has. The other driver has been Jack Graffagnino, a perceptive and smart young man (he took my Chaucer course, which few tutors do), who also proved a skilled driver, and together they have held the program together all the year long. In what I have written both here and elsewhere, I have made it a practice not to describe the persons or the reactions of individual tutors, nor even to identify them (usually). My reasons are various, from an unwillingness to intrude into personal business, as their reasons and reactions often are, to a hesitancy to speak for them, or to predict, or conjecture, what they believe now, or will do, in time to come. Our program operates irrespective of party or person, and the tutors and the learners who make it up are, and have always been, its living heart.

Wednesday April 25, 2017

Our last teaching session, last after forty-seven years, was last night, and I was not looking forward to it, though I told myself that the best thing would be if it could operate as usual, at least as far as possible, and we all would have been left with a memory of that. In the event, however, reality intruded. Noisy from the beginning, the younger children could not be quieted, fell to blows and chasing, such that on any other day would have seen them gone, but I could not bring myself to do so, and shortly thereafter everyone was friends again, though not much less noisy for that. Some, probably most, of the older children clung to their tutors, and made an effort until it was time for the playground, which, not for the first time, came earlier than is our wont. I had a quite possibly psychosomatic stomach ache, but thanks to a helpful group of tutors, our books were packed up and returned, later that evening, to my office, as they have been every year about this time since that fateful April, now more than twenty years gone, when we left them for the summer, hoping they would do some good, and the drugs guys somehow got to them and sold all the new ones. I take comfort, somewhat apprehensively, in the fact that we will return on Thursday for our farewell party, held for the first time ever at Sursum, and hope that we will all survive it.

Friday April 28, 2017

And so at last our program came to end. As we were waiting at Georgetown, before our 6:30pm exit for the last time, two former tutors appeared as well, and happily we made our way down, me trying not to think that this is the last time I'll do this. The day was fine, but the traffic, first of all in Georgetown, was terrible, and it was obvious from the first that we would arrive late, as we did. Our tradition is to end each semester with a reading of our "literary magazine," a whole language writing strategy I learned in Berkeley. The magazine is written by learners and tutors both, and produced at Kinko's. It offers, largely to the community of Sursum Corda, some of the children's writing, and a paragraph from the tutors praising their young learners, and telling the community who they are (home city and state, year, major) for such as are interested (many are). This year, for the first time ever, we printed the photos of tutor and learner in color, not in black and white, and I commissioned a few articles from the tutors about those who have helped us over the years.

As we arrived the sun broke through, or so it seemed, and I urged that we take our reading of the magazine and the accompanying party to Center Point again, a small area at the back of the community center, originally built for community meetings, where three large steps, for sitting, climbed up from an open square, and where only recently we had enjoyed a not very successful tutoring session. Relieved of the requirements of tutoring it suited our needs to perfection, and urged on by two of our larger and louder tutors, the children stood in the center and read their contributions. Very sadly the mother of the two children who had made difficulties at our last tutorial meeting had somehow heard of their transgressions and refused to let them attend, fearing (unnecessarily, I thought) a repetition, but their sympathetic and perceptive tutor brought them food and drink, and they laughed over the magazine together.

Too soon it is time to leave. Having arrived late, we well overstay our hour, and there is nothing precipitous about our exit. More running about, which has become the way, for our younger learners at least, to deal with difficult moments, but there is much cleaning up to be done from the party, and that involves everyone. Tutors and children make their way together to the vans. Goodbyes are exchanged, and I hear one tutor say to his learner, I will see you again, but it may not be for a long time. More hugs, but the majority of the farewells are quick and simple, so as not to break the mood of felt if slightly apprehensive happiness that the reading of the magazine and the party have produced. Then the first van leaves, easily enough I think, but the tutors in ours are slow returning, some having escaped to the playground when the cleanup started, others having gone to bring their very young learners home one last time. More time passes, the children begin to drift away, and the light begins to fail. Now we are together again in the van with the doors closed and the children at a safe distance. A few goodbyes are shouted back and forth, everyone who remains waves vigorously, and we drove out into the warm night.

In the end Sursum Corda will be remembered for its powerful if sometimes twisted charm; for its brave and frightened children, standing up to whatever comes their way; for its independent, self-reliant, and often wounded residents, holding on, as best they can, to their families and their homes; for selfishness and fairness; for sudden hope and long discouragement; and for the paradoxical dignity that, even in this rich and inarticulate republic, continues to attend upon the poor.

GALLERY

For several years the American photographer Harry Mattison worked with the residents of Sursum Corda as a friend and collaborator, recording and helping with autobiographies, and forming a photographic record of the community as a whole. Recently Mr. Mattison returned to Sursum Corda during its last days, both to greet and say farewell (at least for now) to old friends, and to conclude his photographic work there. We have, with Mr. Mattison's generous permission, printed a small selection from this rich archive both in the following Photo Gallery and throughout the book, focusing on the residents and the architecture of the Sursum Corda community.

278

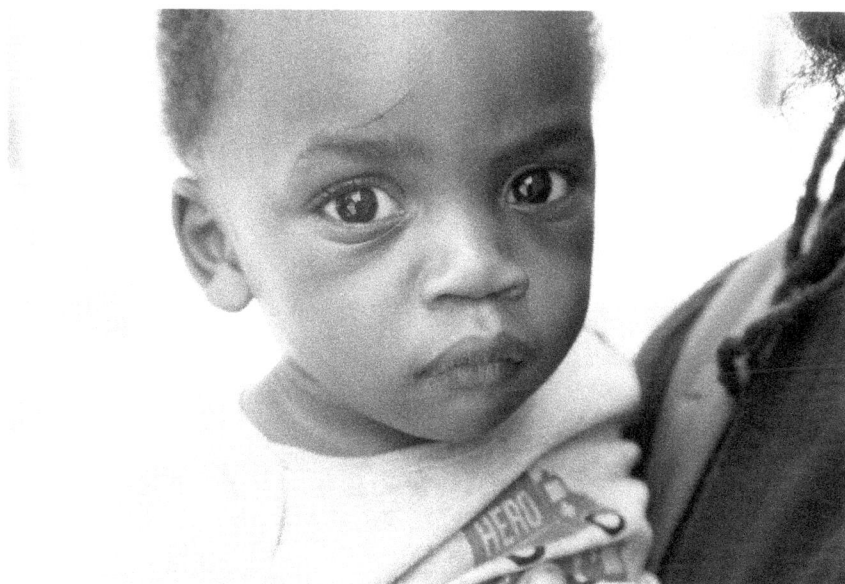

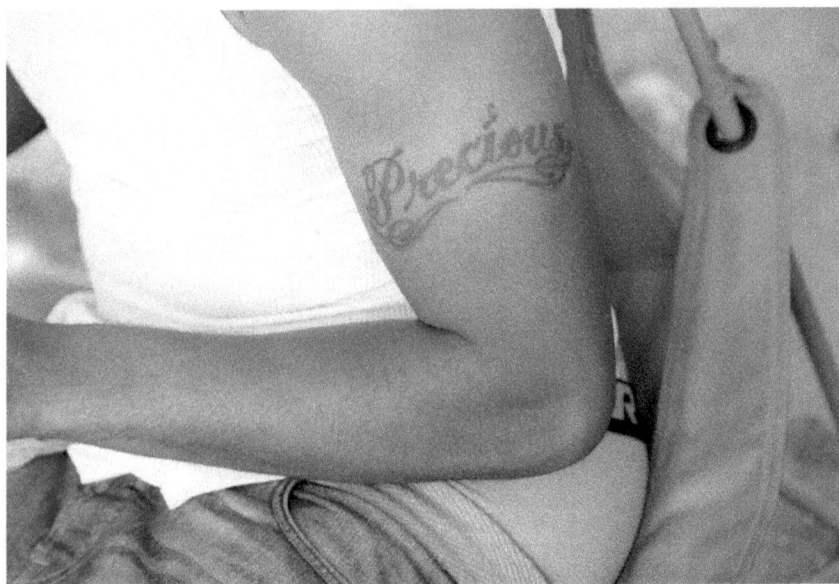

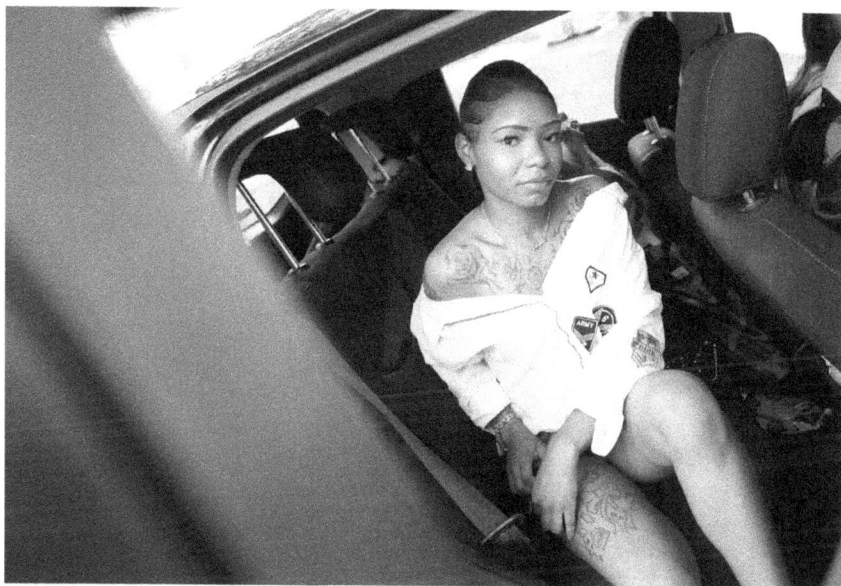

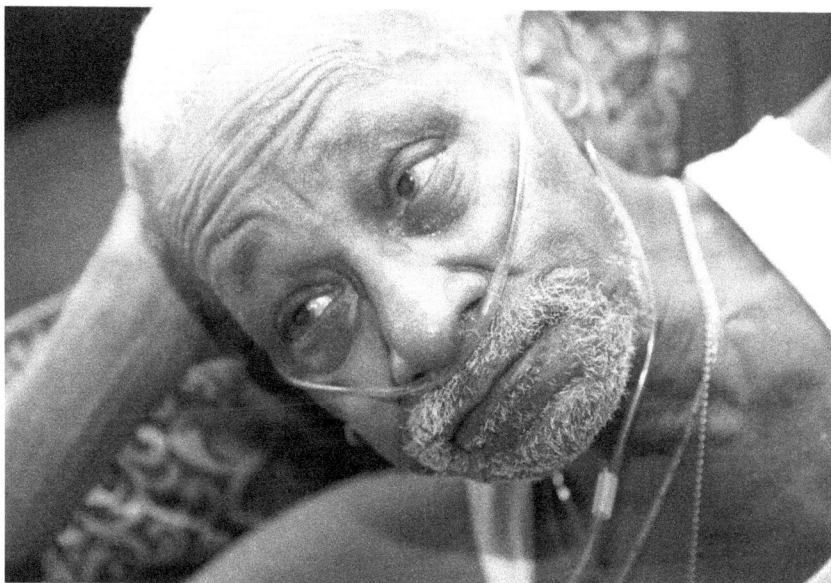

www.ingramcontent.com/pod-product-compliance
Lightning Source LLC
Chambersburg PA
CBHW020656270326
41928CB00005B/144